# Introduction to Tomorrow

# Robert G. Abernethy

# *Introduction to Tomorrow*

## THE UNITED STATES AND THE WIDER WORLD

### 1945–1965

ILLUSTRATED WITH PHOTOGRAPHS AND MAPS

HARCOURT, BRACE & WORLD, INC., NEW YORK

FOR JEAN AND JANE

# Introduction

This is a review of those events and ideas of the last twenty years that seem most important to an American reporter living and working in Washington, D.C.—important at the time they occurred and important as background to whatever happens next. Certainly, there are other points of view, and these same developments probably will appear different to all of us in years to come. But as of late 1965, this is the way they looked to one who had the privilege of either covering or interpreting many of these stories when they were still news.

It is my hope that this account will be of interest to other survivors of these two dangerous decades, especially to those young enough to have no personal memory of the years we used to call "postwar." If reading this book helps create a little tolerance for the changes of the years to come, I will be particularly proud.

I am grateful to all those who helped me with information and advice; to my cousin, Sarah H. Abernethy, who assisted with much of the research; to Joyce Weiner for her encouragement and guidance; and to the staff of the District of Columbia Central Library.

Washington, D.C.
*January, 1966*

7

# Contents

"The present influences the future and, more, it determines it."        —J. Bronowski
*The Common Sense of Science*

"It is easy to prophesy the future because it is a future which began quite some time ago."        —Willi Ley
*Ten Steps Into Space*

"We must deal with the world as it is, if it is ever to be as we wish."        —Lyndon B. Johnson
*Speech at Johns Hopkins University*
April 7, 1965

"The rate of change has increased so much that our imagination can't keep up. There is bound to be more social change, affecting more people, in the next decade than in any before. There is bound to be more change again, in the 1970's."
—Lord Snow
*The Two Cultures*
1959

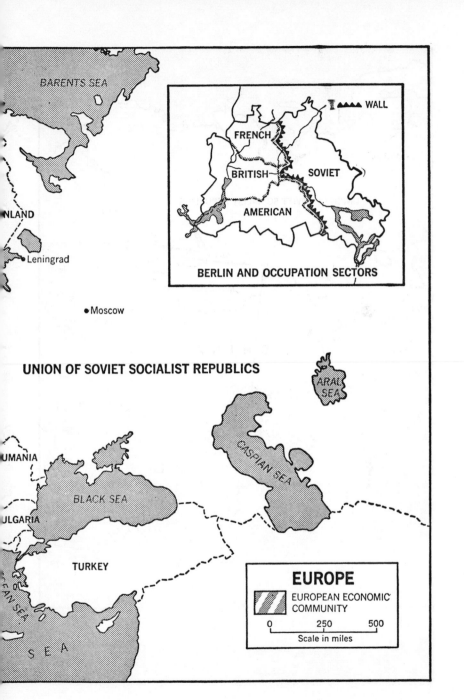

BARENTS SEA

FINLAND

● Leningrad

● Moscow

**BERLIN AND OCCUPATION SECTORS**

FRENCH

BRITISH — SOVIET

AMERICAN

I ▲▲▲▲ WALL

**UNION OF SOVIET SOCIALIST REPUBLICS**

ARAL SEA

RUMANIA

BULGARIA

CASPIAN SEA

BLACK SEA

TURKEY

EAN SEA

SEA

**EUROPE**

EUROPEAN ECONOMIC
COMMUNITY

0     250     500

Scale in miles

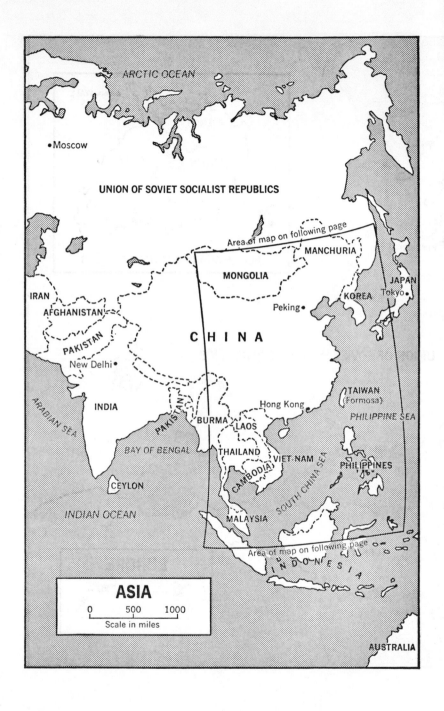

ARCTIC OCEAN

•Moscow

UNION OF SOVIET SOCIALIST REPUBLICS

Area of map on following page

MANCHURIA

MONGOLIA

JAPAN
Tokyo•

IRAN

KOREA

AFGHANISTAN

Peking•

PAKISTAN

C H I N A

New Delhi•

TAIWAN
(Formosa)

ARABIAN SEA

INDIA

Hong Kong

PHILIPPINE SEA

PAKISTAN

BURMA  LAOS

BAY OF BENGAL

THAILAND

VIET-NAM

PHILIPPINES

CEYLON

CAMBODIA

SOUTH CHINA SEA

INDIAN OCEAN

MALAYSIA

Area of map on following page

INDONESIA

## ASIA

0       500      1000

Scale in miles

AUSTRALIA

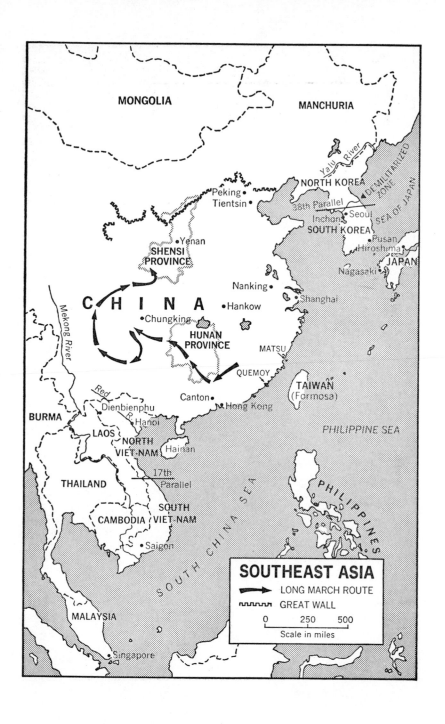

MONGOLIA

MANCHURIA

Yalu River

NORTH KOREA

Peking
Tientsin

38th Parallel

DEMILITARIZED ZONE

SEA OF JAPAN

Inchon
Seoul

SOUTH KOREA

Yenan

SHENSI PROVINCE

Pusan

Hiroshima

JAPAN

Nanking

Shanghai

Nagasaki

C H I N A

Hankow

Chungking

HUNAN PROVINCE

MATSU

Mekong River

QUEMOY

TAIWAN
(Formosa)

Canton

Hong Kong

Red R.

Dienbienphu

BURMA

Hanoi

PHILIPPINE SEA

LAOS

NORTH VIET-NAM

Hainan

17th Parallel

THAILAND

SOUTH CHINA SEA

PHILIPPINES

SOUTH VIET-NAM

CAMBODIA

Saigon

**SOUTHEAST ASIA**

LONG MARCH ROUTE

GREAT WALL

MALAYSIA

0        250       500

Scale in miles

Singapore

*Introduction to Tomorrow*

# Part One
# The New World

# Chapter One

## THE END OF THE WAR

THE President of the United States sat quietly in a large chair to the left of the fireplace, signing papers on a small table in front of him. Two of his cousins were in the room with him, and so was a portrait painter from New York, Mrs. Elizabeth Shoumatoff. The most recent photographs of the President had made the artist concerned about his health, as were those closest to him, but now as she sketched him, she thought he seemed "strangely well." Then, suddenly, he raised his hand to his temple as if he had been stung. "I have a terrific headache," he said, and he fainted.

It was one-fifteen in the afternoon, Central War Time.

The President's valet and a messboy carried him to his bed, but he never regained consciousness. At 3:35 P.M. on Thursday, April 12, 1945, Franklin Delano Roosevelt died of a cerebral hemorrhage. He had been the Thirty-second President of the United States. He was sixty-three years old.

President Roosevelt died at his cottage on top of Pine Mountain in Warm Springs, Georgia, a haven for him and others like him who had been crippled by infantile paralysis. There were more than a hundred patients there at the time, and they were the first to have a chance to show the grief and love millions more in the U.S. and all over the world were to reveal in the next few hours and days. On the morning of Friday, April 13, they hobbled or wheeled

21

themselves or were carried to the front of the Warm Springs Administration Building, where they watched the funeral procession begin its slow journey to Washington.

The Army had sent a band and a thousand infantrymen from Fort Benning, their drums muffled and black streamers flying beside their flags. Next came the hearse bearing the President's body in a mahogany coffin, draped with the American flag. Mrs. Roosevelt, who had been in Washington when the President died, had waited at the White House long enough to see the new President sworn in and then had flown to Georgia. Now, wearing a black fur cape, she rode in the car behind the hearse, her husband's Scotch terrier, Fala, at her feet.

As the procession passed the Administration Building, a Navy Petty Officer named Graham Jackson played his accordion. The day before he was to have entertained the President at a barbecue; now, he played "Going Home," and he wept.

At the bottom of Pine Mountain's red dirt road, the coffin was placed in the lighted last car of the special train for the sad trip north. All through that night, at every station, there were crowds. No one waved. Some cried. Most just stood mute, a little afraid, not yet able to believe the unbelievable. Franklin D. Roosevelt had been the country's leader through depression and war. During the twelve years of his Presidency, an entire American generation had grown old enough to bear arms remembering no other Chief Executive. He had seemed almost permanent.

Franklin Roosevelt was first elected President in 1932, when the country was nearly paralyzed by economic crisis. There had been intensive and unregulated speculation in the stock market, hundreds of thousands of amateur financiers joining the professionals in the hope of striking it rich. Stock values had soared, buoyed not so much by real increases in the value of corporations as by the competition of the hopeful, who often bought with borrowed money. Finally, in October and November of 1929, hope was overtaken by fear, stock prices fell disastrously, lenders called in their money, and the Great Depression began.

By 1932, more than twelve million people who wanted work could not find it—one-quarter of the labor force. The banks were closed in thirty-eight states. Hungry men walked the streets of the cities looking for jobs, or at least for the free "handouts" of bread lines and soup kitchens. In the countryside, corn, wheat, and cotton prices had begun dropping even before there was disaster on the stock exchange, and now farmers were taking the law into their own hands to prevent those to whom they owed money from seizing their land.

Everywhere there was despair and, in some places, panic. Among a sullen few there were mutterings of revolution.

Roosevelt, however, refused to share this gloom. In June of 1932, he had accepted the Democratic party's nomination for President with the words, "I pledge you, I pledge myself, to a new deal for the American people." Reporters afterwards named his administration the "New Deal." On March 4, 1933, the bleak day on which he was inaugurated, Roosevelt insisted, ". . . the only thing we have to fear is fear itself," and then, in a flurry of activity during his first hundred days in office, he tried to use the power of the Federal government to transform depression into recovery.

First came emergency legislation to reopen the banks. By early March of 1933, so many people feared their savings were no longer safe that nearly every bank in the country had been forced to close: to have remained open would have been to risk the sudden withdrawal of all deposits. On March 9, the day Congress convened, Roosevelt sent to the Capitol a bill establishing Federal guarantees and licenses for banks. Both houses of Congress approved the bill within eight hours. The banks reopened.

Farmers had been perhaps the hardest hit by the depression,

their income dropping by more than half from 1929 to 1932. The Agricultural Adjustment Act helped farmers meet their mortgage payments so they could keep their land. Even more important, under the AAA the government paid farmers to cut back their production, on the theory that this would raise farm prices. Ten million acres of cotton, already planted, were plowed up. Six million young pigs were slaughtered.

The Public Works Administration paid for roads and schools and dams and docks and airports and ships, spending about six billion dollars from 1933 to 1939, creating thousands and thousands of new jobs.

The Civilian Conservation Corps provided outdoor work for two and a half million unemployed young men.

The Social Security Act of 1935 began a nation-wide system of insurance for the unemployed and pensions for the aged.

The Home Owners Loan Corporation helped give householders easier mortgage payments so they could keep their property.

And there was much more.

In a sense, the New Deal was a true revolution, for it brought to power in Washington men and women who believed that, far from keeping hands off the economy, the government both could and should play an active part in the achievement of prosperity and the prevention of want.

In his 1932 campaign, Roosevelt had promised to remember "the forgotten man." Of course, there was resentment of Roosevelt's policies and methods, especially by those who believed it dangerous for the government to interfere with business—in effect, taxing the rich to benefit the poor. Some aristocrats called Roosevelt a "traitor to his class." But the great majority of Americans found in the energy of the New Deal and the confidence of its leader hope they thought they had lost. They came to believe that the government was at least trying to do something for them.

In the election of 1936, Roosevelt carried every state but Maine and Vermont, prompting the old Democratic party chief, James Farley, to amend the rule of thumb, "As Maine goes, so goes the nation," to, "As Maine goes, so goes Vermont."

Perhaps it was the experience of pain that permitted this patrician, whose name and wealth brought him all the privileges of the few, to become a man who was admired by so many. Franklin Delano Roosevelt was born January 30, 1882, on an estate near the Hudson River in Hyde Park, New York. His family was old and famous: President Theodore Roosevelt had been a fifth cousin. (T.R.'s side of the family pronounced the name RUSE-a-velt. F.D.R.'s side pronounced it ROSE-a-velt.)

F.D.R., as he became known in newspaper headlines, went to Groton and Harvard and Columbia Law School. He became a New York State Senator, an Assistant Secretary of the Navy, and his party's candidate for Vice-President in 1920. Then, in August of 1921, while he and his wife and five children were vacationing on Campobello Island in New Brunswick, Canada, he was stricken with infantile paralysis and paralyzed from the waist down.

For the next seven years, Roosevelt struggled to overcome his affliction. He never did regain the ability to stand up by himself, but he managed to learn to live and work in spite of his leg braces, and in the process he developed a depth of character and a jaunty confidence his friends had never noticed before. "If you had spent two years in bed trying to wiggle your big toe," Roosevelt said later, "after that anything else would seem easy." [1]

One of Roosevelt's greatest admirers was a young Congressman from Texas named Lyndon Johnson. When he heard the news of the President's death, he told a reporter: "He was just like a daddy to me always; he always talked to

me just that way. He was the one person I ever knew—anywhere—who was never afraid. . . . How he could take it
for us all." [2]

In Washington, D.C., on the morning of April 14, 1945,
half a million people lined the streets along which the President's body would be drawn. It was a military procession,
from Union Station to the White House. The casket bearing
the body of the man who had been Commander in Chief
rode on the kind of two-wheeled ammunition carrier the
French called a caisson, pulled by six white horses. There
were troops and two bands and black limousines carrying
the Roosevelt family and government officials. There was a
riderless horse with its stirrups reversed, the symbol of a
fallen warrior. There was the strange near-silence of a mourning crowd, the irony of sadness on a sunny spring day. "It
was a processional of terrible simplicity," wrote a *New York
Times* reporter, "and a march too solemn for tears except
here and there where someone wept alone." [3]

Mrs. Roosevelt had asked that no flowers be sent, but they
were anyway, rising ten feet high along the wall of the East
Room in the White House. Two hundred people crowded
that room, singing two of the President's favorite hymns,
"Eternal Father, Strong to Save" and "Faith of Our Fathers,"
listening to the minister recall that "the only thing we have
to fear is fear itself." Then they followed the caisson back
to Union Station for the last part of the journey, to the grave
in the garden at Hyde Park.

Never before had an American been so internationally
mourned, for Roosevelt had become the symbol of all the
U.S. had done to help win World War II. Long before most
Americans shared his opinion, he came to believe that even
though the U.S. was isolated by two oceans, it was still directly threatened by the new militarists in Germany and
Japan. Gradually, he had fought the isolationists who in-

sisted the U.S. remain neutral. Eventually, he helped change the country's major goal from economic recovery to military victory. "Doctor Win-the-War," as he put it, replaced "Doctor New Deal."

So in April of 1945, as they fought toward Berlin and the mainland of Japan, American soldiers and sailors paused for services in honor of their dead leader. In London, the House of Commons adjourned for the first time in history in honor of an American. There were stately memorial services in London and Paris, and in Moscow the Russians proclaimed two days of mourning and raised their national banner of mourning over the Kremlin.

In Washington, Robert A. Taft, a Republican Senator from Ohio who had often been a Roosevelt opponent, called the President, simply, "The greatest figure of our time." He was, said Senator Taft, "a hero of the war, for he literally worked himself to death in the service of the American people." [4]

The train from Washington arrived at Hyde Park on the morning of April 15. Again, there were the caisson, the six horses, and the riderless horse. This time, West Point cadets escorted the body—up the hill and into the garden. There was a twenty-one-gun salute. A frail seventy-eight-year-old clergyman recited, "Now the Laborer's Task Is O'er, Now the Battle Day Is Past." A bugler blew taps, and the body was lowered into the ground.

The job of leading the United States through war to victory and, hopefully, peace now fell to Harry S. Truman, who, on the day Roosevelt died, had been Vice-President for just eighty-two days. That afternoon of April 12, 1945, Truman had been presiding over the United States Senate and then at five-fifteen had walked to the other side of the Capitol to visit his old friend, Sam Rayburn, Speaker of the House of Representatives. (Almost every afternoon Rayburn invited a few friends to come and talk politics with him at what he called his "Board of Education.") When Truman got to Rayburn's room, he was told the White House had been trying to reach him. He telephoned and was asked to come downtown as quickly as possible.

At the White House, Truman was taken upstairs to Mrs. Roosevelt, who told him that the President had died.

Truman's first words were of sympathy for Mrs. Roosevelt. "What can I do?" he asked.

The First Lady's reply was a mark of her graciousness. "Tell us what we can do," she said. "Is there any way we can help you?" [5] She knew then, perhaps better than he, the demands of the Presidency.

A little after seven that evening, when his family and friends had gathered at the White House, Harry Truman was sworn in as President. The next day he expressed to reporters some of his feelings. "Boys," he said, "if you ever pray, pray for me now. I don't know whether you fellows ever had a load of hay fall on you. But when they told me yesterday what had happened I felt like the moon, the stars, and all the planets had fallen on me. I've got the most terribly responsible job a man ever had."

A reporter said, "Good luck, Mr. President."

Truman replied, "I wish you didn't have to call me that." [6]

Truman was a genuinely humble man, and his critics said he had a great deal to be humble about. But as they learned more about him, most Americans grew to understand that Harry Truman was no ordinary man.

He had been born near Kansas City, Missouri, on May 8, 1884. His parents gave him no middle name, just a middle initial, "S." He was a frail boy who had to wear glasses before he was nine, but he read a great deal and learned to play the piano well. Since he could not pass the eye examination, he could not accept an appointment he received to West Point; so when he finished high school, he went to work first

as a timekeeper for a construction gang, then later as a bank
clerk and a farmer. He joined the National Guard, and when
the U.S. went into World War I Truman went to France as
a First Lieutenant in the Field Artillery.

In 1917, many army units, such as Truman's regiment,
were composed of men from the same home town. A generation later, in the early days of World War II, such units
were abolished because it was too hard on the town if the
unit were wiped out; but Truman fought side by side with
his neighbors, rising to Captain and making life-long friends.

After the war, Truman and an Army buddy became partners in a Kansas City men's store, only to go broke in 1921
when times turned bad. So Truman, married by then and
needing work, accepted an offer from the political boss of
Kansas City, Thomas J. Pendergast, to run for County Judge.
In Kansas City, this office is not a judicial one but an admin-
istrative one, requiring not so much legal training as good
sense in awarding road-building contracts. Pendergast guessed
that Truman's popularity with his wartime friends would
make him a useful vote getter, and he was right. Truman was
elected in 1922 and said later, "My whole political career is
based upon my war service and war associates." [7]

Even though the Pendergast machine developed a reputation for corruption, Truman did his job so well that he
was able to run successfully for the U.S. Senate in 1934. There,
again, he worked hard enough and made a good enough name
for himself so that in 1940 he was reelected, even though
his old benefactor, Tom Pendergast, had been sent to jail
for cheating on his income tax.

Those were the days when the U.S. was beginning to spend
more and more money on armaments. Truman wanted the
money to be spent carefully, and he became chairman of a
committee to investigate the National Defense Program. It
was estimated that this Truman committee saved the tax-
payers fifteen billion dollars, earning for its chairman such

a national reputation that in 1944, when Roosevelt wanted a new man as Vice-President, he chose the Senator from Missouri.

On the morning of April 13, 1945, when Harry S. Truman walked into the oval office so long occupied by Roosevelt and sat down in the President's chair, he seemed to a Roosevelt assistant who brought him letters and papers "almost sacrilegiously small." [8] Across the country, millions more wondered about this former haberdasher with the thick glasses, Tom Pendergast's piano-playing friend. Was he big enough for Roosevelt's chair? Certainly, Roosevelt had not prepared him for it, giving him no special briefings or responsibilities: since the inauguration in January, Roosevelt had been in Washington only about one day in three. Therefore, Truman's first job as President was to find out in detail what was going on. The first day after he was sworn in he had his first meeting with the Chiefs of Staff and the Secretaries of War and Navy, who began telling him of the war that had to be won and of the twelve million men of whom he was now Commander in Chief.

World War II was fought by fifty-seven nations on every ocean and on every continent except North and South America. Germany, Italy, and Japan started it; the U.S., Britain, Russia, and the other Allies, as they called themselves, finished it. The war was a global slaughter in which, not counting the millions of civilians who died because of air raids and persecution, more than fifteen million men were killed fighting. Moreover, although it began as a classic struggle for power among individual nations, the war grew to be a clash of fundamental ideas about the nature of human beings —freedom and democracy mortally challenged by what came to be called totalitarianism.

In the 1920's and 1930's, in much of the world, it proved possible for ruthless leaders to twist the longings of their countrymen into powerful and aggressive mass movements. Through propaganda, on the one hand, and terror, on the other, these leaders acquired total control, their will and their word overriding law, tradition, ethics, and individual rights. Always the total dictator preached that his people and nation should dominate, by force, at least that part of the rest of the world closest to them: might, said the totalitarians, made right.

In the years since World War II, Communism has been the most dangerous form of totalitarianism, but before World War II the threat came from Fascism.

The name "Fascist" came from the Latin word *fasces,* which were bundles of wooden rods with the head of an ax sticking out, all tied together by red straps. In ancient Rome, they were carried in processions as symbols of authority. In modern Italy, in 1919, Benito Mussolini, who wanted to revive for his countrymen the past glory of Rome, formed a political party with the fasces as its symbol. Devoted to violence and power, by 1922 the Fascists and their black-shirted strong-arm squads had so intimidated all their rivals that Mussolini became Italy's Prime Minister. Then, by means that included murder, Mussolini became Italy's dictator, "Il Duce" (ill DOO-chay), the leader, he and he alone running the country, glorifying conquest, craving war.

Halfway around the world, the people of Japan were hearing similar ideas. Japanese Army officers, especially, believed their country should seize an empire. They had been impressed by the military power of Europe and America. Only with comparable power and the empire it could bring, they argued, could Japan's crowded people have the raw materials and markets they needed to prosper.

In 1931, Japanese troops in northeast China, in Manchuria, started a war, taking over the whole area by force, renaming it Manchukuo. China protested to the League of Nations, which had been established after World War I to keep the peace, but the League merely appointed a commission to investigate. It did not physically intervene. So, the Japanese military men went on to take over their own government and then plan the conquest of every other Asian government from Korea to Burma. They called what they wanted the "Greater East Asia Co-Prosperity Sphere," but it was really just another name for empire. By 1941, General Hideki Tojo was top man.

Formidable as were Mussolini in Italy and Tojo in Japan, however—as great a testament as each man's career was to the apparent effectiveness of force—both paled in comparison to Hitler in Germany. If ever there was a question about whether one man could change history, this man's life should answer it.

Adolf Hitler was born near the German border in Austria on April 20, 1889. He grew up lonely and unsuccessful, a poor student whose grades were not good enough for him to become an artist or architect, as he wanted. When he moved to Vienna at the age of twenty, he earned a living painting advertisements.

In 1913, Hitler emigrated to Munich, in Germany, and in 1914 he enlisted in the German Army. He became a messenger on Germany's Western Front in World War I, where he was shot in the leg and gassed but where, somehow, he felt at home, serving well enough to be awarded the Iron Cross, First Class.

After that war, Hitler went back to Munich and into politics, shouting his ideas at all who would listen, shouting down any who tried to argue. Like many other Germans, Hitler believed that his country had had to endure the humiliation of the Treaty of Versailles—the treaty ending World War I—not so much because the Army had been defeated in battle as because of betrayal by the new democratic government in Berlin. In fact, as even the high command of the Army admitted, the German government had been faced with the choice of accepting the terms of Versailles or of inviting invasion, and it had chosen the treaty. But, to Hitler,

the politicans had given the Army a "stab in the back." Defeat of Germany for any reason, of course, was intolerable
to Hitler because he thought the Germans were a "master
race" who were the rightful rulers of Europe and the world.
He also thought the Jews, in every country, were Germany's
enemy, and he hated them with a blind passion. Like Mussolini, Hitler believed that all life was struggle and that the
strong should rule and the weak serve. Hitler was contemptuous of democracy and Christianity, with their concern
for the individual person. He was, in fact, contemptuous of
everything gentle and tender. He believed no one should be
trusted, that ruthlessness and willpower could accomplish
anything, that lying, cheating, stealing, murdering—any
means at all—were permissible in the fight for power.

In Munich, in 1919, Hitler helped organize the National
Socialist German Workers' party, abbreviated to the Nazi
party from the sound of the first two syllables of the German word for "national." Its symbol was the swastika, the
twisted cross. As a party leader and organizer, Hitler seemed
at first glance an unimpressive man, with his dirty trench-
coat, a falling lock of black hair, and a square little mustache. But Hitler was one of the greatest orators and propagandists the world has ever known, his harsh voice repeating, repeating, repeating the lies and the hatred and the
dreams on which the Nazis built a following. Otto Strasser,
who worked with Hitler, wrote: "I have been asked many
times what is the secret of Hitler's extraordinary power as
a speaker. I can only attribute it to his uncanny intuition,
which infallibly diagnoses the ills from which his audience
is suffering." [9] Others spoke of Hitler's "hypnotic" eyes, of
his ability as an actor, of his hysterical rages. Whatever his
lure, the Germans took it. Humiliated by defeat in World
War I, impoverished by the inflation and then depression
that followed, intimidated by brown-shirted Nazi bullies,
they permitted Adolf Hitler, in 1933, to become their Chancellor.

Quickly, by terror and propaganda, Hitler transformed

Germany into a dictatorship in which he alone was the leader, "Der Führer." The secret police, the *Gestapo,* shot or imprisoned anyone who challenged Hitler's authority. German soldiers took this vow: "I swear by God this holy oath: I will render unconditional obedience to the Führer of the German Reich and People, Adolf Hitler, the Supreme Commander of the Armed Forces, and will be ready, as a brave soldier, to stake my life at any time for this oath." [10]

(In Hitler's view, Germany had had two previous Reichs, or empires. He boasted that his Third Reich would last for a thousand years.)

In 1924, long before he became Chancellor, Hitler had spent nearly a year in jail because he had tried to take over the government in Bavaria. While in jail he had written a book called *Mein Kampf*—My Struggle—in which he described in detail what he felt was his mission—to create a militant Germany strong enough to enlarge her borders to include German people living in neighboring countries and to give to all Germans *Lebensraum*—living space. But hardly anyone outside Germany took him seriously until it was almost too late.

The problem was that Britain and France had suffered such terrible losses in the trenches of World War I that the people of those countries found the idea of another war all but unthinkable. Hitler understood this, constantly talking peace even though he planned attack. Therefore, in 1934, when Germany began rearming—violating the terms of the Versailles Treaty—Britain and France protested, but they did not act.

In 1935, Italy invaded Ethiopia, in Africa. The Ethiopian Emperor, Haile Selassie, appealed for help to the League of Nations, but the League had no military forces and could not intervene.

In 1936, Hitler sent his troops into the Rhineland, on the border with France, violating that part of the Versailles Treaty which specified that the Rhineland be demilitarized. No one even threatened force to stop him.

In 1936, Germany and Italy practiced for the battles to come by helping General Francisco Franco win a civil war in Spain and become dictator there. The rest of the world was troubled but not outraged. (It was during the Spanish Civil War that a famous Fascist technique was given its name: Franco's Army attacked Madrid with four columns of troops and with what a Spanish general called a "fifth column" of sympathizers inside the city.)

Nineteen thirty-six was also the year in which Germany and Italy agreed on common aims, Mussolini likening the partnership to an axis " 'round which all those European states which are animated by a desire for collaboration and peace may work together." [11] To those who fought them, Germany and Italy and, later, Japan, too, were known as the Axis powers.

In 1937, Japan went to war against all China. The United States did not even stop selling Japan oil and scrap iron.

In 1938, Germany marched into Austria and part of Czechoslovakia.

With hindsight, it seems that World War II might have been prevented had Hitler's aggression been stopped, by force, earlier. But Britain and France made the mistake of hoping that if they permitted Hitler to have just a little of what he wanted—if they appeased him—he would be satisfied. Instead, achievement of a little just increased his desire for more.

In 1938, Hitler threatened war unless he could take over part of Czechoslovakia called the Sudetenland, in which there were many German-speaking people. The "master race," as he saw it, must be united. The Prime Minister of Britain, Neville Chamberlain, and the Prime Minister of France, Edouard Daladier, flew to Munich for a conference with Hitler and there agreed that he could take the Sudetenland if he would promise not to take anything more. The deal was made.

At the time, the Munich Agreement was popular. Czechoslovakia might have been "sold down the river," but no one

in Britain or France wanted war, and when Chamberlain
returned to London, he leaned out a second-story window of
Number Ten Downing Street, the British White House, and
told a crowd of admirers that he had come home from Germany bringing peace with honor. "I believe," he said, "it is
peace in our time."

Few words seem more hollow today, which is why
Munich and the umbrella Chamberlain usually carried be-
came bitter symbols of the fundamental lesson of World War
II: that appeasement of a dictator does not pay.

Hitler demonstrated the worthlessness of his word in the
spring of 1939 when he broke the Munich Agreement and
took over all Czechoslovakia. In August of 1939, Germany
and Russia signed a ten-year agreement not to fight each
other and divided Eastern Europe between them. On September 1, 1939, Germany invaded Poland, and that, at last,
brought a reaction: on September 3, 1939, Britain and
France declared war.

Hitler's new planes and tanks brought quick victory in
the East: *blitzkrieg,* it came to be called, "lightning war."
Germany took Denmark and Norway, too—her invasion
plans of Norway actually drawn up, in part, by the traitor
Vidkun Quisling, a Nazi at heart whom the Germans installed as top man during their occupation and whose name
became the despicable synonym for one who collaborates
with an enemy. (His countrymen tried, sentenced, and shot
Quisling immediately after the war.) Then, on May 10, 1940,
Germany turned west to attack France, Holland, Belgium,
and Luxembourg. German power—especially her tanks and
divebombers—produced a break-through to the sea, almost
trapping the best British and French divisions. The British
assembled eight hundred and fifty ships and small boats,
and from May 26 to June 3, 1940, although under constant
air attack, they evacuated more than 300,000 men from the
port and beaches of Dunkirk in France, near the Belgian
border. These troops had to leave behind all their equip-

ment, but they lived to fight again, and the British called Dunkirk a miracle.

By June of 1940, the Germans were in Paris, where Hitler danced a little jig of joy and ordered to be brought from a museum the same old railroad dining car in which France had dictated surrender terms to Germany at the end of World War I. It was placed in a forest northeast of Paris on the exact spot at which the 1918 surrender had taken place, but this time, on June 23, 1940, it was France that surrendered to Germany.

Now with her ally on the European continent fallen and the U.S. not yet ready to join the fight, Britain faced Hitler's power by herself. But the British people had both great courage and a great leader, one of the most accomplished men of his time, a soldier, an author and orator, an artist and bricklayer, a statesman with a long view of history and the powerful capacity to inspire, Winston Leonard Spencer Churchill.

Churchill was born at Blenheim Palace in Oxfordshire on November 30, 1874. One of his ancestors, John Churchill, was a soldier so distinguished that he was made the Duke of Marlborough and given an estate named for his most famous victory, over the French and their allies, in 1704, at Blenheim on the Danube River in what is now Germany.

Winston Churchill was a slow student, but his family was sufficiently influential so he was admitted to Harrow, one of Britain's great "public" schools, even though he had written nothing on his Latin entrance examination. At Harrow, he did well in English but so poorly in Latin and mathematics that his father had to give up all hope that his son would become a lawyer, settling on soldiering instead. Twice Churchill failed the entrance exams to Sandhurst, Britain's West Point, but he finally passed, and having done so, he did well. As a young officer he served in Cuba and India, and in the Middle East, at a place in the Sudan called Omduran, he participated in one of the last great cavalry charges in history.

Churchill's mother was an American, Jeanette Jerome, whose father was the owner of *The New York Times*. Perhaps in part because of his influence, perhaps just because of his own aptitude, Churchill the soldier also became Churchill the journalist, reporting on his military campaigns for London newspapers. By the time he was twenty-five years old, Churchill had written three books—one, *The Story of the Malakand Field Force* (based on his Indian service), a best seller. Then he decided on still a third career—as a politician. He resigned from the Army to stand for Parliament but was defeated and went off to South Africa and more adventures as a correspondent, covering the Boer War. He was captured; he escaped; and in 1900, better known and now something of a war hero, Churchill stood for Parliament again, and this time he won, going on to devote the rest of his long and productive life to all three of his professions.

In Britain, the top men of the majority party in the House of Commons run the government, the Majority Leader being the (King's or Queen's) Prime Minister. With one party or another, Churchill served in most of the key government ministries: twice he was First Lord of the Admiralty (in the U.S. its equivalent is Secretary of the Navy) and twice he was Prime Minister.

He prepared the British Navy for World War I and then commanded a battalion of the Royal Scots Fusiliers in France. He wrote biography and history and won the Nobel Prize for Literature (in 1953); he learned to fly an airplane; he became a good enough bricklayer to get a union card; some of his landscapes were exhibited at the Royal Academy; but above all, Churchill was a leader whose long cigar and two fingers upheld in a "V" for Victory sign became worldwide symbols of courage and whose unexcelled command of the English language—spoken and written—inspired free men everywhere.

"He is History's Child," said the President of the United

States on January 24, 1965, when Churchill died, "and what he said and what he did will never die."

When Germany invaded France in May of 1940 and all who had practiced appeasement were discredited, Churchill became Britain's Prime Minister. He had been one of the few to sound a warning about Germany's rearmament and Britain's weakness, calling Munich a "defeat without a war." As Prime Minister, Churchill told the House of Commons the war would not be easy. "I have nothing to offer," he warned, "but blood, toil, tears, and sweat." [12] He knew Britain was next on Hitler's list, and just after Dunkirk he said: "Let us therefore brace ourselves to our duties, and so bear ourselves that, if the British Empire and its Commonwealth last for a thousand years, men will say, 'This was their finest hour.' " [13]

Hitler decided that if he were going to conquer Britain, he would have to invade, and if he were to invade successfully, he would have to control the air. The Battle of Britain, therefore, was fought in the air.

The German Air Force, the Luftwaffe, tried to destroy Britain's airfields and planes and the factories in which they were built. Britain's Royal Air Force tried to prevent it.

The battle began in July of 1940, and the RAF did its job well, shooting down nearly two German bombers for every plane it lost. So by September, the Germans shifted their objective from the airfields and factories to the British people themselves. Beginning on the night of September 7, 1940, London was bombed every night for fifty-seven nights, by an average of two hundred planes per night.

But the RAF and the people survived what came to be called "the Blitz," prompting Churchill to say of the brave young pilots, "Never in the field of human conflict was so much owed by so many to so few," [14] and to write of all his countrymen, ". . . the British people held the fort ALONE till those who hitherto had been half blind were half ready." [15]

The British endured much for many reasons, not the least Churchill's staunch example. Speaking to the boys at his old school, Churchill said, "Never give in, never give in, never, never, never, never—in nothing, great or small, large or petty—never give in except to convictions of honor and good sense." [16] To Parliament on June 4, 1940, he said: "Even though large tracts of Europe and many old and famous States have fallen or may fall into the grip of the Gestapo and all the odious apparatus of Nazi rule, we shall not flag or fail. We shall go on to the end, we shall fight in France, we shall fight in the seas and oceans, we shall fight with growing confidence and growing strength in the air, we shall defend our island, whatever the cost may be, we shall fight on the beaches, we shall fight on the landing grounds, we shall fight in the hills; we shall never surrender, and even if, which I do not for a moment believe, this island or a large part of it were subjugated and starving, then our Empire beyond the seas, armed and guarded by the British Fleet, would carry on the struggle, until, in God's good time, the New World, with all its power and might, steps forth to the rescue and liberation of the Old." [17]

The outcome of the Battle of Britain forced Hitler to postpone his plans for invasion. He turned east again, attacking Russia—despite the nonaggression pact—on June 22, 1941.

The Battle of Britain also had an effect in the United States, helping kill isolationism. During the 1930's, most Americans had thought they could stay out of war simply by refusing to become involved in the arguments of the older nations. Protected by two oceans, they thought at first that Hitler and the war in China were other people's worries. Congress passed a series of laws designed to keep the U.S. neutral.

By the time of the Battle of Britain, however, most Americans were neutral no more. In September of 1940, the U.S. traded Britain fifty destroyers for some West Indian bases.

"Give us the tools," Churchill had said, "and we will finish the job." [18] American convoys began steaming to Britain loaded with materials that made the U.S., as Roosevelt had put it, "the great arsenal of democracy." [19] The "half-blind" became "half-ready," and in December of 1941 the U.S. went to war.

Most Americans had decided long before 1941 that the Axis was the enemy and Britain the friend. Still, enough of the old isolationism lingered for it to take a dramatic event to change sympathy into alliance. The Japanese supplied it.

The Japanese dream, the Greater East Asia Co-Prosperity Sphere, was to stretch from Korea and Manchuria through China, down into French Indo-China, out to the Philippines and the Dutch East Indies, and around to Malaya and Burma. This was to be Japan's empire.

Possibly because of all they had taken freely before, possibly because of the history of appeasement in Europe, the military men running Japan thought they could get and keep this empire by occupying it quickly and by destroying the American fleet in the Pacific.

On the Sunday morning of December 7, 1941, much of the U.S. Pacific fleet was at anchor in Pearl Harbor near Honolulu, in Hawaii. Suddenly, with no warning, at 7:55 A.M., 353 Japanese planes from six aircraft carriers attacked. Of eight American battleships in Pearl Harbor, four were sunk and each of the others damaged. Two auxiliaries were sunk and eight other ships severely damaged. One hundred and eighty-eight U.S. planes were destroyed. Two thousand four hundred and three American servicemen and civilians were killed and 1,178 wounded.

When Franklin Roosevelt asked Congress the next day for a declaration of war against Japan, he called December 7 "a day that will live in infamy." Congress approved a state of war with Japan and, three days later, with Germany and Italy.

At first after Pearl Harbor, the story of the war was one of unbroken Axis victories, the Germans penetrating to the outskirts of Moscow and the Japanese occupying all their empire. But then American shipyards and production lines began operating around the clock, and as a result, the Allies gradually came to dominate the world's sea and air. With this freedom they could begin taking back land.

In 1942, in the Pacific, the U.S. defeated the Japanese Navy at the Battle of Midway and began "island hopping" west toward Tokyo.

In Russia, the great turning point came in the winter of 1942–43, when 200,000 Germans were encircled and captured at the battle of Stalingrad.

In North Africa, in 1942 and 1943, the Allies pushed out the Germans and Italians and set the stage for the invasion of southern Europe.

In 1943, the Allies invaded Sicily and Italy, and the government of Italy surrendered.

In 1944, the Allies invaded France. D-Day, the day of invasion, was June 6.

In 1945, the war ended—on May 7 in Europe and on August 14 in the Pacific.

It is easy to dramatize war but hard to report it. The strategies of headquarters can make it seem a thrilling game, which it is not. The courage of an infantryman can make it seem noble, which it is not. It is true that war's adventure and comradeship have made many veterans look back on their service with nostalgia. But, on balance, war remains as the Civil War General William Tecumseh Sherman is said to have described it—"hell."

Bill Mauldin was a cartoonist for the U.S. Army newspaper, *Stars and Stripes,* in Italy. He knew about fear and mud and the life and death of the G.I.—the ordinary American soldier, so nicknamed from the initials for Government Issue, which referred to everything standard, the Army way.

Mauldin wrote this: ". . . you don't fight a kraut by

Marquis of Queensbury rules. You shoot him in the back, you blow him apart with mines, you kill or maim him the quickest and most effective way you can with the least danger to yourself. He does the same to you. He tricks you and cheats you, and if you don't beat him at his own game you don't live to appreciate your own nobleness. But, you don't become a killer. No normal man who has smelled and associated with death ever wants to see any more of it. . . . The surest way to become a pacifist is to join the infantry." [20]

The pilot and the marine and the seaman and the prisoner and the widow and the mother all had their own points of view.

For years after the war, there were rumors that Hitler was still alive, but the best evidence points to his having taken his own life on April 30, 1945. As the Russians closed in on his underground bunker in Berlin, Hitler shot himself in the mouth. He was fifty-six years old.

Two days before, in Italy, Benito Mussolini was caught by some of his countrymen, who shot him and hung up his body in the city of Milan.

Japan had agreed to surrender on August 14, after two of her cities had been leveled by atomic bombs. The formal surrender ceremony took place on the deck of the battleship *Missouri* in Tokyo Bay on September 2. General Tojo attempted to shoot himself but failed; he was tried as a war criminal, found guilty, and hanged.

There is one last part to the grisly record of Fascism: the almost unbelievable story of what the Nazis did in their concentration camps. At first these camps were just prisons for Hitler's enemies, but during the war they became the scenes of organized mass execution, especially of the Jews Hitler hated. In fulfillment of Hitler's order of what he called "the final solution of the Jewish problem," Nazi officials shipped to Buchenwald and Dachau in Germany, to Mauthausen in Austria, to Auschwitz in Poland, and to the other camps, locked freight cars packed with Jewish people.

At these camps the Jews were ordered into large rooms to take "showers." But instead of water they got poison gas.

Camp commandants competed with each other to see who could develop the most efficient gas chambers. At Auschwitz they could kill two thousand people at a time, three times a day. By 1945, the Nazis had killed about six million Jews.

Not counting civilians, World War II had cost the Allies roughly 10,650,000 men killed or missing, and the Axis, 4,650,000. But the war had also taught some lessons, such as the folly of appeasement: American foreign policy after the war would be solidly based on that belief. Another lesson was the need for some kind of new international peace-keeping machinery. In Moscow in 1943, the leaders of the U.S., Britain, Russia, and China had agreed that there should be a United Nations organization. Diplomats planned the U.N. at conferences in Washington in the late summer of 1944, and Harry Truman's first decision as President was that the conference in San Francisco to found the U.N. would open on schedule in spite of President Roosevelt's death.

Therefore, on April 25, 1945, the representatives of forty-six nations gathered to write a charter that might keep the peace so newly and dearly won. They assembled in the late afternoon in the San Francisco Opera House, built as a memorial to those who died in World War I. There was a moment of silence and then a message of welcome from President Truman, who said, "We must build a new world, a far better world. . . ."

The rise of Fascism . . . the brutality of dictatorship . . . the tragedy of war . . . the concentration camps . . . all these facts had helped dispel some of the hopeful illusions of the would-be peacemakers of the early 1920's. Now, in 1945, a *New York Times* reporter looked down from the balcony of the San Francisco Opera House and wrote: "The mood of the assembly was so like the mood of the war—a war without parades, without slogans, without songs—that one had the feeling that men were getting down to the business of making peace in the same grim spirit of determination of soldiers making war. . . ." [21]

Some people insist that the only way to prevent nationalistic wars is for the individual nations of the world to give up some of their power over their own affairs to a world government, just as the thirteen original American states gave up some of their sovereignty to the new Federal government. But this was not possible at San Francisco: the U.S., for one nation, would not permit it. So the U.N. Charter put peace-keeping power in the hands of the five principal allies who had just won the war. The hope was that the U.S., Britain, France, Russia, and China would continue to be a Grand Alliance; at least, no one held out much hope for peace if the big five did not cooperate. Over the objections of many of the smaller nations, each of the big five was given a veto in the U.N. Security Council, which meant that the U.N. would be able to act to keep peace only if none of the big five voted "no."

The Charter proved far from perfect, but at least it ended the war with a peaceful promise. The delegates signed the Charter on June 26, 1945, followed by five others later but still in time to be considered original members (fifty-one in all). As they signed, President Truman told them: "If we had had this Charter a few years ago—and above all, the will to use it—millions now dead would be alive." It was a happy moment but, in retrospect, a bittersweet one because the Grand Alliance so quickly disintegrated. The great challenge of the years since has been to keep peace not through but among the big five, with the price of failure now many times even that of World War II.

*Chapter Two*

# THE BOMB

JUST before five-thirty on the morning of July 16, 1945, a sphere of tightly fitted prisms of high explosive was detonated on a one-hundred-foot-high steel tower in the desert about fifty miles from Alamogordo, in southern New Mexico. Inside this sphere was a hollow core of plutonium, about the size of a baseball. Inside this was a hollow core of beryllium, about the size of a ping-pong ball, coated with a layer of polonium. The high explosive implosion, as the scientists called it, hit the plutonium ball from every direction simultaneously, so squeezing it that in less than a hundredth of a millionth of a second there was begun the world's first atomic explosion. The beryllium and polonium, nicknamed the "urchin," combined to form a kind of trigger, guaranteeing the plutonium enough energy to start a chain reaction.

The plutonium sphere weighed only about ten pounds, and in the explosion only about a gram of this—less than half the size of a dime—actually was transformed into energy. Yet that energy was nearly twenty thousand times greater than the force that would have been produced by the explosion of a ton of high explosive, such as TNT. The bomb's temperature, in the center, was about a hundred million degrees Fahrenheit. The cloud it created went eight miles high. Its light was seen four hundred and fifty miles away.

*46*

It rattled windows two hundred miles away. It destroyed all life within a mile of it, and for four hundred yards around it, it burned the sand into green glass.

In their reinforced shelters or trenches ten thousand yards away from what they called "Zero," many of the scientists and engineers who had built the bomb could describe its effect only in the language of poetry and religion. Dr. J. Robert Oppenheimer thought of Hindu scripture: "If the radiance of a thousand suns were to burst at once into the sky that would be like the splendor of the Mighty One," and, "I am become death, the shatterer of worlds." [1]

Brigadier General Thomas F. Farrell reported to the Secretary of War: "It was golden, purple, violet, gray and blue. It lighted every peak, crevasse and ridge of the near-by mountain range with a clarity and beauty that cannot be described but must be seen to be imagined. It was that beauty the great poets dream about but describe most poorly and inadequately. Thirty seconds after the explosion came, first, the air blast, pressing hard against the people and things; to be followed almost immediately by the strong, sustained awesome roar which warned of doomsday and made us feel that we puny things were blasphemous to dare tamper with the forces heretofore reserved to the Almighty." [2]

The only reporter present wrote: "It was a sunrise such as the world had never seen, a great green super-sun climbing in a fraction of a second to a height of more than 8,000 feet, rising ever higher until it touched the clouds, lighting up earth and sky all around with a dazzling luminosity. Up it went, a great ball of fire about a mile in diameter, changing colors as it kept shooting upward, from deep purple to orange, expanding, growing bigger, rising as it expanded, an elemental force freed from its bonds after being chained for billions of years." [3]

Another scientist said: "I am sure that at the end of the world—in the last millisecond of the earth's existence—Man will see what we have just seen." [4]

The terrible beauty of Alamogordo was a spectacular warning that all-out war was about to become all-out suicide. It
also revealed perhaps the most important revolution of our
time—the staggering increase there has been in the total
amount of knowledge about the physical world. The nuclear
chemist Dr. Glenn T. Seaborg said in 1962: "Man has
progressed further in the fields of science and technology in
the past several decades than in all of previous history." [5]

By the middle sixties, the U.S. government was spending
more than fifteen billion dollars a year on research and
development—more than it spent on such purposes in all
the years from 1789 to 1945, including the cost of the bomb.
Worldwide, in the first half of the twentieth century, the
total number of scientists and engineers doubled about
every twelve years, permitting science writers to estimate
that "90 percent of all the scientists who ever lived are
alive today." The accomplishments of this growing army
were recorded in perhaps fifty thousand publications printing what may have been a million articles a year.

The scientific revolution had its beginnings in the astron-
omy of Babylon and ancient Greece, but it began to accel-
erate only about four hundred years ago. Up until that
time, churchmen had speculated and craftsmen had tinkered,
but the same men had not done both. In the late sixteenth
and seventeenth centuries, however, it began to be acceptable for educated gentlemen to use not only their brains but
also their hands, and with this development modern science
began.

The word "science" comes from the Latin word for knowledge, but we now mean by it not just a collection of facts
and ideas but also a way of getting them. Science is the
systematic search for the kinds of truth that can be measured,
a marriage of the experimental and the theoretical, pro-
gressing by reliance first on one, then on the other—observ-
ing, theorizing, testing, and testing again.

The results of this measured search for order increase

constantly: unlike a poet or artist, a scientist has available to him the accumulated knowledge of all his predecessors, which permits him to begin where they stopped. This is why this method of pursuing truth has had such conspicuous success and why one of its devotees has called it "the most beautiful and wonderful collective work of the mind of man." [6]

Since its beginnings, modern science has been an international community whose members have paid little attention to barriers of boundary or politics. Galileo, Copernicus, and Kepler lived in what are now Italy, Poland, and Germany. On their work, the great Englishman, Sir Isaac Newton, built. In our time, perhaps the greatest scientist was a man who was himself first a German, then a Swiss, then an American . . . a man who was a pacifist, a musician, a humanitarian, and—beyond all else—a theoretical physicist, Albert Einstein. Had it not been for his insight, the bomb could not have been built.

Einstein was born in southern Germany, in Ulm, on March 14, 1879, and he grew up in Munich. As an adult, he remembered the sense of wonder he had had when his father gave him a compass when he was a boy. In school, Einstein refused to learn what did not interest him, but he taught himself more geometry and calculus than even his teachers knew.

Einstein studied mathematics and physics in Zurich, in Switzerland, and while working for his Ph.D., he got a job examining patents for the Swiss government. He discovered that he could do his job with just a few hours' work each day, so he spent the rest of the time doing what he loved— trying to understand the physical world.

In 1905, at the age of twenty-six, Einstein published five major scientific papers, one of them his Special Theory of Relativity. According to this theory, the speed of light is always the same; size—or, in the physicist's more precise

term, "mass"—and even time vary depending on their rela-
tion to the speed of light.

One consequence of the Theory of Relativity was that
energy and mass were interchangeable expressions of the
same reality. It was almost as if matter were "solid" energy
and energy "liquid" matter. Einstein's famous formula for
this was $E = mc^2$. E is energy, m is mass, and c is the speed
of light. According to this formula, whenever even a little
m is lost, a lot of E is released. This is the underlying theory
of the bomb and the theory that explains how just one gram
of matter can create the "radiance of a thousand suns."

In 1921, Einstein won the world's greatest scientific honor,
the Nobel Prize. It had been established by Alfred Nobel,
a Swedish chemist who made a fortune from his invention
of dynamite and other explosives. When he died in 1896,
he left his money in trust to be used to honor achievement
in five fields: physics, chemistry, medicine or physiology,
literature, and peace.

After his Special Theory was published in 1905, Einstein
taught in Switzerland, Czechoslovakia, and Holland, and beginning in 1913 he was director of the Kaiser Wilhelm
Institute in Berlin. Germany then was plunging into World
War I, fiercely patriotic, but Einstein was a pacifist. He considered war despicable and nationalism infantile. None of
these ideas endeared him to his countrymen.

When World War I was over and Hitler's Nazi party began attacking German Jews, Einstein's life was threatened
and one of his friends was murdered. So in 1933, when Hitler came to power, Einstein moved to the United States, to
the Institute for Advanced Study in Princeton, New Jersey,
saying, ". . . as long as I have any choice, I will stay only
in a country where political liberty, tolerance and equal-
ity of all citizens before the law prevail." [7]

A French physicist wrote of Einstein's emigration: "It's
as important an event as would be the transfer of the Vatican
from Rome to the New World. The Pope of Physics has

moved and the United States will now become the center of the natural sciences." [8]

To those who knew him, Einstein was a gentle, beautiful character, eccentric but almost saintly. In the winter he covered his long white hair with a stocking cap. In the summer he rarely wore socks. Once he used a $1,500 check for a bookmark and then lost the book and the check with it.

But Einstein's simplicity was part of his genius: he devoted his time only to what he considered most important. He wrote: "I am a horse for single harness, not cut out for tandem or team work. I have never belonged wholeheartedly to country or state, to my circle of friends, or even to my own family. These ties have always been accompanied by a vague aloofness, and the wish to withdraw into myself increases with the years." [9]

Einstein lived quietly in Princeton with his secretary and stepdaughter, his piano and violin and books and pipes and Chinese puzzles, cherishing what he called "that solitude which is painful to youth but delicious in the years of maturity." [10] But he cared enough about the world from which he had withdrawn to give violin concerts during World War II to help raise money for those the war had impoverished, and after the war Einstein worked for world government and total disarmament.

His life, however, remained science. In 1952, when he was asked to become president of the new state of Israel, he refused, with thanks, in order to continue the almost religious quest to which he had devoted the last half of his long life—trying to find laws that would apply equally to all parts of the universe. Einstein's theories had explained the behavior of much of the world, but they had not proved correct for the tiniest parts of it, where only the laws of chance and probability seemed applicable. Einstein could not accept such an apparent lack of order, saying he could not believe that God plays dice with the Cosmos. But Einstein was never successful in his search.

Albert Einstein died in his sleep at the age of seventy-six on April 18, 1955. His brain was removed for scientific study, and then his body was cremated. As he had wished, he has no grave, and his only monument is his work.

The insight of Einstein and others made physics, especially nuclear physics, the frontier of science in the 1920's and 1930's, men and women in every major center of research trying to discover the fundamental structure of matter. They began with the elements of which everything in nature is made—ninety-two of them, from hydrogen, the lightest, to uranium, the heaviest. Each element is a collection of molecules, and each molecule is made of atoms, each atom formed like a tiny solar system with its sun called the nucleus and the planets called electrons. The nucleus of each atom consists of one or more tiny particles called protons and—in all but hydrogen—at least one particle called a neutron. A hydrogen atom's nucleus is just one proton; the nucleus of an atom of the most common kind of uranium has 92 protons and 146 neutrons, the sum of which gives the element its mass number, $U^{238}$.

The word "atom" comes from a Greek word meaning "indivisible," and until our time this was apt: no one knew that an atom could be split. But in 1934, in Rome, a brilliant young Italian named Enrico Fermi split the atom in half—without knowing what he had done. Like many other physicists then, Fermi was fascinated by the phenomenon of radioactivity by which some chemical elements, such as radium, decay gradually, giving off tiny particles and rays of energy. In France in January, 1934, Frederic Joliot and his wife, Irene Curie, had created radioactivity artificially, and Fermi was doing the same thing, adding neutrons to the nuclei of atoms of every element, trying to make them unstable. When Fermi bombarded uranium with neutrons, he created what he thought was a group of wholly new elements but which was revealed for what it really was four years later in Berlin by the Germans Otto Hahn and Fritz Strassmann. They dared to write that whereas other experimenters had chipped a few pieces off the "indivisible" atom, what Fermi had achieved and what they had repeated was to split the atom roughly in half.

At Christmastime in 1938, news of what came to be called nuclear fission traveled fast. Hahn and Strassmann wrote to Sweden to their former colleague, Lise Meitner, a brilliant physicist whose religion had forced her to flee Hitler's Germany. She told her nephew, Otto Frisch. (It was an American biologist friend of Frisch who suggested the name "fission," the description of what had been done to the atom reminding him of the fission, the dividing, of a living cell.) Frisch told the great Danish scientist with whom he worked in Copenhagen, Niels Bohr, and in early 1939 on a visit, Bohr took the news to the United States.

It was part of America's great good fortune that it could attract to its shores some of the most brilliant refugees from Fascism. In early 1939 Fermi had just arrived at Columbia University in New York, having become so uncomfortable living under Mussolini that when he went to Stockholm to receive a Nobel Prize in late 1938, he took his family with him and kept right on going. Another top physicist, newly arrived from Germany, was Leo Szilard, and there were many more. To Szilard and others it seemed probable that the splitting of one uranium atom would release enough new neutrons to split other uranium atoms and that the result would be a "chain reaction." If this chain reaction took place very quickly, they reasoned, there would be an explosion of almost unbelievable power. No one knew whether an atomic bomb could be built, but if it could be, the European refugees—especially—were fearful of what it might mean in the hands of a dictator such as Hitler. So in 1939, when the Nazis imposed a blackout of all news about German experiments with uranium, Leo Szilard decided that the time had come for someone to talk about atomic fission to the President of the United States.

Szilard and others persuaded Albert Einstein to write a

letter to Roosevelt, which he did on August 2, 1939. It referred to the possibility of ". . . a nuclear chain reaction in a large mass of uranium," and then it said: "This new phenomenon would also lead to the construction of bombs, and it is conceivable, though much less certain, that extremely powerful bombs of a new type may thus be constructed. . . ."

Szilard chose Einstein to write the letter partly because he thought his famous name would be the best lure, but even so, he was not certain the President would read the letter. Therefore, Szilard enlisted the support of Alexander Sachs, a brilliant New York economist and a friend of Roosevelt's. Sachs got an appointment with the President for October 11, 1939, and did his best to explain what Einstein had written, but he was not satisfied that he had made the President understand. He stayed up all that night wondering how he could best present the atomic idea, and just before dawn, on a park bench in Lafayette Square across the street from the White House, Sachs decided on a plan.

At breakfast, Roosevelt teased him, asking, "What bright idea have you got now?"

Sachs replied, "All I want to do is tell you a story."

Sachs told the President how Napoleon Bonaparte had wanted to invade Britain but could not because of the uncertain winds of the English Channel. One day, said Sachs, an American living in Paris came to Napoleon and told him it was possible to propel boats by steam. The American was Robert Fulton, but Napoleon did not listen.

Did you ever wonder, Sachs asked President Roosevelt, how history would have been changed if the Emperor Napoleon had built steamships and been able to cross the Channel and conquer Britain?

Roosevelt said nothing but sent out for a bottle of old French brandy. When it arrived, Roosevelt poured two glasses and said to Sachs, "Alex, what you are after is to see that the Nazis don't blow us up?"

Sachs said, "Precisely."

Roosevelt called in one of his aides, handed him Einstein's letter, and said, "This requires action."

Many physicists felt certain a nuclear chain reaction was possible, but theory and proof are two different things. So, all through 1940, 1941, and 1942, experiments continued aimed at producing a real, not just a theoretical, chain reaction. With government guidance and support, Fermi and his co-workers from Columbia University pooled their talents with another group at the University of Chicago, and there, in a squash court under the West Stands of Stagg Field, Fermi built what came to be called a nuclear reactor, or "pile." It was the shape of a doorknob, lying on its side, about twenty-six feet across. It was made of natural uranium and graphite.

The physicists knew from their earlier experiments that no quantity of natural uranium would sustain a chain reaction by itself. But they also knew that if lumps of natural uranium were dotted in a precise way in a huge stack of graphite, the reactor might go "critical" and a chain reaction begin.

At noon on December 2, 1942, the pile contained about 12,000 pounds of uranium. Every calculation indicated that with just a little more, the work would be done. But Fermi was a man of habit. He ordered everyone to quit for lunch, so it was not until they had come back to work that they were successful—at three-thirty that afternoon.

The squash court and the West Stands have been torn down, but on the wire fence by the sidewalk near the spot where the pile went critical a large plaque reads:

ON DECEMBER 2, 1942
MAN ACHIEVED HERE
THE FIRST SELF-SUSTAINING CHAIN REACTION
AND THEREBY INITIATED THE
CONTROLLED RELEASE OF NUCLEAR ENERGY

Fermi had proved that an atomic bomb might be possible and that power for peaceful purposes might be released from the atom, too.

On that afternoon, wartime security forced those who knew what Fermi had done to use the most guarded language in telling others who needed to know. One such report began: "The Italian navigator has arrived in the new world."

On August 16, 1942, even before Fermi's successful chain reaction, a special section of the Army's Corps of Engineers was created to try to build an atomic bomb. It was called the Manhattan Engineer District, and it was commanded by a self-confident builder, General Leslie R. Groves.

Groves's double job was to manufacture the stuff from which a bomb could be made and to design and build a bomb. In strict secrecy, in just under three years, with the direct and indirect help of more than a half a million people, at a cost of about two billion dollars, the job was done.

The raw material of the atomic bomb was natural uranium from the Belgian Congo and from Canada. Natural uranium is a mixture of three uranium types, or isotopes: one part of $U^{235}$ for every 139 parts of $U^{238}$, plus a tiny fraction of $U^{234}$. In the years since Fermi unwittingly split a uranium atom in Rome, physicists had learned that when natural uranium is bombarded with neutrons, only the atoms of $U^{235}$ split. The $U^{238}$ absorbs neutrons.

But physicists also had learned that when atoms of $U^{238}$ absorb neutrons, they create as a by-product a heavy element called plutonium. Like atoms of $U^{235}$, when atoms of plutonium are hit with neutrons they split. It is $U^{235}$ or plutonium that is the essential fuel of a fission bomb.

In 1942, there was not one millionth of a pound of pure $U^{235}$ or plutonium in existence, no one knew how to get enough, and no one knew which might be produced quicker. General Groves, therefore, tried for both. At Oak Ridge,

Tennessee, he built plants to separate $U^{235}$ from natural uranium. In Hanford, Washington, he built reactors to make plutonium.

Creating the raw stuff of the bomb, however, was just part of the problem, for the bomb still had to be designed and built. This was done at a special laboratory in the isolation of what had been a boy's school on top of a mesa in Los Alamos ("the Cottonwoods"), New Mexico. There were gathered two thousand military men and four thousand civilians, including many of the leading scientists of the U.S. and Britain. The man in charge was a brilliant young physicist named J. Robert Oppenheimer.

Oppenheimer was born in New York City April 22, 1904. As a boy, he was a sheltered prodigy far more interested in geology, mathematics, and the classics than in sports and playmates. His father, a wealthy textile importer, was able to provide special tutors and trips to Europe, which made the boy even more learned.

Oppenheimer devoured Harvard, graduating summa cum laude in three years, absorbing not only physics and chemistry but also philosophy and poetry and Sanskrit, too. He became one of those intense, rare men who was precocious in many fields besides his own.

Oppenheimer studied physics in England, Germany, and Holland and then came home in 1929 to teach in California. He divided his time between the California Institute of Technology in Pasadena and the University of California at Berkeley, learning to teach well, developing the ability to inspire students, training men who went on to lead American physics. When the war came, he was the one chosen to build the bomb.

Oppenheimer helped General Groves choose the Los Alamos site. Then he circled the country persuading scientists to come to work with him, leading them with patience, insight, and success.

The total Oppenheimer story, however, was not without blemish. After World War II, in order that nuclear development in the U.S. could be managed by civilians rather than by the military, all the government's nuclear programs were transferred to a new agency called the Atomic Energy Commission. Oppenheimer was one of the most distinguished scientific advisers to this commission, but on April 12, 1954, the A.E.C. suspended his clearance to see secret information, judging him a security risk. On June 1, 1954, a special review board found Oppenheimer loyal to the United States but still a risk.

The A.E.C. charged Oppenheimer with having had many friends who were Communists. It said his brother and his brother's wife, as well as the woman he almost married and the woman he did marry, were all Communists or former Communists. The A.E.C. accused Oppenheimer of having given generously to Communist-backed causes and of having hired Communists or former Communists at Los Alamos. Most important, it accused him of having lied to security officials.

Oppenheimer admitted his prewar sympathy with some Communist objectives long before he went to Los Alamos, but he denied that he was ever a member of the Communist party or that he had ever accepted Communist theory. He explained that he had become aware of politics and political ideas late in life, after Hitler had come to power in Germany, and that he was just one of many people who supported Communist causes because they seemed genuinely anti-Fascist. Oppenheimer also admitted that he had been slow to report a friend's suggestion that he pass atomic secrets to the Russians and then had invented stories to try to protect his friend. But Oppenheimer insisted he was guilty of nothing more criminal than naïveté.

The A.E.C. did not restore Oppenheimer's clearance, but nearly ten years later, on April 5, 1963, it did give him its highest award for contributions to atomic energy. This was the Enrico Fermi award, named for the "Italian navigator" who had died of cancer November 28, 1954.

Oppenheimer, Fermi, and the others at Los Alamos from 1942 to 1945 were independent spirits who did not take easily to the strict secrecy the Army would have liked to impose. One scientist wrote his wife letters torn into tiny pieces, so the censors would have to fit them all together before they could read them. The same man also broke into the laboratory's most secure combination safe and left inside a slip of paper reading, "Guess who?" It was no wonder that General Groves once said to his Los Alamos security officers, "At great expense we have gathered on this mesa the largest collection of crackpots ever seen." [11]

It was in the spirit of the letter-tearer and safe-cracker that the Los Alamos scientists named their bombs. They had developed two designs. Partly to describe their shapes, partly with Roosevelt and Churchill in mind, they called them: the Thin Man and the Fat Man.

Like Fermi's pile at Chicago, a mass of fissionable material has to be a certain size before a chain reaction will begin, before it becomes critical. Otherwise, too many neutrons escape into the air. The Thin Man bomb, therefore, is a gun in which one piece of pure $U^{235}$ is fired at another. When the two are apart, they are safe, but when the two come together, quickly, they make more than a critical mass.

The Fat Man bomb is based on the principle that a mass of plutonium at normal pressure is safe, even though it is one sphere, but under high pressure, with a compressed surface area, the same mass becomes critical. High explosive crushes the plutonium; the beryllium core furnishes extra neutrons to guarantee that the chain reaction begins. The

Fat Man bomb was the more difficult to build, but because it used less fissionable material than the Thin Man, it was ready to go first. It was the bomb of Alamogordo.

When Harry Truman became President, he knew nothing of the Manhattan project. Investigators for his Senate committee overseeing defense spending had discovered that something important was going on at Oak Ridge and at Hanford. But Secretary of War Stimson paid a personal call on Senator Truman, asking him to call off the investigation, and Truman did. It was only after his first Cabinet meeting, at the White House the night he became President—April 12, 1945—that Truman found out about the bomb. Fittingly, it was Stimson who lingered behind after the others left and broke the news.

About this time, as Allied troops fought their way into Germany, they were accompanied by special teams whose mission it was to discover how close Hitler was to building an atomic bomb. Long before the war was over the answer was known: Germany was at least two years behind the U.S.

Germany surrendered two months before the first bomb was tested, but the war with Japan went on. Therefore, it was President Truman's job to decide whether to use the bomb, and if so, how.

Many of the atomic scientists thought the bomb was too terrible to be used or that it should be demonstrated peacefully before being used against human beings. Among those who felt this way were some of the men who had led the campaign to get the U.S. to build the bomb in the first place. Leo Szilard, for instance, wrote: "During 1943 and part of 1944 our greatest worry was the possibility that Germany would perfect an atomic bomb before the invasion of Europe. . . . In 1945, when we ceased worrying about what the Germans might do to us, we began to worry about what the government of the United States might do to other countries." [12]

Szilard sent an appeal to Roosevelt just before he died urging that the U.S. not use the bomb in the war.

To Truman, however, the decision to use the bomb was justified because of the American lives that might be saved. U.S. officers estimated that the price of invading the Japanese mainland might be as high as half a million Americans killed, and Truman had this price very much in mind. "I don't mind telling you," he recalled on a television program in 1965, "that you don't feel normal when you have to plan hundreds of thousands of complete, final deaths of American boys who are alive and joking and having fun while you are doing your planning. You break your heart and your head trying to figure out a way to save one life." No one could be sure that a peaceful demonstration of the bomb would persuade Japan to give up. Truman, therefore, ordered use of the bomb, hoping to hurry Japan's surrender and prevent the costs of invasion.

On the morning of August 6, 1945, a B-29 bomber called the "Enola Gay" took off from the island of Tinian, in the western Pacific, for Japan. (The pilot, Colonel Paul Tibbets, had named the plane for his mother the day before.) In the bomb bay was a Thin Man bomb, incompletely assembled in order to avoid any danger of explosion should the Enola Gay crash on take-off. The final assembly took place during the flight.

Over Hiroshima, Japan, the bomb was dropped. Sixty percent of the city was destroyed.

There is wide variation in figures on the number of casualties caused by the Hiroshima bomb, but according to the Atomic Energy Commission, there were about 256,000 civilians in the city that day. Of these, 68,000 were killed and 76,000 injured. Other estimates include Japanese military men present and are higher.

On August 9, 1945, another B-29 named "Bock's Car" (flown by Major Charles W. Sweeney but named for its regular pilot, Captain Frederick C. Bock) dropped a Fat

Man bomb over Nagasaki. According to the A.E.C. nearly 174,000 civilians were in the city. Thirty-eight thousand of them were killed and 21,000 injured. Other estimates place the total number killed and injured in Nagasaki at nearly 100,000.

Einstein said of the bomb, "The world is not ready for it." [13] He also said, "If I had known that the Germans would not succeed in constructing the atom bomb, I would never have lifted a finger." [14]

Oppenheimer said, "In some sort of crude sense which no vulgarity, no humor, no overstatement can quite extinguish, the physicists have known sin; and this is a knowledge which they cannot lose." [15]

The pilot whose reconnaissance helped choose Hiroshima as the target said, "I often see in my dreams women and children running in and out of fires, and it's just hell." [16]

President Truman said, "We have spent two billion dollars on the greatest scientific gamble in history—and won." [17]

The atomic bomb raised the most fundamental questions of morality and responsibility and changed the world's basic concepts of strategy and national power. But its effects were merely the most dramatic of all the changes of the Scientific Revolution. In the fifties and sixties, the measured search for truth and order continued and accelerated throughout the world—chemists and biologists working closer and closer to an understanding of the essence of the life process itself, astronomers probing the distant universe, and astronauts training to explore the moon.

It was Robert Oppenheimer who offered one of the best and earliest descriptions of what was happening. He said in 1954: "One thing that is new is the prevalence of newness, the changing scale and scope of change itself, so that the world alters as we walk in it, so that the years of man's life measure not some small growth or rearrangement or moderation of what he learned in childhood, but a great upheaval." [18]

And in 1963, after he had become Chairman of the Atomic Energy Commission, Glenn Seaborg foresaw a future of great upheavals. "I am not hesitant to predict," said Dr. Seaborg, "that man's knowledge of nature and himself will more than double in the next three decades—that is, the scientific discoveries and advances of the next thirty years will be more than equal to all those of past years and centuries." [19]

crutch of what he learned in childhood, but a great city
beyond."

And in 1873, there is little circumstantial evidence to the

Franklin Delano Roosevelt, April 4, 1939. *(Wide World Photos)*

Chief Petty Officer Graham Jackson plays "Going Home" as President Roosevelt's body leaves Warm Springs, Georgia, April 13, 1945. *(Ed Clark,* © Life *Magazine, Time Inc.)*

Caisson carrying President Roosevelt's body passes the White House, April 14, 1945. (*United Press International Photo*)

Harry S. Truman on one of his morning walks,
February 1, 1956. *(Wide World Photos)*

Adolf Hitler, 1939. *(United Press International Photo)*

Hitler addresses a rally at Nuremberg, Germany, 1937. *(United Press International Photo)*

Winston Leonard Spencer Churchill, in his uniform as an honorary Air Commodore of the Royal Auxiliary Air Force. *(British Information Services)*

Hitler rejoices over the fall of France, June, 1940. *(European Picture Service)*

U.S. troops wade toward the beach at Normandy, D-Day, June 6, 1944.
*(U.S. Coast Guard)*

U.S. Marines raise flag on Mount Surabachi during the battle for Iwo Jima, February, 1945. (© *The Associated Press*)

U.S. Secretary of State Edward R. Stettinius, Jr., signs United Nations Charter, June 26, 1945. President Truman stands beside him. *(United Nations)*

Albert Einstein. *(Photo by Alan W. Richards)*

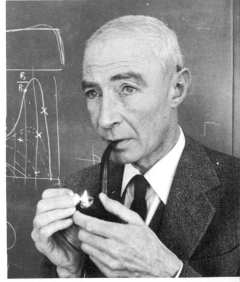

J. Robert Oppenheimer, April 5, 1963. *(Wide World Photos)*

# Part Two
# East and West

*Chapter Three*

# THE REVOLUTION IN RUSSIA

THE same day the U.N. Conference opened in San Francisco, on April 25, 1945, another significant event took place 7,500 miles to the east, in Germany, in the middle of the Elbe River, about seventy-five miles south of Berlin. The Russian and American armies met. They had begun about 2,300 miles apart; the Russians in the ruins of Stalingrad, the Americans on the beaches of Normandy. They had defeated the Germans. Now on this day, at four-forty in the afternoon, two of their men touched hands.

The American was a young second lieutenant from Los Angeles, William D. Robertson. He had started out that morning in a jeep with three of his men, under orders to clear the roads of refugees. When he found his way into the city of Torgau, on the Elbe, he heard shots from across the river and was told that the Russians were there.

Robertson broke open a German drugstore and took some dyes with which he colored a cloth and made a crude American flag. He climbed to the top of a tower overlooking the river, waved his flag, and shouted the only Russian word he knew, "Tovarich" (Comrade).

This moment had been anticipated. Allied officials had worked out a recognition signal; and when the Russians saw Robertson's flag, they fired colored flares into the air. Robertson was supposed to do the same thing, but he had no flares. He tried to explain, shouting in English across the river. But the Russians could not understand and were suspicious, thinking this might be a German trick. They opened fire on the tower, and Robertson left in a hurry, going back into Torgau, where he managed to find an English-speaking Russian just released from a German prisoner-of-war camp, whom he took back to the tower and who confirmed to his countrymen that Robertson's greeting was genuine. When they were convinced, the Russians ran out of the woods and began crawling down the sagging spans of a blown-up bridge. Robertson started across the bridge from his side, and in the middle they met, pounding each other on the back and shouting, "Hello, hello."

Robertson's unit was the 69th Division, First Army. The Russians were of the 58th Guards Division, Soviet First Ukrainian Army.

The Russians took the Americans back to their side, produced wine, sardines, biscuits, and chocolate and began a celebration. After about an hour, Robertson recrossed the river, loaded his jeep with his own three men and four Russians, who had crossed with him—eight in all—and set out for his headquarters. There the party kept going and growing.

Then they all moved back to Russian headquarters. Everywhere there was handshaking and backslapping and toasts to each country, to their leaders, to victory, and to lasting peace in the world. Several Russians played their accordions. The Americans sang "Old Folks at Home" and the Russians sang "If There Should Be War Tomorrow," both at the same time. A correspondent who heard the effort commented that it was "a greater social than a musical success." [1] But there was nothing the matter with the spirit of the celebration. An American jeep driver said, "These Russkys are pretty good boys," and the Russians referred to "Tovarichii Amerikanskii."

When word of the meeting on the Elbe got back to Washington, London, and Moscow, the Allied leaders agreed to make simultaneous announcements. They did, on Friday, April 27. In Moscow, trains stopped to let passengers hear the news coming over the street-corner loudspeakers, and that night, as the sun set behind the Kremlin, 324 antiaircraft guns fired 24 salvos in honor of the occasion. Green, red, orange, and yellow balls of fire burst in the Moscow sky.

The meeting in the middle of the Elbe symbolized the end of Hitler's Germany, formal surrender coming two weeks later. It also symbolized one of the great facts of the postwar world: the U.S.A. and the U.S.S.R. had become the two strongest nations on earth. Had the leaders of those two nations been able to maintain the spirit of their happy infantrymen, a generation and more might have been spared the fear of sudden nuclear annihilation. But they could not. The two principal reasons why they could not were the nature of Russia and the ideas of Marx.

Karl Marx was a brilliant, proud, angry German, born in the Rhineland on May 5, 1818. Like so many other men of his time, he learned to hate the abuses of the Industrial Revolution: the new machines brought wealth to the few, but they also brought misery to the many.

Marx studied philosophy in Berlin and then became a newspaperman, but he was not content to observe. "The philosophers hitherto have only interpreted the world," he wrote. ". . . the thing is, however, to change it."

Marx wandered over much of Western Europe, talking to other disciples of change. Eventually, he settled in London, and there, in 1847, he and another restless German named Freidrich Engels wrote a document that did change the world. They called it *A Manifest for the Communist Party*.

The word "Communist" comes from a Latin word meaning "belonging to all." The idea that members of a com-

munity should share their property was centuries old. What
Marx and Engels did was insist that Communism not only
could come about but would come about, inevitably, because
of what they said were the laws of history.

They saw the past and present as a battle between the
social classes. "The history of all hitherto existing society,"
says the *Communist Manifesto,* "is the history of class
struggles." In feudal times, wrote Marx and Engels, there
were just two classes: nobles and serfs. Then the growth
of trade produced a new class of capitalists, the French word
for which was *bourgeoisie.* The bourgeoisie then produced
its opposite, the workers, with nothing to sell but their labor.
This class was called the *proletariat.*

As Marx and Engels saw it, the bourgeoisie would get
richer and smaller, the proletariat poorer and bigger, until
—inevitably—the proletariat would revolt, seizing the mills
and the factories, the means of production. There would be
just one class.

Until the last of the bourgeoisie had been eliminated,
there would have to be what Marx and Engels called a dictatorship of the proletariat. But eventually there would be
no government at all. Marx and Engels thought the sole
purpose of government in any country was to protect the
top social class; therefore, when the proletariat had become
the only class, the state could and would wither away. The
rules of the new society could be, merely, "From each according to his ability, to each according to his need."

When Marx died in London on March 14, 1883, Engels
said of him: "Marx was a genius. The rest of us were talented
at best." Yet what a collection of contradictions Marx was!
He loved the works of Shakespeare and Aeschylus. "Nothing human," he liked to say, "is alien to me." On the other
hand, he thought and wrote best when he was attacking
some other person's work.

He was a devoted family man. Yet he hated much of the
world. He told his wife when they were married: "Jenny, if

we can but weld our souls together then with contempt shall
I fling my glove in the world's face, then shall I stride through
the wreckage a creator."

Marx insisted that the key to history was the way in which
men made their livings, yet he himself seemed oblivious
to economic pressure. He wrote occasional articles for Hor-
ace Greeley's *New York Tribune,* but only once in thirty
years in London did he try to find a steady job. He preferred
to study and write. Creditors hounded him. Much of the
time his family lived in poverty. Three of his six children
died. He endured carbuncles, boils, an enlarged liver, rheu-
matism, and a variety of other ills.

Yet he may have had more influence on more people than
any other human being since Jesus Christ and the Prophet
Mohammed. In a sense—even though he was an atheist—
Marx created what became almost a religion, setting down not
just a collection of ideas, but a call to action as well. The
last words of the *Communist Manifesto* are: "Let the ruling classes tremble at a Communist revolution. The prole-
tarians have nothing to lose but their chains. They have a
world to win. Workers of the world, unite!"

Had he lived to see it, Karl Marx probably would have
been surprised at the location of the world's first Communist
revolution. He had taught that such an uprising would come
in one of the world's most advanced industrial nations, where
the struggle between bourgeoisie and proletariat was most
advanced. But instead of a Marxist revolution in France or
Britain, it happened first in Russia—vast, backward, largely
peasant Russia.

The Union of Soviet Socialist Republics is the biggest
country in the world. China has the most people, but the
Soviet Union has the greatest area: 8,602,700 square miles.
The U.S.S.R. covers one-sixth of the earth's land surface.
It sprawls across half of Europe and a third of Asia.

It borders twelve nations and twelve seas.

It is bigger than all of South America and more than twice as big as the U.S.

It spans eleven time zones.

It has almost every useful mineral, nearly a third of the world's forests, 100,000 rivers, and nearly 225 million people.

Of the Russians, one scholar has asked: "How could a people not be great and not aspire to greatness, whose horizon was as unlimited as this Eurasian Plain?" [2]

The Russian people have been molded not only by their land but also by more than a thousand years of war and oppression. In the ninth century, they were conquered by Vikings from Scandinavia. Then, out of the East rode Genghis Khan and his Golden Horde. These Mongols ruled Russia cruelly, absolutely, for three hundred years.

Next came the Czars—a succession of kings who were native Russians, not foreigners, but who, like the Mongols, were cruel tyrants. There was no election and no congress and no constitution; the Czar's word was absolute law.

Until the nineteenth century, Russia was a feudal, Oriental backwater, untouched by the great streams of history that had nourished Western Europe, such as the Renaissance and Reformation. Then, in the early 1800's, Western ideas of liberty and justice began to trickle in, and many Russians came to want the freedoms Western Europeans had.

Russia's serfs—slaves tied by law to the land they worked or the landowner they served—had been freed in 1861. But almost every other demand for elementary reform brought only strict repression by the Czar: arrest, exile to Siberia, perhaps execution. Therefore, some Russians came to believe the only way to get the changes they wanted was by conspiracy and revolution.

It was into this climate on April 22, 1870, that Lenin was born. His real name was Vladimir Ilyich Ulyanov. He was probably the greatest revolutionist the world has ever known.

Lenin's father was a respected school administrator who had been rewarded for his work with the title, "Excellency." The Ulyanov home was orderly and respectable, hardly the kind of place from which a revolutionist would seem likely to come.

But then, when Lenin was sixteen, his secure world began to come apart. First, his father died. Then his older brother, Alexander, was caught in an amateurish student plot to assassinate the Czar and was hanged. Then Lenin himself, because of his brother's record, was expelled from the university he had just begun to attend.

In those days, students expelled from Russian universities were forbidden to live in university towns or in big cities. So at the age of seventeen, Lenin went into exile, under police supervision. This is when he began reading Marx, and this is when he decided to give his life to revolution.

In 1893—his exile over—Lenin moved to Russia's capital city, St. Petersburg (now Leningrad), to begin his revolutionary career. Trying to avoid the Czar's police, Lenin came to believe that only if disciplined, totally dedicated Marxists such as himself led the revolutionary movement, could it succeed. He also insisted that his revolutionary party be secret and authoritarian, that democracy and publicity were luxuries it could not afford.

Lenin gave his cause all his time. One man who knew him said: "There is no other man who is absorbed by the revolution twenty-four hours a day, who has no other thoughts but the thought of revolution and who, even when he sleeps, dreams of nothing but revolution." [3]

Lenin also made secrecy and deceit part of his everyday life. He learned to write in code. He used seventeen different pseudonyms before he finally settled on Lenin. Apparently, the name grew from one of his previous pseudonyms, Ilyin, which, in turn, was derived from his middle name, Ilyich.

Thus did the strict, authoritarian regime of the Czar not only create a revolutionary movement but also determine how it was to be organized. Even in our time, imitating the Russians, all Communist parties still remain secret and authoritarian, ruled from the top down.

For his subversive activities, Lenin was sent to prison in 1895 and to Siberia in 1897; then in 1900 he left Russia.

In London, in 1903, at a conference of Russian Marxists, there was a battle for leadership that Lenin won. From the Russian word for majority came the name "Bolshevik"; from the Russian word for minority came the word "Menshevik." Lenin, the propagandist, never let anyone forget that he was a Bolshevik.

In the early 1900's, Russia was just beginning to become a nation of industry as well as of farms, and as in every other country to which it had come, this Industrial Revolution was accompanied by great unrest. On January 22, 1905, more than 200,000 workers and their families marched to the Czar's Winter Palace in St. Petersburg to ask for some basic reforms. But instead of being permitted to present their petition, they were fired on at close range by the Czar's troops, and the day became known as "Bloody Sunday."

There were massive strikes, workers organizing councils called "Soviets" to represent them.

But, once again, the old Russian pattern prevailed: the Czar promised reform and instead substituted terror. Perhaps 15,000 persons were killed, 20,000 wounded, and 70,000 put in jail.

This repression worked for a while, but then came World War I and, with it, an unbearable strain on Russian society. Russia suffered more casualties in that war—dead, wounded, and missing—than any other nation involved on either side. There were humiliating defeats and mass desertions from the army, drastic food shortages, and then—to the surprise even of those who wanted it most—an almost spontaneous revolution. Peasants began seizing the land from those who owned it. In the capital city, by then called Petrograd, workers were so hungry that they went out on strike and soldiers refused to fire on them. It became clear that the "Dear Father Czar" had lost the loyalty of his people. He abdicated, and a reform government took his place, headed by Alexander Kerensky.

This new government was to be a democratic one, but it did not move quickly enough to give the Russian people the things they demanded. So, it became possible for the Bolsheviks to take over. Lenin had hurried home from Western Europe as soon as the revolution began, promising peace to the war-weary, bread to all, land to the peasants, and all power to the Soviets. In the chaos of Russia in 1917, these promises and Lenin's discipline let the Bolsheviks prevail. They took control of the Petrograd Soviet; they persuaded key military units to support them, or at least not to oppose them, and on November 7, 1917, this minority seized power by force. It was, in fact, what the French call a "coup d'état," but it has become known as the world's first successful Communist revolution.

Lenin became head man of the new Bolshevik government, the Chairman of the Council of People's Commissars. He and his fellow revolutionaries moved the capital city to Moscow, where their headquarters became the old fortress, the Kremlin. They renamed their country the Union of Soviet Socialist Republics, and they chose a new flag: a field of red, the traditional color of European revolutionary banners, on which were crossed a hammer and sickle, to symbolize the union of workers and peasants.

But then began, in a sense, a great betrayal. None other than Friedrich Engels had predicted it: "People who imagined that they had made a revolution always saw next day that they did not know what they had been doing, and that the revolution which they made was nothing like the one they had wanted to make." [4] Step by step, Lenin brought to Russia a totalitarianism as cruel as that of the Czars whose evils he had devoted his life to wiping away. One reason was Lenin's own character: twenty-four years as a Marxist conspirator had made him intolerant of any opposition. Another reason was the real threat to his authority: from 1918 to 1920 there was civil war, with the anti-Communist "White Russians" fighting the Bolsheviks, and Britain, France, the U.S., and Japan also sending in troops to oppose Bolshevik rule.

In the name of Karl Marx, Lenin's new government had abolished private ownership of land and taken over the banks, all the means of production, the factories and mills, and even most stores. Now, to hold on to power, Lenin created not a dictatorship of the proletariat, but a dictatorship over the proletariat. When he discovered that his Bolsheviks did not have a majority of the assembly elected after the Czar abdicated, Lenin ordered his troops to break it up. Then he banned all political parties but his own. He even outlawed opposition groups within the Communist party. During the Civil War, the Czar and all his family—by then prisoners—were shot.

With such repression Lenin clung to power, and his Red Army eventually won the war. But Russia's economy was in chaos. During the winter of 1921 and 1922, perhaps five million people died of hunger. During the summer of 1922, Herbert Hoover's American Relief Administration fed ten million Russians a day.

To try to recover, Lenin retreated from his "War Communism" and prescribed an un-Marxist dose of capitalism in all but the biggest industries. Some private ownership returned. But Lenin maintained his own tight rule, setting the stage for the even more ruthless dictator waiting in the wings.

Lenin died on January 21, 1924, of a burst blood vessel in his brain. Trying to create a better life for most Russians, he had made a revolution. But he had been willing to use and permit any means to that end, often quoting the proverb,

"Promises are like piecrusts: made to be broken." Therefore, the end Lenin achieved was a totalitarian dictatorship, and the Bolshevik government became a tyranny as great as any the Russians had ever known.

This ancient conflict between means and ends remains basic to all Communism. Dictators cannot give their people freedom without undermining their own rule. Revolutionaries cannot condone murder and still remain dedicated to human welfare. Lenin himself once expressed one part of this dilemma, describing his love of music, which he felt compelled to abandon because of his cause. Of Beethoven he said: "I know nothing that is greater than the Appassionata; I'd like to listen to it every day. It is marvelous superhuman music. I always think with pride—perhaps it is naïve of me —what marvelous things human beings can do. But I can't listen to music too often. It affects your nerves, makes you want to say stupid nice things and stroke the heads of people who could create such beauty while living in this vile hell. And now you mustn't stroke anyone's head—you might get your hand bitten off. You have to hit them on the head, without any mercy, although our ideal is not to use force against anyone. Hm, hm, our duty is infernally hard." [5]

Lenin's successor was Joseph Vissarionovich Dzhugashvili, better known by the name he chose, Stalin, "Man of Steel." He was born in the town of Gori, in southern Russia, on December 21, 1879. Both his parents had been serfs, legally bound to the land they worked until emancipation in 1861. Stalin's father became a shoemaker, but he died when the boy was eleven. Stalin's mother took in washing to help pay her son's way in a church school.

Stalin did well and got a scholarship to a seminary, where he studied to become a priest. But he read Marx as well as the Bible; he sneaked away from the seminary to preach Communism, not Christianity, and in 1899 he was expelled. He became a full-time revolutionist, and Lenin's man. He spent about half of his twenties and thirties in jail, in Siberia, or on the way to or from both.

Stalin was neither a brilliant orator nor a distinguished thinker but an organizer, a detail man, an administrator. With the revolution he became a Commissar in Lenin's government and, in 1922, Secretary-General of the Communist party. He controlled all government machinery, promoting those loyal to him, downgrading those who might serve a rival.

Lenin became concerned, writing in 1923: "Stalin is too rude, and this failing . . . becomes intolerable in the office of Secretary-General. Therefore, I propose to the Comrades that they think of a way of removing Stalin from this post and appointing to it another person. . . ." [6] But before he could see his proposal carried out, Lenin died.

In the struggle for Lenin's job, Stalin allied himself first with one group, then with another. By 1928 he had eliminated all rivals and was in absolute control.

Lenin and some of the other leading revolutionists who had known Western Europe believed that only if there were Communist revolutions there could the revolution in Russia succeed. But Stalin represented peasant, Oriental Russia, and he proclaimed a doctrine called "Socialism in One Country." Russia would secure its revolution by itself.

In 1928, Stalin began a reign of Czarlike terror to make his backward country a modern power. "We are fifty or a hundred years behind the advanced countries," Stalin explained. "We must make good this distance in ten years. Either we do it or they crush us." [7]

Stalin's revolution began in Russia's countryside, on her twenty-five million private farms. Stalin ordered the wealthier landlords destroyed and small farms merged into huge collective farms, state-owned and state-run. The peasants resisted, slaughtering half their cattle rather than hand them over to the state, but the peasants were slaughtered in turn. By Stalin's own estimate, five million of them were killed.

By 1930, half Russia's farms had been collectivized. By the end of Stalin's rule, nearly all.

Simultaneous with the revolution on the land, Stalin decreed the first Five Year Plan for industry. Each factory was given a production goal; each worker was told where to work.

A generation endured too little food and clothing and shelter, but Russia became a modern power, training engineers and scientists, building dams and power plants and tractors. Steel production went up to six million tons in 1932 and eighteen million in 1938.

Stalin took no chances with real or imagined opposition. There were waves of terror. Again and again, like an ancient Czar, Stalin ordered purges of those he distrusted. It has been estimated that during the thirties, two million Russians were killed and seven million more arrested, among them all the old Bolsheviks with whom Stalin had started in power.

As World War II approached, Stalin saw that his country would need more time to prepare if it were to survive. He invited Britain and France to join Russia in a pact that might have prevented Hitler's aggression, but when they were unwilling to adopt the idea, Stalin reversed his position and signed a non-aggression pact with Hitler—on August 23, 1939. This had the effect of permitting Hitler to concentrate his attack on the democracies to the West, but it also gave Russia the extra time she required. On June 22, 1941, when Hitler ignored his agreement and invaded Russia, the Soviet Union had gathered strength enough to survive.

Russia lost at least seven million and perhaps ten million men killed in action in World War II—about one person in twenty. Another ten million civilians died. But even with such losses, the Soviet Union in 1945 was still the greatest power in Europe.

That power had been achieved by both Marxist and traditional Russian methods. Now Stalin put it to use for both Marxist and Russian ends, the foremost of which was expansion. Stalin's Russia had first begun to expand in 1939 following the Nazi-Soviet pact, part of which granted Germany's permission for Stalin to invade and take over a portion of Rumania and all of Latvia, Lithuania, and Estonia. The pact also had permitted Russia to occupy eastern Poland, after the Nazi invasion from the west.

After the war, Russian control followed the Red Army, Soviet agents building up local Communist parties in each country the Army occupied in Eastern Europe, then forcing these parties into power. Seven countries, supposedly independent, became in fact "satellites" of the Soviet Union: Poland, East Germany, Czechoslovakia, Hungary, Rumania, Bulgaria, and Albania. This meant nearly one hundred million Eastern Europeans brought under Russian rule. (Yugoslavia also had a Communist government, but it had come to power on its own, not with Russian help, so its leaders refused to take orders from Moscow. This independence was to become a pattern whenever Communists came to power without Soviet assistance.)

Not only were there Marxists loyal to Moscow in charge of every government on Russia's eastern border, there were other disciplined followers of Marx and Lenin eager to take charge in other European countries. The Communist parties of France and Italy were particularly strong.

During the 1920's and 1930's, most Americans had paid little attention to other nations, still convinced that their country's best interests were served if she kept to herself, isolated by two oceans. Even during the war the people of the U.S. had thought little about Russia, except to be grateful that Soviet troops, too, were fighting the Germans. But now, after the war, as the U.S. disarmed, the alliance with the U.S.S.R. crumbled, and many free men began casting worried looks abroad, wondering what kind of force they faced.

Part of the challenge, they decided, grew from the ideas of Marx and Lenin, ideas that held revolution inevitable, everywhere, but that also justified any means to hurry it along.

Part of the challenge, they concluded, was also Russia and Russians—persevering, long suffering, patriotic—with a deep suspicion of the foreigners who had so often invaded her and with an ancient inferiority complex toward the West. Now the Communism and the Russianness had been combined with the world's second greatest industrial and military power. What should the free nations do?

Winston Churchill thought he knew. On March 5, 1946, he journeyed to Westminister College in Fulton, Missouri, to receive an honorary degree and make a speech he chose to call "The Sinews of Peace." With President Harry S. Truman on the platform with him, Churchill said the supreme task of free statesmen was to protect "the haggard world" from the "two gaunt marauders—war and tyranny." But tyranny was again on the march, he said, and that made war a threat. "From Stettin in the Baltic to Trieste in the Adriatic," said Churchill, "an iron curtain has descended across the Continent." What should be done? The U.N. should have an international armed force, and the English-speaking people should forge a "special relationship," a new military alliance to stand firm against Russian power. "From what I have seen of our Russian friends and allies during the war," said Churchill, "I am convinced that there is nothing they admire so much as strength . . . and there is nothing for which they have less respect than for weakness, especially military weakness."

The history of most of the next twenty years was dominated by each side's search for strength, the Communists trying to expand and the free nations trying to contain them in a struggle that came to be called the cold war.

*Chapter Four*

# CONTAINMENT

O N SEPTEMBER 17, 1796, George Washington published in the *American Daily Advertiser* his "Farewell Address" to the people whose President he had been for seven and a half years. The President warned against letting loyalty to a particular region or political party divide the new country. He also advised that the U.S. not become entangled in the alliances of Europe. He asked: "Why quit our own to stand upon foreign ground? Why, by interweaving our destiny with that of any part of Europe, entangle our peace and prosperity in the toils of European ambition, rivalship, interest, humor, or caprice? It is our true policy to steer clear of permanent alliances with any portion of the foreign world. . . ."

That was in 1796. By 1946, just one hundred and fifty years later, the world had changed so much that the U.S. had sent troops to Europe in two world wars and was about to become deeply and constantly involved not only in the affairs of Europe but with those of most of the rest of the world, as well. By the 1950's, the U.S. had military alliances with forty-two nations of Europe, South America, and Asia. By the 1960's, more than a million American soldiers, sailors, marines, and airmen were regularly on duty abroad or at sea, from Berlin to South Viet Nam.

The principal reason America was so entangled with the

rest of the world was the cold war with Russia. The phrase, "cold war," had been common in France in the late 1930's: just before World War II began, Hitler's threats and pressures had been called "the white war" or "the cold war." In 1947, when it had become obvious that the U.S. and Russia were in a new kind of fight, the columnist Walter Lippmann recalled the phrase of the 1930's and chose it as the title of a book about the postwar world. In April of 1947, in a speech to the South Carolina legislature, the financier and statesman Bernard Baruch said: "Let us not be deceived— today we are in the midst of a cold war."

There was also another phrase that became more and more common in those days: the cold war, it was said, was a struggle between East and West.

Joseph Stalin was head man in the East; the West was led by Harry S. Truman, and their first battlefield lay in the chaos and misery that was postwar Europe.

For five hundred years, the history of the world had been dominated by the power and the money and the spirit of the people of Western Europe. Now World War II had left Europe poor and weakened, and the power she once enjoyed had slipped away to Moscow and to Washington. Again, it was Winston Churchill who best described the wreck the war had left: over wide areas of "this noble continent," he said in Switzerland in 1946, "a vast quivering mass of tormented, hungry, care-worn and bewildered human beings gape at the ruins of their cities and homes and scan the dark horizons for the approach of some new peril, tyranny, or terror." [1]

And the next year, Churchill called Europe ". . . a rubble heap, a charnel house, a breeding-ground of pestilence and hate." [2]

From Washington the view was equally alarming. Europe's weakness might invite Russian attack just as her misery already was creating sympathy for Communist ideas.

In 1945, with most Americans impatient to enjoy the luxuries of peace, most U.S. troops were brought home and
discharged; by the middle of 1947, the total number of U.S.
military personnel was just 13 percent of what it had been
two years earlier. U.S. leaders hoped the atomic bomb and
the wartime alliance could keep the peace for many years,
but now they discovered that Soviet Russia was no longer
their ally and that despite the bomb there was the threat of
a Communist Europe.

The people of Britain had had "their finest hour" in 1940.
Now the leaders of America rose to the threat they faced.
The U.S. used its power and its money and its spirit first to
"contain" the Russians, then to help build a new Europe in
which Communism could not prevail.

"Containment" was the word of George Kennan, an
intense, scholarly foreign service officer who had spent most
of his career studying the Soviet Union. In 1946, from his
post in the American embassy in Moscow, Kennan sent
back to the Secretary of State a famous report, part of which
he published in 1947, under the pen name "X." In his analy-
sis, Kennan warned that Russia's hostility to the West grew
both from her dictatorship and from the dictator's Communist ideas. He wrote, also, that both their Russianness
and their belief that Communism will win in the long run
permit Soviet leaders to retreat in the face of superior force.
"In these circumstances," Kennan concluded in the published version of his report, "it is clear that the main element of any United States policy toward the Soviet Union
must be that of a long-term, patient but firm and vigilant
containment of Russian expansive tendencies." [3]

Actually, U.S. containment of Russia had begun before
there was a word for it. There had been move and countermove in Iran and Turkey. Then, in early 1947, came the
first real battle. Britain had been using its money and its
troops to help Greece and Turkey, but in February of 1947,
Britain told the U.S. it could no longer afford to give this

aid. President Truman decided the U.S. would have to take Britain's place, and he called in the top men from the Congress to try to get their support. Truman described the civil war in Greece, where Communists were trying to overthrow the government. He outlined Turkey's need for help to pay its bills and keep its army. He estimated that the job the U.S. should do would cost 400 million dollars.

In March of 1947, most Americans were conscious of Russian pressure; but they were not yet convinced of the need for an expensive American response. To command public attention to the crisis, therefore, Truman made a personal appearance before Congress, on March 12, 1947, to appeal for Greek-Turkish aid. In just three days Congress voted the money. Turkey was strengthened, the Greek government won its civil war, and the idea that the U.S. should help other free people fight Communist attempts to take them over became known as the Truman Doctrine.

Next came the Marshall Plan, in the President's words, "the other half of the walnut." That plan bore the name of a soldier who won the Nobel Prize for Peace, a quiet, dedicated, brilliant military planner, a man President Truman called "the greatest living American," George Catlett Marshall.

George Marshall was born December 31, 1880, in Uniontown, Pennsylvania. He grew up wanting to be a soldier but could get no appointment to West Point. One reason was that his father was a Democrat in a Republican Congressional district.

Marshall was determined, however, so he went to the Virginia Military Institute. He was tall and gawky and shy. But he earned the respect of all who knew him.

In those days, newcomers to V.M.I. were "hazed" by the upperclassmen. Usually there were no problems, but with Marshall there was an accident. He was gored with a bayonet. Marshall was in the hospital for weeks, but he lived and he refused to report the name of the cadet who had nearly killed him.

Marshall was elected senior officer of his class each year he was at V.M.I., and in his final year, he was First Captain. Also during his last year, Marshall went out for football and not only made the team but was also named an All-Southern tackle.

Second Lieutenant Marshall was ordered to the Philippine Islands, to several Army schools, then back to the Philippines, acquiring all the while an unusual ability to make plans. One day during maneuvers, the chief of staff became ill and Marshall was called, suddenly, and asked to write a defense plan for Manila. What Marshall dictated so impressed the commanding general that he told those near him: "Keep your eyes on George Marshall. He is the greatest military genius of America since Stonewall Jackson." [4]

Marshall was on General Pershing's staff in France during World War I, again making plans. Slowly, he rose in rank and in the respect of his colleagues, developing a quiet, almost aloof dignity. The same general who had compared him to Stonewall Jackson called him ". . . one of those rare men who live and dream in their profession—a soldier who is not satisfied with daily duty superbly done. . . ." [5]

In 1939, even though he had not graduated from West Point and even though others outranked him, George Marshall became Chief of Staff of the Army. Two days later Germany invaded Poland, and World War II began.

Marshall fought for the draft of soldiers and for a general build-up in American strength. He saw the Army grow from fewer than 200,000 men in 1939 to more than 8,000,000 in 1945. He helped make all the basic Allied decisions about how to fight World War II. It was his view that the war against Germany should take first place, the war against Japan, second. It was he who helped resist Churchill's idea that the Allies should invade southeastern Europe and advance through the Balkans. Churchill, like a good statesman, was thinking about the postwar world and about who would control what territory. Marshall, like most American officers, had been trained to see his mission solely as "success in battle" and to leave politics to others. He once said: "War is the most terrible tragedy of the human race and it should not be prolonged an hour longer than is absolutely necessary." [6]

Marshall wanted to command troops, to go to Europe and lead the Normandy invasion. But, as had been his lot most of his life, he was ordered to make plans, instead. President Roosevelt told him: "I wouldn't sleep at night with you out of the country." [7]

When the war was over, President Truman called Marshall "the greatest military man that this country ever produced—or any other country, for that matter." When Marshall resigned as Chief of Staff in November of 1945, the President cited him with these words: "In a war unparalleled in magnitude and horror, millions of Americans gave their country outstanding service. General of the Army George C. Marshall gave it victory. . . ."

After his retirement, Marshall went home to his farm in Virginia to get a rest, but it was just six days before President Truman asked him to go to China to try to settle the civil war there. He went. Then, early in 1947, the President called him home to become Secretary of State.

As Secretary of State, Marshall's most pressing problem was what to do about Europe. He asked George Kennan and others for their ideas. On June 5, 1947, in a speech at Harvard University, Marshall revealed a plan for European recovery. In less than a year it was in operation.

The fundamental idea of the Marshall Plan was that the U.S. would give Europe money to rebuild if Europe—as a whole—would decide how the money should be spent. The purpose touched many basic elements in the American character. It defended freedom and it helped others. It

25 88                                  INTRODUCTION TO TOMORROW

was also good business: after all, only a recovered Europe could once again become what it had been before the war, America's best customer.

The Foreign Assistance Act became law on April 3, 1948. From that day to the end of June, 1951, the U.S. gave Europe more than twelve billion dollars. The Europeans put the money into seed and fertilizer and tractors, generators and locomotives, cotton and new textile machinery —most of it bought in the U.S. The Plan worked. Europe became productive again. General Marshall called it "a near miracle."

Because of the Plan, Marshall was given the Nobel Prize for Peace in 1953.

The story of the cold war includes blunders as well as triumphs. In 1947, Russia made what now seems a monumental mistake. At Harvard, Secretary Marshall had said, "Our policy is directed not against any country or doctrine, but against hunger, poverty, desperation, and chaos." He left it up to the Europeans to decide who would benefit. Had Russia and her Eastern European satellites joined the Plan, they might have prevented it from working. Certainly, they would have made its approval by Congress less likely. But in June of 1947, Russia refused to have anything to do with the idea. She also insisted that her satellites reject the plan, too.

So, the Marshall Plan involved the U.S. and eighteen other free countries. It strengthened each of them, and by requiring that they work together in distributing the aid, it helped move them a little closer to the ancient dream of a United States of Europe.

While the Marshall Plan was evolving, a crisis developed in Germany. It was the first of many dangerous confrontations between East and West that revealed Germany as the main battlefield of the cold war.

Had President Roosevelt and General Marshall followed

Prime Minister Churchill's advice and agreed to an invasion of southeastern Europe, the Allied armies might have occupied all Germany, and the cold war might have developed very differently. But by 1944, Churchill had been overruled, and in that year the U.S., Britain, and Russia agreed that after the war Germany should be divided three ways, each ally occupying one zone. (Later, Russia agreed that France could have a zone, too, as long as it was carved out of the territory previously assigned Britain and the U.S.)

This division of Germany put the capital city, Berlin, 110 miles inside the Russian occupation zone. So, it was agreed that the four allies should occupy Berlin together.

But, quickly, the agreements of wartime became the arguments of peace. In conference after conference, the Western allies could not agree with Russia on how either Germany or Berlin should be administered. During the war, the Allies had decided that postwar Germany should be run as a whole, but now, as the cold war developed, the Western zones gradually became one unit and Russia's another. Also, the Western sectors of Berlin became one unit and Russia's another.

On June 20, 1948, the West made it clear it intended to make a working unit of its zones, even if Russia's zone was separate: it distributed new money all over West Germany. Apparently in reply, on June 24, 1948, Russia tried to force the West out of her zone by blockading Berlin, stopping all traffic in and out by land or canal. To the U.S., this was a clear violation of wartime understandings. It also threatened the freedom of the two million West Berliners.

President Truman understood that if the Russians had been able to force the Allies out of Berlin, they might have been able to force them out of all Germany. He rejected as too dangerous the idea that the West try to crack the blockade on the ground, by force, but he approved an alternative. On June 26, 1948, the Berlin airlift began.

For 328 days, 24 hours a day, in all weather, the Allies

flew into Berlin more than 2,000,000 tons of coal, medicine, dehydrated potatoes, powdered eggs, and powdered milk. Before it was over, there had been more than 250,000 flights. The men flying the planes became so good at their jobs that they made 1,398 trips in one 24-hour period, landing a plane every 30 seconds.

During the airlift, nearly a hundred airmen were killed. The Berliners endured short rations and high unemployment. They cut down many of their famous linden trees for firewood. But the airlift worked.

After negotiations at the U.N. in New York, the Russians lifted their blockade on May 12, 1949. In Berlin, street lights went on again, the autobahn was reopened, and from West Germany—pulled by a Russian locomotive—a train full of British soldiers and Western correspondents rolled across what was becoming a Communist state into what had remained a free city.

Whatever the West's resolution during the Berlin blockade, it was also true that Western Europe was almost defenseless. Even though the U.S. had the bomb, Western strategists measuring the balance of European power were afraid that Russia had enough men and enough power in Eastern Europe to march to the Atlantic in two weeks. One observer said: all the Russians need to get to the English Channel is shoes.

In the winter of 1947, the tough British Foreign Secretary, Ernest Bevin, urged Secretary Marshall to consider finding a way to join the power of the U.S. and Canada to that of Western Europe. The negotiations were delicate: George Washington's advice still carried great weight with many Americans. But early in 1948, the Communists themselves helped decide the outcome. In Czechoslovakia, where they shared power with non-Communists, the Communists staged a coup d'état on February 24, 1948, and took over power completely. The body of the pro-Western foreign minister, Jan Masaryk, was found in the street underneath the window of his office. Apparently, he had committed suicide.

This coup in Czechoslovakia intensified Western fears that the Communists would push west in Europe wherever they could. So, on April 3, 1949, the U.S. and eleven other nations signed the North Atlantic Treaty. They agreed that an armed attack against any one of them would be considered an armed attack on all. In other words, if Russia moved into Western Europe, the U.S. would fight.

Under the Treaty there was created a North Atlantic Treaty Organization, with headquarters just outside Paris. Of course, there were problems with authority and with numbers. Someone commented that never in history had so few been commanded by so many. But before long, as part of NATO, 250,000 American soldiers were on duty in Europe ready to help delay or perhaps repel any Communist attack, and as of fifteen years after NATO's creation, no attack has come.

NATO and the Marshall Plan, containment and aid. There were, in addition, two other major American responses to Communist power in the years before the cold war suddenly became hot. Both were new types of aid.

One was technical aid, expert advice on how to do such things as build sewers and stop malaria. To the surprise of nearly everyone but himself, Harry S. Truman had won the Presidential election of 1948, and in his Inaugural Address of January, 1949, the President proposed what he called "a bold new program" to teach underdeveloped countries American skills. This was the fourth foreign policy point in the President's address. The program came to be called "Point Four."

There was, too, military aid. This began with the aid to Greece and then to the NATO allies. It grew to include assistance to nearly every country sharing a border with

the Communists: it was containment, world-wide. By the
mid-sixties, the U.S. had given more than thirty-three billion dollars to help train and equip and pay the armies
of its allies.

Containment's greatest test came in the summer of 1950,
when Communist attack, which had been prevented in
Europe, occurred in Asia.

At 4 A.M. on Sunday, June 25, 1950, the North Koreans
began a mortar and artillery barrage across the 38th parallel into South Korea. Then, behind heavy Russian tanks,
the North Koreans invaded. Suddenly, that rainy Sunday,
there were refugees and confusion and panic and retreat.
The "Land of the Morning Calm" was anything but.

Korea sticks down from the mainland of Asia like a
crooked, mountainous thumb. Most of its thirty-five million
people are poor. But they are proud of their ancient history: their ancestors were the first in the world to build
an observatory and the first in the world to use moveable
type.

For centuries, Korea had been a battlefield between China
and Japan. Japan ruled Korea from 1909 until 1945. Then
U.S. troops occupied Korea south of the 38th parallel, Russian troops occupied the North, and Korea became a battlefield in the cold war.

Just as in Germany, the U.S. and Russia could not agree
on how Korea should be run as a whole, the Russians wanting an all-Korean government at least sympathetic to Communism, and the U.S. insisting that the country be free.
So, again as in Germany, Korea was split. Under U.S. and
U.N. sponsorship, the Republic of Korea was created in
the South. Under Russian sponsorship, North Korea became Communist. By 1950, both Russia and the U.S. had
withdrawn their troops, but the North Koreans were left
equipped for war.

One reason war came may have been Communist doubt

that the U.S. would fight. U.S. officials were committed, publicly, to the defense of the island chain running from the
Aleutians to Japan and Okinawa and on to the Philippines,
but they had not made it clear that Korea was part of this
commitment.

On Sunday, June 25, after the attack, U.S. officials re-
quested and were granted an emergency meeting of the
U.N. Security Council, which Russia had been boycotting
for several months. That day she continued to stay away,
and because she did, the Council could and did vote without threat of a Soviet veto. This may have been another
classic cold-war mistake. It permitted the Council to order
an immediate cease fire.

The North Korean attack, however, was not something
that could be stopped by a vote in New York, so the U.S.
and the U.N. had to decide whether the problem was
worth war. No one was sure what the choice would be.
Observers recalled Munich in 1938 and noted that the U.N.
was precisely five years old. Would it be able to keep peace?
Or would this be its last birthday?

President Truman decided that whatever had to be done
to stop the North Korean attack must be done. He sought
and received U.N. support, and on June 27, 1950, the
United Nations became the first world organization in the
history of mankind to vote the use of armed force to stop
the use of armed force. It called on its member nations to
"furnish such assistance to the Republic of Korea as may
be necessary to repel the armed attack. . . ."

President Truman called it a "police action," and by
the end of the week he had ordered in U.S. troops. They
were green to battle and soft from occupation duty in Japan.
They were heavily outnumbered. They fell back, and
farther back, often surprised and sometimes surrounded. But
they held, in what was called a "perimeter," around the
southeastern port of Pusan—held while help came and their
Supreme Commander planned a counterattack. That Com-

mander was one of the most proud, colorful, brilliant, brave, and uncompromising soldiers in American history, General of the Army Douglas MacArthur.

MacArthur was one of those rare men who seemed led by destiny from one success to another. His father was a famous general who had won the Medal of Honor in the Civil War. The boy's birthplace was an Army post in Indian territory, near Little Rock, Arkansas. His birthday was January 26, 1880.

MacArthur wanted to go to West Point, and he did. He became First Captain and graduated first in his class—handsome, disciplined, and confident.

He served in the Philippines and in Mexico. Then he helped organize the famous 42nd Division and went to France with it, in 1917. Later MacArthur wrote of this "Rainbow Division": "The outfit soon took on a color, a dash, and a unique flavor that is the essence of that elusive and deathless thing called soldiering." [8]

In World War I, MacArthur displayed the patterns of the rest of his life. He was a great troop commander, the best the U.S. had, according to the Secretary of War. He became a general. Regularly, he courted danger and death. Once when he was transferred from one assignment to a better one, his old colleagues gave him as a going-away present a silver cigarette case on which was engraved, "To the Bravest of the Brave." The citation for his second Distinguished Service Cross read: "On a field where courage was the rule, his courage was the dominant feature." But with MacArthur's excellence, there went a theatrical kind of vanity, and with his daring, there went an independence that made him sometimes do as he saw best, not as his orders directed.

The sum of these qualities brought MacArthur growing fame. After World War I, he became Superintendent of West Point and then the Army's Chief of Staff. It was

Douglas MacArthur, on horseback, who—on orders of President Herbert Hoover—cleared out the army of unemployed men that camped in Washington during the depression in the summer of 1932.

MacArthur went to the Philippines again in 1935 to help train the army there. (It was as Field Marshal of the Philippine Army that he designed his special cap, so rich with gold leaf.) When World War II began, MacArthur's forces in the Philippines were overrun, but for his defense of the islands he won the Medal of Honor, and even though he was ordered out as the Japanese advanced, he managed to leave behind some hope. His parting words to the people he had tried to protect were, "I shall return."

In Australia, MacArthur began planning his counterattack, and he did return to the Philippines, wading ashore on October 20, 1944. It was he who received the Japanese surrender in Tokyo Bay, he who successfully and compassionately oversaw the rebuilding of postwar Japan, and he who commanded the U.N. forces in Korea.

MacArthur was aloof and proud, as if he saw himself a part of history. He was colorful: with the "props" that became his symbols—the special cap, the corncob pipe, the sunglasses—he seemed to behave almost like an actor playing the part of MacArthur. And, like Churchill, he had a gift with words. To him there were few "grays," few compromises. Everything was black or white, right or wrong. Nor was he shy about speaking of the things in which he believed. He summed up much for which he stood when, on May 12, 1962, at the age of eighty-two, he returned to West Point to accept its highest award and speak, without notes, to the Corps of Cadets. His theme was their motto, Duty-Honor-Country. He said:

"Those three hallowed words reverently dictate what you ought to be, what you can be, and what you will be. They are your rallying points: to build courage when

courage seems to fail; to regain faith when there seems
to be little cause for faith; to create hope when hope
seems forlorn. . . . Duty-Honor-Country. . . ."

At first, the cadets had listened merely respectfully. Now,
as this man who had been a general in three wars stated
his creed, they realized this was a rare occasion. Mac
Arthur continued:

". . . your mission remains fixed, determined, invio-
lable—it is to win our wars. All other public purposes,
all other public projects, all other public needs, great
or small, will find others for their accomplishment; but
you are the ones who are trained to fight; yours is the
profession of arms—the will to win, the sure knowledge
that in war there is no substitute for victory; that if you
lose, the nation will be destroyed; that the very obses-
sion of your public service must be Duty-Honor-Country. . . ."

The General had spoken for nearly forty minutes. Now,
as he closed, his voice became a whisper.

". . . the soldier, above all other people, prays for
peace, for he must suffer and bear the deepest wounds
and scars of war. But always in our ears ring the ominous
words of Plato, that wisest of all philosophers, 'Only the
dead have seen the end of war.'

"The shadows are lengthening for me. The twilight
is here. My days of old have vanished tone and tint; they
have gone glimmering through the dreams of things that
were. Their memory is one of wondrous beauty, watered
by tears, and coaxed and caressed by the smiles of yesterday.

"I listen vainly, but with thirsty ear, for the witch-
ing melody of faint bugles blowing reveille, of far drums
beating the long roll. In my dreams I hear again the

crash of guns, the rattle of musketry, the strange, mournful mutter of the battlefield.

"But in the evening of my memory, always I come back to West Point. Always there echoes and re-echoes Duty-Honor-Country.

"Today marks my final roll call with you, but I want you to know that when I cross the river my last conscious thought will be The Corps—and The Corps—and The Corps.

"I bid you farewell." [9]


". . . in war there is no substitute for victory." MacArthur was determined to win in Korea, and he almost did.

On September 15, 1950, he surprised his enemies with a landing halfway back up the Korean peninsula, at Inchon. Simultaneously, his army around Pusan counterattacked, and the North Koreans were routed.

In October of 1950, U.N. forces recrossed the 38th parallel and headed for Korea's border with China, along the Yalu River. It was then that the first hints of danger came, reports that Chinese troops had joined the North Korean fight. Communists had come to power in China the year before.

For some reason, MacArthur did not heed the intelligence reports. U.N. troops moved closer and closer to China's border. Then, on November 25, the Chinese struck, bugles blowing, a massive thirty-division attack pushing the U.N. forces back below the 38th parallel again, trapping the First Marine Division, nearly destroying it.

". . . in war there is no substitute for victory." General MacArthur could accept no stalemate, no halfway success. He had overwhelming power in the air and at sea. His country had nuclear weapons. He wanted to use this power to offset China's numbers. He wanted to bomb across the Yalu.

But in Washington, General MacArthur was overruled. To the President, Russia—not China—was still the major foe. There was the fear, as General Omar Bradley put it, that MacArthur's strategy would have invited the wrong war, with the wrong enemy, at the wrong time, in the wrong place. Besides, there was no sanction from the U.N.

Still, General MacArthur wanted victory. He carried his campaign to the public, becoming openly critical of U.S. and U.N. policy. So, on April 11, 1951, President Truman fired him. The highest ranking officer in the American army came home for the first time in fifteen years.

MacArthur received a hero's welcome from coast to coast, but behind him remained a new kind of war with objective in neither space nor time: there was no guarantee of victory if troops could hold on until a certain date or advance to a certain place. Hills changed hands again and again as truce talks dragged on. Finally, on July 27, 1953, an armistice was signed. Its symbol became a lonely two-and-a-half-mile-wide strip winding 155 miles across central Korea, the "Demilitarized Zone," or "DMZ," where the only signs of life were an occasional patrol and the wild game that found it a sanctuary.

Sixteen nations sent armed forces to Korea and five others sent medical aid units. As a result, Communism was contained. Communist casualties were enormous, but so were the South Koreans', civilian and military, and so were America's. According to the U.S. Department of Defense, 33,629 Americans died, 103,284 were wounded, and 4,753 were missing and presumed dead. In all more than 400,000 U.N. troops were killed or wounded.

There was little rejoicing when the Korean War ended. It seemed to most Americans as if there had been neither victory nor a substitute. True, the Communists had not taken all Korea, but neither had they been defeated. Moreover, the "volunteers" who poured across the Yalu in the autumn of 1950 were massive evidence that Communists were now in power not only in the world's biggest country but also in the country with the most population.

Containment had been successful—there was no doubt of that. Nevertheless, with the Chinese Communist victory in their civil war, the disciples of Marx and Lenin had come to control almost a quarter of the earth's surface and almost a third of its people.

*Chapter Five*

# THE REVOLUTION IN CHINA

IN AN important sense, especially to Americans, the major events of the past twenty years have revealed an incomplete picture of the world as it is, and—even more important—as it probably will be, because so many of those events have taken place as if China did not exist. Except for their entry into the Korean War, the Chinese, until recently, have been too busy with civil war and revolution at home to play a major role in international affairs. Moreover, since 1949, the U.S. has had with China no formal diplomatic relations and few contacts of any kind, making that great and ancient country perhaps the only one in the world about which Americans know less today than their parents did a generation ago.

Like fighting blindfolded, this ignorance may prove a dangerous handicap. Always in the past, China has expanded whenever she was united and strong, her people convinced that they were superior to all others. Now China is united and growing strong again, and this time her new leaders consider the West, especially the U.S., an enemy. Therefore, it would seem not only possible but also likely that, just as the past twenty years have been dominated by U.S. relations with Russia, so the next twenty years will bring a similar struggle with China. The "sleeping giant," as Napoleon Bonaparte called her, is waking up and, as he prophesied, she is beginning to shake the world.

China has more people than any other nation on earth. No one knows the precise number, but the best estimates are about 700 million now and perhaps a billion by 1980. China's population is growing by perhaps 15 million people a year, which means that there is another Chinese in the world about once every two and a half seconds. Therefore, of all the men, women, and children on earth, nearly one out of every four is Chinese.

China is also big—not as large as the U.S.S.R. or Canada but the third largest country in the world, with about a third more area than the U.S. The trouble is that only about 15 percent of this land is good for growing food, so even though there are nearly four times as many Chinese as Americans, the U.S. has more land under cultivation.

This ancient pressure of people on land has shaped all Chinese history, molding the Chinese into a race accustomed to hardship and hunger, making China's greatest natural resource the muscles of her people for whom life has been a constant struggle to apply to "the good earth" work and water enough to make it productive.

But whatever their material shortcomings, the Chinese are a proud people, the products of the world's oldest continuous civilization. In 1923, in a cave near China's capital city, archaeologists discovered remains of a creature they named Peking Man, who lived at least 500,000 years ago. Chinese history goes back perhaps thirty-five centuries. Paper and printing and gunpowder and the compass and the wheelbarrow—all were known in China long before they were known in Europe. Moreover, long before North America was anything but forest, the Chinese came to believe that theirs was the great "Middle Kingdom" and that all those around it were "barbarians." It is true that China was supremely isolated: the world's widest ocean on the east and south, the world's highest mountains to the west, nearly a thousand miles of desert to the north. Until recently, her people knew little of the rest of the world.

Nevertheless, the achievement of Old China was so impressive that Chinese emperors expected all foreigners to pay tribute, and visiting barbarians performed in the Emperor's presence what was called a "kowtow": kneeling three times and prostrating themselves nine times, their noses flat to the floor.

Chinese history is measured in dynasties, generations of rule by one family, like the Stuarts or Tudors in England. Long before the time of Christ, there were the dynasties of Shang and Chou and Ch'in. It was one of the Ch'in Emperors in the third century B.C. who finished building the Great Wall, a 1,500-mile-long barrier across north and northwestern China, the purpose of which was to keep out "barbarians."

There were other great dynasties: Han, Tang, and Sung. Then, despite the wall, Genghis Khan, with his mounted archers, swept out of Mongolia to found a dynasty that ruled from 1260 to 1368 A.D. (In Mongolian, Genghis meant "Emperor Within the Seas." Khan meant "King" or "Lord." From the name of Genghis Khan's elite bodyguard, his "ordo," we get the word "horde.") Kublai Khan, Genghis's grandson, rebuilt the city of Peking, conquered south China as well as north China, and ruled the greatest empire the world had ever known, spreading from the Yellow Sea to the border of Poland and from Siberia to India and the Middle East. Marco Polo, that adventurous merchant of Venice, was for seventeen years one of the Khan's officials, serving for part of that time as governor of a small Chinese city.

The Mongol dynasty was succeeded by the native Chinese Ming dynasty until 1644. Then came another period of foreign rule, by the Manchus, until China's revolution began in 1911. The Manchus were from Manchuria, now north-eastern China.

Whoever the ruler, foreigner or native, the Chinese people saw him as halfway between heaven and the people, enjoying what was called the Mandate of Heaven: as long as he behaved himself, heaven supported him; but when and if he misbehaved, heaven withdrew its mandate, and the people could revolt.

How could a ruler make sure he did not misbehave and risk losing the Mandate of Heaven? The answer was to do what Confucius said. Confucius was a philosopher who lived five hundred years before Christ and who developed for the Emperor and officials of China elaborate rules of good conduct. In time, Confucianism also became a system of rules of daily life for everyone. In essence, people were to do unto others not what they would like done unto them but what was required by their relationship: a son should behave toward his father differently than toward his brother or his friend. Confucianism was one key to harmony among a crowded people.

Another key was the family: among old China's peasants, the family, not the individual and not the party, was what was important. Each family looked after its own, dividing its land among the sons of each generation, arranging marriages, and honoring its aged.

Most peasants were all too familiar with hunger, disease, and debt, but a few families owned enough land to rent some to those who owned none. These were the gentry, who helped run the villages and who might afford to let at least one promising son stay out of the fields in order to study. In Western countries, the way to wealth and power has been through invention and investment and exploration, but in China it was through study. Study enabled a boy to learn to read and write, no easy job in a language with no alphabet and perhaps 40,000 different picture characters, and knowing how to read and write made a young man eligible to take the examinations that could open the door to the Emperor's civil service. Like Marco Polo, he might become an official—a mandarin—helping rule part of the Middle Kingdom. He would collect taxes and keep order and settle disputes and build dams and control floods. He would become Governor and Senator and Judge and Jury—all in one—his badge of privilege being long fingernails, to prove he did not have to labor with his hands.

This ancient system—the peasants, the gentry, the scholar-mandarins, the Emperor, Confucianism, and the family—had survived flood and famine for so many years no one knows the exact beginning. But it could not survive the influence of the West. European and U.S. missionaries and merchants, backed by modern military power, created in China an impatience that could be satisfied only by revolt.

The first leader of that revolution was an eloquent doctor named Sun Yat-sen.

To Westerners, much that is Chinese has long seemed both figuratively and literally backwards: men used to wear pigtails; soup is often served at the end of the meal; and the family name comes first. The man who became the first President of the Chinese Republic was called Dr. Sun. His "first" name was Yat-sen.

Because Sun was a child of Old China, it is not surprising that no one knows the exact day of his birth. But the year was 1866, and the place was a village near Canton in south China.

Sun's mother had the traditional "lily feet," bound when she was still a baby so they would not grow. These tiny feet on adult women were considered especially attractive by Chinese men. They were also painfully effective in keeping the women at home.

Sun's father was a peasant, but apparently he was one of the top men in his village and could afford to let Sun's older brother leave home and go to Hawaii as a laborer.

This brother did well in Hawaii, so, at age twelve, Sun followed him. He learned English; he attended a Church of England school; he became so incurably exposed to Christian and Western ideas that when he went back to his village, at age sixteen, he was appalled at what he considered the superstition there. So he, in turn, appalled the people of his village by breaking off part of one of the idols in the temple, trying to prove that a god who could not protect himself could not protect others. Because of this sacrilege, the village elders invited Sun Yat-sen to leave home.

He went to Hong Kong, where he was baptized a Christian and enrolled in an English college to study medicine. Sun became a doctor in 1892, but almost immediately he gave up that profession for another. Like Lenin, the lawyer turned revolutionary, Doctor Sun took up the practice of rebellion.

Sun Yat-sen had grown up during a time of great unrest caused by floods and famine, but above all by foreigners. Western missionaries and traders had been coming to China for three hundred years, but in the nineteenth century they came in force. They taught and they healed and they bought and they sold. (One of the things they sold most profitably was opium.) In the process, they made the Chinese feel inferior: China had remained isolated and agricultural while Europe had experienced an industrial revolution, so the "barbarians" had industrial and military power the Middle Kingdom could not match.

Britain was the leader in wanting to do business with China. But other countries, the U.S. among them, were eager followers.

From 1840 to 1842, there took place what came to be called the Opium War. The Manchu Emperor wanted to restrict most trade and to ban all opium trade, but the British wanted as much trade as possible. So, with their modern ships and guns, the British forced China's Emperor to grant, by treaty, to them and to other foreign powers the right to do business in certain ports along China's coast. The "powers" even demanded that parts of the treaty ports be territory in which they, not the Chinese, ruled. There was a famous sign in a park in Shanghai that read: No Dogs or Chinese Allowed. The embarrassment of China's defeat in the Opium War helped produce a peasant uprising in the 1850's. Just before Sun Yat-sen was born, a fanatical south China schoolmaster, Hung Hsin-ch'uan, who had learned just a little Christianity, believed himself called by God to overthrow the Manchus. In what was called the Taiping rebellion, he led his people almost to Peking before he was stopped.

Like so many other young Chinese of that time, Dr. Sun was fascinated by the ideas behind Western power. He became convinced that what China needed to become modern and self-respecting was the overthrow of the Manchus, the departure of all other foreigners, and the establishment of a republic.

In 1895, Sun Yat-sen tried to organize a rebellion in Canton, but the government discovered a shipment of pistols he had ordered and arrested most of his helpers. Sun fled to Japan with a price on his head, cutting off his pigtail, growing a mustache, and passing for a Japanese.

In Japan and all over the world then, there were young Chinese studying the things they hoped could strengthen their country. For sixteen years, Sun moved among these people, preaching revolution and raising money for it. In America, in Europe, in Southeast Asia, in Japan, Sun wore disguises, escaped kidnaping, faked his passport.

In New York in 1905, he set down what he liked to call the "Three Principles" of the people, the goals of his revolution. These were: Nationalism, Democracy, and the People's Livelihood. Nationalism meant China for the Chinese, a Middle Kingdom independent of foreigners, beginning with the Manchus. Democracy meant that there should be government by the people, not by an Emperor. The People's Liveli-

hood meant land reform—ownership of land by more people
--and some socialism.

From 1906 to 1911, even from abroad, Sun played a part
in eleven armed uprisings in China. The last one succeeded.

Anti-Manchu, antiforeign feeling had been growing deeper
and deeper. In 1894 and 1895, Japan used her new "Western"
industrial and military power to defeat and humiliate China
in a war.

Then, in 1900, came the Boxer Rebellion, an anti-Chris-
tian, antiforeign uprising of village militia. "Boxer" was a
loose English translation of the Chinese name for these
militia, who murdered thousands of Chinese Christians,
several foreign missionaries, and one foreign diplomat before
the armies of eight nations put down the revolt by capturing
Peking.

Then in 1904 and 1905 came Japan's victory over Russia
in a war. The Chinese were elated by this, for they thought it
proved that a modernized Asian nation could win.

On the tenth day of the tenth month in 1911—"Double
Ten"—a revolt broke out in the city of Hankow. The army
there mutinied, and the revolution quickly spread all through
south China, men cutting off their pigtails as a sign of their
freedom from old Manchu ways. It was all deceptively easy.

Sun Yat-sen was in the U.S. at the time, but by the end
of the year, he was back in his country and was elected Pro-
visional President of the new republic.

The next step was to unify the country and create a government of the people where there had never been such a
thing before. But this job proved too big. By 1916—as so often
in the past between dynasties—China had shattered into little
pieces, each region ruled by a "warlord." Democracy seemed
a "will-o'-the-wisp," and Sun became disillusioned. "If we
speak of liberty to the average man," he said in 1924, "he
surely will not understand us. . . . The Chinese do not
know anything about liberty. . . . We have too much liberty,
no cohesion, no power of resistance; we are 'loose sand.' " [1]

To Dr. Sun, the answer to the problem seemed the cement of discipline and authority. Looking to Russia and seeing that Lenin and the Bolsheviks, with their new Communist party, were holding onto the power they had taken, Sun tried to apply the same techniques in China.

In 1913, he had reformed his old secret society into a new political party, the Kuomintang, the National Peoples party. Now, in 1922, he began remodeling the Kuomintang after the Communist party of the Soviet Union.

Russia sent agents to advise him, and Sun sent to study in Moscow his most trusted lieutenant, a lean young soldier named Chiang Kai-shek.

Chiang Kai-shek was born October 31, 1887, a son of the gentry in eastern China. His father died when he was nine, so he was sent to live with relatives, but he ran away to become a soldier.

When he was about fifteen, his relatives arranged his marriage. (In typical Old Chinese fashion, he never saw the girl before the ceremony.) By the time Chiang passed the examinations for China's West Point, he was already a father.

Chiang stayed at military school in China for one year, then went abroad to Japan, to the Imperial Defense College in Tokyo, where he chose for himself the name "Kai-shek," meaning "Immovable Stone." It was there also that he first heard Dr. Sun speak and joined Sun's revolutionary movement.

Chiang Kai-shek developed into a wiry, five-foot-ten-inch, aloof, but politically astute officer, tough and ruthless enough to rise to the position of Commander in Chief of the Kuomintang army. He became the Generalissimo, or for short, the "Gimo."

Dr. Sun sent Chiang to Russia in late 1923 to study the Red Army. Then Chiang came back to be commandant of the new Whampoa Military Academy in Canton, training an officer corps for the Kuomintang army. With these men, Chiang spent most of the rest of his long life fighting, retreating, and making plans to fight again.

In China in the teens and twenties, there was great ferment and great disillusionment. The Double Ten revolution had brought not democracy but a nation of from fifteen to thirty feuding warlords. Moreover, despite the promises of self-determination, World War I had brought no end to foreign influence.

Sun Yat-sen spoke for millions of his people when he said, just before he died on March 12, 1925—at the age of fifty-eight—". . . the revolution is not yet finished." [2] He could have had no idea how right he was.

Chiang Kai-shek succeeded Dr. Sun as leader of the Kuomintang. With Russian help, he carried on its organization into a party disciplined enough to keep power once it seized it. His dream was to unify China again, to achieve Dr. Sun's first principle, a China independent of foreign rule. Then, unified, China might grow toward democracy and economic reform.

But in the disappointment of the twenties, many other Chinese concluded that Dr. Sun's methods were a failure and that only in some other way could China become a great and modern Middle Kingdom. For many of them, that other way lay in the teachings of Marx and Lenin. The Chinese Communist party was organized in Shanghai in the summer of 1921.

For a few years, the Communists and the Kuomintang worked together, jealously but successfully. As a result, in 1927, with Communist agents going ahead to preach reform, Chiang Kai-shek led his army north from Canton, defeating every warlord in his path until he had in fact unified the country once again. He chose Nanking for his capital and renamed the city of Peking "Peiping." (Peking means Northern Capital; Peiping means Northern Peace.)

Then, as soon as he had taken power, Chiang turned on

the Communists. He admired their discipline and their
methods, but he had learned in Russia and in China that
they were dangerous allies. He decided to rid himself of
them before they got rid of him.

There is no denying that Chiang Kai-shek was a dictator,
his word absolute law enforced by the army and his secret
police. But, especially in Peiping, education flourished.
Chiang and Madame Chiang, his vivacious U.S.-educated
second wife, led attempts at revival and reform with the
goal of democracy. The number of treaty ports diminished.
Had there been peace, Chiang might have been able to
achieve his and Sun Yat-sen's dream; but there was no
peace.

Japan invaded Manchuria in 1931. More important,
Chiang could not rest while Communism remained a force
in his land. When his Blue Shirts, his secret police, cracked
down on Communists in the cities, those who survived fled
to the countryside. There they joined Communist strong-
holds founded not on the proletariat but on the peasants,
and there they encountered the leader of peasant-based Communism in China—a tall, austere, ruthless, persuasive, chain-
smoking, poetry-writing former peasant himself, Mao Tse-
tung.

The province of Hunan, in south-central China, is famous
for its sturdy and hard-working peasants. Mao Tse-tung was
of such stock, born December 26, 1893. His father was a
particularly hard worker whose stern discipline Mao learned
to loathe.

Mao's father arranged his son's marriage when the boy
was about fifteen. But Mao did not like his bride, nor did he
want to work as his father demanded. He wanted to go to
school. He and his father argued, he won, and he left home
and began studying to be a teacher.

Like so many other young Chinese students then, before
and during World War I, Mao looked for a road by which

China could become modern and independent. For him, Communism seemed the answer.

He was one of the founders of the Chinese Communist party in 1921. Then he went back to his native Hunan to try to organize workers for revolution.

In 1927, when Chiang Kai-shek and his Kuomintang army defeated the warlords, there was a peasant uprising in Hunan, the peasants taking advantage of the defeat of their warlord to seize land from the village gentry and become their own rulers. Far from being a gentle change, this was a reign of terror. Mao Tse-tung was impressed. He wrote in a famous report on the revolt: "What Dr. Sun Yat-sen wanted to do in the forty years he devoted to the revolution but failed to accomplish, the peasants have accomplished in a few months." [3] Nor was Mao troubled by the violence that made such achievement possible. In the same report he said: ". . . a revolution is not the same as inviting people to dinner, or writing an essay, or painting a picture, or doing fancy needle-work; it cannot be anything so refined, so calm and gentle, or so mild, kind, courteous, restrained or magnanimous. A revolution is an uprising, an act of violence whereby one class overthrows another." [4]

Mao also said, "Power grows out of the barrel of a gun." [5]

Mao decided that the peasants—90 percent of China's people—were those on whom a Communist revolution should be based and that the peasants—as they had demonstrated in Hunan—had much to teach. Mao's slogan became: "Learn from the masses."

In Spanish, the word for war is "guerra," and the word for little war is "guerrilla": its use dates from the early 1800's when Spanish troops harassed Napoleon's army after the main Spanish force had been defeated. Mao Tse-tung became a guerrilla leader, organizing a peasant army in the mountains of Hunan, developing and perfecting hit-and-run methods by which to survive Chiang's attacks. His famous formula for guerrilla warfare was: The enemy advances: we retreat. The enemy halts: we harass. The enemy tires: we attack. The enemy retreats: we pursue.

Mao's tactics worked, and so did his treatment of the peasants around his stronghold. Other warlords had looted and ruined, but Mao ordered his soldiers to be polite and to pay for whatever they took. Mao did not want to alienate those he hoped to lead.

From Shanghai, the leaders of the Chinese Communist party looked with suspicion at Mao's peasant stronghold, his Soviet. Marx and Lenin had taught that revolution must be based on the proletariat in the cities, and Russian Communists ordered the Chinese Communists to follow this formula.

But Mao stood firm. Even though he was dismissed from the top leadership of the party, he continued to insist that China's revolution be peasant-based. Of the experiences of Communists in Russia, Mao said: "If we copy them and apply them mechanically and allow no change whatsoever it will be like whittling down the feet to fit the shoes." [6] Besides, Mao had on his side the argument of success: his peasant Soviet remained intact while Communist groups in the cities were broken up by Chiang's police.

Though the Japanese had occupied Manchuria, Chiang Kai-shek considered Mao's growing Red army an even greater danger. Chiang retreated before the Japanese, but he mounted five major offensives against the Communists. By the time of the fifth one, in 1934, Mao's rivals from the cities had been forced to take refuge in his Soviet. They then over-ruled Mao and ordered a traditional, not a guerrilla, defense. So a million Kuomintang troops managed to surround the Soviet, and nearly a million of Mao's men were killed or starved to death. The survivors decided they had to try to escape.

In October of 1934, two columns of men broke out of the trap and began the almost incredible—now legendary—Long

March. They walked a zigzag route six thousand miles from Hunan to northern Shensi, near the Great Wall. It was like going from Alabama to North Dakota, by way of New Mexico, except that roads were scarce. The marchers crossed 18 mountain ranges and 24 rivers in 368 days.

The whole march was conducted under nearly constant attack, the Kuomintang forces harassing by land and air. There were fights with the armies of ten different warlords and threats from primitive tribes. In all, those on the Long March fought more than 200 battles. Of 100,000 men in the main column, which Mao commanded, 80,000 died en route from wounds or starvation or drowning or exposure.

So, it was understandable that the lucky few who reached the city of Yenan were bound together for the rest of their lives by the comradeship forged in the suffering of 1934 and 1935. Nor was there any longer any question about who led Chinese Communism. It was the man who had led the Long March, Mao Tse-tung.

Looking back afterwards, Mao saw the Long March as far more than mere escape. He saw it as a lasting piece of propaganda. He wrote: "It is a manifesto, an agitation corps and a seeding machine. . . . It proclaims to the world that the Red Army is an army of heroes." [7]

In the new capital of what was called the Chinese Soviet Republic, Mao and everyone else lived with no more than the basic necessities in dusty caves carved into the sides of Yenan's one-thousand-foot-high brown cliffs. There, by candlelight at night, Mao studied and wrote poetry and developed the theories by which he intended to rule the New China. Visitors were impressed by the simplicity of life in Yenan; they were not aware of the terror Mao was planning.

Meanwhile, more and more of Chiang Kai-shek's own officers were getting restless about the war on the Communists rather than the Japanese. In December of 1936, when Chiang flew to the city of Sian in southern Shensi Province to supervise another offensive against Mao, one of his own marshals arrested him and held him prisoner for twelve days, demanding above all else that Chiang promise to stop fighting his fellow Chinese and begin fighting the invader.

On Christmas Day in 1936, Chiang was released, and shortly thereafter there was formed again a united front between the Kuomintang and the Communists, Chiang turning his major attention on the Japanese. It became possible again to travel to Yenan, and Mao's cave city began getting supplies and new recruits from all over China. The territory it controlled expanded to 100,000 square miles.

One of those who came to Yenan was a Shanghai movie star named Lang Ping. Mao fell in love with her and made her his fourth wife. His first wife had been the one given him when he was still a boy. His second was the daughter of a professor under whom he had studied in Peking; she had been executed by the Kuomintang. His third wife had accompanied him on the Long March, had nearly died of the wounds she received during the March, and had borne Mao a baby girl shortly after the March ended. Nevertheless, Mao chose Lang Ping.

The turning point in the struggle between the Communists and the Kuomintang was probably the new attack by Japan in July of 1937. Both Chiang and Mao were now fighting the invader more than each other, but Chiang's armies took the brunt of the attack, losing battle after battle, giving up the cities near the coast—Peking, Tientsin, Shanghai, Nanking, Canton—retreating inland to set up a new capital at Chungking.

Meanwhile, the Communists expanded their territory. By 1944, Mao ruled about a hundred million people.

Mao's guerrilla tactics were one reason his territory grew while Chiang's contracted. Mao's forces established bases in the mountains and in other hideouts. Then they moved out among the peasants, preaching courage and reform, organizing new guerrilla units. Officers lived as simply as the men, and all of them lived among the people, as Mao put it, like fish in water. Against both the Japanese and the Kuomintang armies, Mao's doctrines succeeded. He had written: "In guerrilla warfare select the tactic of seeming to come from the east and attacking from the west; avoid the solid, attack the hollow; attack; withdraw; deliver a lightning blow, seek a lightning decision." [8]

Mao encouraged defection from Chiang's armies, caring for Kuomintang wounded, promising no punishment to those who came over to his side. Moreover, with all recruits —peasants, bandits, former Kuomintang soldiers, whoever— Mao applied the techniques of propaganda and persuasion he had been studying and developing ever since the peasant uprising in Hunan in 1927. Through a careful combination of threat and public confession of former "errors," a process that came to be called "brainwashing," Mao and his lieu-tenants turned their supporters into fanatics.

But perhaps the major reason for Mao's success was Chiang's failure. Madame Chiang had come to the United States in 1942 and, with her fragile eloquence, had touched the hearts of the country, especially of Congress, which she had been invited to address. The U.S. gave Chiang massive aid. Then, after the war, from 1945 to 1949, the U.S. saw Chiang as the only alternative to Communism and gave him two billion dollars more, the bulk of it in the form of military supplies, most of which were captured by the Com-munists.

When Japan surrendered to the Allies in 1945, what happened in China was that Chiang and the Kuomintang returned to the cities and the Communists took the country-side. But then, like a sickness, defeat took Chiang. His top officials, once so idealistic and energetic, had grown tired during the war. Some of them had become corrupt. Others were aware that China demanded massive reforms, especially in the countryside; but they did not know how to bring this about. Finally, there was inflation. In the two and a half years from January, 1946, to August, 1948, prices doubled sixty-seven times. By 1948, compared to what they had been before the war, prices were up three million times. Middle class savings were destroyed.

As more and more people became disillusioned with the Kuomintang, Chiang tightened his control. This just made more and more people disillusioned. Communist agents, preaching order and stable prices and honest administration, became heeded more and more.

The U.S., through General Marshall, tried to stop the Chinese civil war and prevent the government from falling, but it was too late. Chiang had lost the Mandate of Heaven.

In late 1948, Chiang's armies suffered a major defeat near Nanking. One by one, Chiang's generals began making deals with the Communists, surrendering to them. Soon the cities began to fall: Tientsin and Peking in January of 1949, Nanking in April, Shanghai in May, Canton in October.

Chiang and the remains of his army withdrew to the island of Taiwan, which the Portuguese had named Formosa, in their language, "beautiful island."

On February 3, 1949, Mao's troops entered Peking, the city they wanted to be their capital. (The Communists changed the name back again from Peiping.) In a cold dust storm, they marched past the great south gate and then, symbolically, through what had once been the foreign part of the city. It took them all day.

Mao Tse-tung himself made his triumphal entry into Peking on March 25, 1949. Then on October 1, from the top of the Gate of Heavenly Peace, he formally proclaimed the People's Republic of China. Perhaps Mao knew what was coming: the executions, the brainwashing, the fear, the hunger. But the people did not, and they were happy. They believed that foreign humiliation was at last ended, believed the promises of Mao's agents, believed that the revolution that had begun in 1911 had finally been successful, that they might now have peace and land of their own and a house to live in with their families. In the Tien An Men Square, they sang and watched a parade of the army, the peasant guerrillas, cavalry, sailors, actors, dancers, doctors, and veterans of the Long March. They looked up at the huge, smiling picture of Mao and wished him 10,000 years of life.

---

# Chapter Six

# THE BRINK OF WAR

For the twentieth of January, Inauguration Day in 1953 was unusually mild and sunny in Washington, D.C. In the Capitol plaza, a bigger crowd than ever before on such an occasion—more than 100,000 persons—waited for the President-elect to take the oath of office. Across the country, about half the people were in areas that could receive the first coast-to-coast television broadcast of an inauguration.

For thirty-two minutes that day, the United States, technically, had no chief executive. Harry S. Truman's term expired, by law, at noon, and it was not until 12:32 P.M. that Dwight David Eisenhower held his right hand in the air, placed his left hand on two Bibles, one that had once belonged to George Washington and the other that had been his since he was a cadet at West Point, and repeated what the Constitution required:

"I do solemnly swear that I will faithfully execute the office of President of the United States, and will to the best of my ability preserve, protect, and defend the Constitution of the United States."

Ever since the inauguration of Franklin Pierce one hundred years before, it had been the custom for the dignitaries at such ceremonies to wear high silk hats, but Eisenhower decreed a change. At his inauguration, he and nearly everyone else wore black Homburgs. Top hats had often been associated with both elegance and fun, but no one had ever implied that there was anything frivolous about a Homburg.

Nor was there anything but the most solemn tone to the new President's Inaugural Address. Customarily, such a speech is a key to the style and concerns of an incoming administration, and this address was no exception. It began with a prayer the President himself had written that morning in his hotel suite. It continued with a realization that in the 1950's a President's most important responsibilities were diplomacy and defense. Wearing heavy horn-rimmed glasses, the President read slowly and distinctly. "How far have we come," he asked, "in man's long pilgrimage from darkness toward the light? Are we nearer the light—a day of freedom and of peace for all mankind? Or are the shadows of another night closing in upon us?"

Dwight Eisenhower was a man of compelling sincerity, conspicuously devoted to the peace and freedom of which he spoke so longingly, so often. It is one of the many ironies of our time that he should have been the President of the United States during years in which science and the cold war combined to produce the most dangerous arms race in history.

When the Inaugural Address was over and the Marine Band had played "The Star-Spangled Banner," then and only then did joy displace solemnity. The crowd burst into the applause from which it had been restrained by the subject and phrasing of the President's speech; "Ike" responded with the radiant grin for which he was so famous, raising both arms above his head to form a "V"; and—in a few minutes—the parade began.

Seven hundred and fifty thousand persons watched as the President and Mrs. Eisenhower rode from Capitol Hill to the reviewing stand in front of the White House. More than 25,000 others marched or rode behind them. There were fifty floats, sixty-five musical units, three hundred and fifty horses, an Alaskan dog team, and three elephants. The parade lasted two and a half hours longer than planned, until well after nightfall, but among those participating there was a spirit of exultation. Were not the Republicans back in power for the first time in twenty years? Whatever the mood of the President's speech—whatever the facts of life and power with which he would have to deal—now was the time for a party.

A California cowboy named Monte Montana expressed the informal exuberance of the afternoon, halting his horse from time to time along Pennsylvania Avenue to lasso a policeman, a Naval officer, or a pretty girl. When he arrived at the reviewing stand, Montana asked the President's permission to lasso him. Mr. Eisenhower stood up and Montana threw. On his first try he missed, but he made it the second time.

Dwight David Eisenhower was perhaps the most popular President, both at home and abroad, that the United States had had in this century. His great gift was the ability to unify, to make men of different temperaments and interests work together. He was capable of icy anger and unrestrained impatience, but his most memorable expression was his smile, sudden and infectious, a reminder that in spite of a lifetime of military service, he seemed to bear none of the disagreeable traits that sometimes accompany great rank and honor. He rose early always and stood straight, as a career officer must. But in conspicuous contrast to some of his colleagues, he was a modest and tactful man of simple tastes and sometimes boyish enthusiasms. He liked golf, bridge, painting, outdoor cooking, and pulp Westerns.

Eisenhower was born in Denison, Texas, on October 14, 1890. His father and mother had been Kansans, and they moved back to settle near Abilene, Kansas, when "Ike"— as he was known nearly all his life—was two. Dwight was the third of seven Eisenhower sons, one of whom died. His father, who had been less than a success in farming and business, worked as a night watchman and mechanic in a creamery run by an offshoot of the Mennonite sect, the River Brethren. The Eisenhowers were faithful members of this sect, adhering even to its insistence on pacifism.

Poor and numerous, all the Eisenhower boys worked hard. For a time after he had finished high school, "Ike" had a job at the creamery from six at night to six in the morning. From such duties, from his capable mother, from his church, from the near-frontier atmosphere in which he was raised, the future President accumulated his disciplines and beliefs.

It was almost an accident that he went to West Point. Certainly, he got no encouragement from his pacifistic parents. But a friend was interested in Annapolis, "Ike" went along to take the entrance examination with him, took the exam for West Point as well, and went to the latter when it turned out he was too old for the former.

His record at the Military Academy was not outstanding, but he graduated in June of 1915 and entered the long, slow-motion routine of the peacetime army. He did not get overseas during World War I, but—gradually—in one staff job after another, he rose in rank and reputation. During most of the thirties, he served General Douglas MacArthur in both Washington and Manila, then came home to be Chief of Staff of the Third Army, which "won" the important and much-publicized Louisiana maneuvers of 1941, on the eve of war.

Just after the Japanese attacked Pearl Harbor, the new head man of the Army, Chief of Staff George C. Marshall, sent for Colonel Eisenhower. Trying to find the best men in the Army, the General asked the Colonel what strategy he would choose to win the war in the Pacific. Eisenhower knew he was being tested and asked for a few hours to think. When he returned and outlined his plan to General Marshall, the Chief of Staff said simply, "I agree with you." [1]

Eisenhower was ordered to the War Plans Division of the War Department General Staff.

In 1942, Eisenhower prepared a thirty-page order setting up one unified command for all American forces—Army and Navy—in the European theater of operations. Three days later, finally satisfied that he had found the right if not the most senior man for the job, General Marshall named Eisenhower the commander of these troops. Later, Eisenhower was chosen Supreme Commander of all Allied forces in Europe. Through the invasions of North Africa, Sicily, Italy, and finally France, it was Eisenhower whose delicate job it was to make American admirals and British generals, British admirals and American generals, Canadians, Australians, New Zealanders, Free French, Belgians, Dutch, South Africans, Norwegians, Poles, Czechs, and Greeks all work together. "Eisenhower has been slightingly called a 'politician-general,' " wrote one of his biographers, John Gunther. "It was lucky for the world that he was." [2]

The high point of Eisenhower's military career came in June of 1944 with the climax of the war in Europe, Operation OVERLORD, the massive invasion of Normandy in northwestern France. An assault force of 200,000 men waited to cross the English Channel in 5,000 ships under cover of nearly 11,000 aircraft in the greatest invasion armada of all time. Meteorologists reported that the best combination of daylight, moonlight, and tidal conditions would be on June 5, 6, and 7, but then came the worst Channel weather in twenty years. Eisenhower ordered D-Day postponed from June 5 to June 6, but that just forced another crucial decision. Should he give the order to go on the sixth and risk destruction by the weather as well as by the Germans or wait for the next favorable period two weeks away, a wait that might permit the Germans to discover OVERLORD's date and place? On the night of June 5, the weather forecast improved slightly, and Eisenhower said, "O.K. We'll go."

One of the most poignant communiques of World War

II is the one General Eisenhower wrote but never had to issue at the time of D-Day in Normandy. No one knew whether the assault forces could get and stay ashore. What if they could not? The Supreme Commander prepared the following message: "Our landings in the Cherbourg-Havre area have failed to gain a satisfactory foothold. I have withdrawn the troops. My decision to attack at this time and place was based upon the best information available. The troops, the air, and the Navy did all that bravery and devotion to duty could do. If any blame or fault attaches to the attempt it is mine alone." [3]

The invasion did not fail; the communique became merely a memento; and General Eisenhower—the man who oversaw the defeat of Nazi Germany—became the greatest American hero of World War II.

Late in 1945, Eisenhower succeeded George Marshall as Chief of Staff of the Army; he became President of Columbia University in 1948; then he returned to Europe early in 1951 to become the first commander of the North Atlantic Treaty Organization forces.

The combination of Eisenhower's personality and accomplishments made him a natural possibility for the Presidency, and he probably would have won either party's nomination. But he chose the G.O.P., letting his many Republican champions enter his name in the first primary election of 1952. He was nominated at the Republican convention in Chicago in July of that year, and in November he won a landslide victory. The Democrats had nominated the able and articulate Adlai Stevenson, but neither he nor, perhaps, any other man could compete with the Eisenhower legend. In electoral votes, the count was 442 to 89, with Republicans also taking control of both houses of Congress.

By January of 1953, many persons in the U.S. were uneasy about the nature of the new world in which they lived. Up until the 1930's, Americans had been accustomed to think-

ing that nearly every important international trend reinforced their own national directions. History seemed on their
side. But World War II had left the U.S. fighting a cold
war with the Soviet Union in which by no means everything seemed to be going its way.

China had "gone" Communist.

The war in Korea dragged on.

The Soviet Union had recruited and planted spies in the
United States, the most effective of whom probably was a
physicist named Klaus Fuchs, who admitted that he had
passed information to Russia all the time he had been doing
nuclear weapons research at Los Alamos.

Then, on August 29, 1949, Russia tested her first atomic
bomb—years before most American scientists had predicted
she could.

Clearly, the new President's major responsibility would
be national defense.

Eisenhower had said once: "I hate war as only a soldier
who has lived it can, only as one who has seen its brutality,
its futility, its stupidity." [4] Now the question was: How
should major war be prevented?

In December of 1952, on the way home from an inspection trip to Korea, the President-elect conferred with his
top advisers on over-all military strategy. They decided on
what came to be called a "New Look." They agreed that
the U.S. had to be strong enough to prevent—to deter—Russian attack. But in keeping with traditional Republican
economic doctrine, they also agreed that unless government
spending were reduced and the Federal budget balanced,
the U.S. could be weakened at home just as effectively as if
it were attacked from abroad. As Eisenhower saw it, the
key to the "New Look" was to try to equip fewer men with
greater firepower, and the key to that was to rely more
and more heavily on the growing quantity and variety of
nuclear weapons. Of these, by far the most awesome was
the then newly-created hydrogen bomb.

The hydrogen bomb was the younger cousin of the first nuclear bomb set off in the New Mexico desert in 1945. But whereas the force of the fission bombs of Alamagordo, Hiroshima, and Nagasaki was measured in kilotons (KT's)—the equivalent of an explosion of thousands of tons of TNT—the power of the H-bomb was measured in megatons (MT's) —millions of tons.

The first hydrogen bomb was tested on a little island called Elugelab, near Eniwetok in the Pacific Ocean, about halfway between Hawaii and Australia. It was set off at 7:15 A.M. local time on November 1, 1952.

The Alamogordo bomb had a force of 19 KT's. The first H-bomb was 10 MT's—more than five hundred times as powerful.

The mushroom cloud at Alamogordo rose nearly eight miles. At Elugelab it went up twenty miles. The fireball at Elugelab grew to a width of three and one-half miles within four seconds, and beneath it—where the little island had been—there was nothing but a mile-wide, 175-foot-deep crater in the ocean floor.

In November of 1952, no one knew much about the precise effects a ten-megaton bomb might have if exploded over a city. But during the fifties, as more and more nuclear tests were measured, scientists developed a clearer understanding of just what the cost might be. At low altitude on a clear day, a ten-megaton bomb would blast away most buildings in every direction for ten miles. The flash of heat from the bomb would give third-degree burns out to about twenty miles, second-degree burns to twenty-five miles; it might blind anyone who looked at it even from as far away as one hundred miles; it would start thousands of fires and might gather them up into one great firestorm that could burn everything combustible, including the oxygen in the air. Moreover, for years and years afterwards, the tiny radioactive particles created by the explosion and swept up in the mushroom cloud would fall out from the

sky to poison the earth and the sea and whatever creatures
struggled there to survive.

The energy of the Alamogordo bomb came from the
fission process, the splitting of heavy atoms. When they
split, they lost a tiny bit of their mass, mass that "became"
energy. But Albert Einstein's famous statement of the relationship between mass and energy, $E = mc^2$, applies not
only to the fission of heavy atoms but also to the fusion of
light ones. It was fusion that was tested at Elugelab.

Just as uranium or plutonium are used in a fission bomb
because they are heavy, so hydrogen is used in a fusion
bomb because it is light. In the H-bomb, high enough temperatures are created to fuse atoms of hydrogen, or varieties
of it. In the process, just as in fission, mass is lost and vast
energy released. It is because of the intense heat required
for fusion that this type of bomb is called thermonuclear.

The man who became known as the "Father of the
Hydrogen Bomb," a nickname he disliked intensely, was
a dark, brilliant, intuitive, persuasive former Hungarian—
a physicist and chemist adept at both theory and engineering—Edward Teller.

Teller was born in Budapest on January 15, 1908. His
father was a successful lawyer who had his son tutored privately until he was ten.

"For as long as I could remember," Teller wrote in 1962,
"I had wanted to do one thing: to play with ideas and find
out how the world is put together." [5]

Teller went to school in Budapest until he was eighteen,
but in Hungary in the 1920's, it was difficult for a Jew, as
Teller was, to overcome prejudice and get a higher education. So, in 1926, Teller went to Germany.

One Sunday in Munich, in 1928, Teller was running for
a street car to begin a trip to the mountains where he
could do some climbing when his right foot slipped under

the wheel of the car and had to be amputated, just above the ankle. The rest of his life Teller would have to wear a leather foot and walk with a limp.

When Hitler came to power with his anti-Semitic ideas, Teller moved on again. He studied and worked in Copenhagen and London, then came to the United States in 1935. It was at George Washington University in Washington, D.C., that Teller began his thermonuclear research.

What Teller and others wanted was nothing less than a way in which the energy created in the stars—in our sun—also could be created on earth. In 1938, the Cornell University physicist Hans Bethe—another refugee from Nazi Germany—theorized that the source of the sun's light and heat was a thermonuclear fusion of hydrogen into helium. But to achieve this would require temperatures then unknown on earth: 100 million degrees centigrade.

At Columbia University in 1941, the year Teller became an American citizen, Teller and Enrico Fermi were discussing fusion. Both men knew the likelihood of a fission bomb. Fermi asked Teller: Why not use such a bomb to create heat enough to trigger the kind of thing that happens in the sun?

In 1943, Teller went to Los Alamos to work almost exclusively on the bomb of Alamogordo. But Teller never lost interest in Fermi's suggestion and in what the physicists called the "Super."

After Hiroshima, U.S. nuclear weapons research was put into low gear. Most of the physicists wanted to get back to their universities and have no more to do with what many of them had come to feel was the "dirty" business of Los Alamos. Moreover, the U.S. government felt that its monopoly of the fission bomb would continue for many years. Then came August 29, 1949, and unmistakable evidence that the Soviet Union had tested its own atomic bomb. Teller was convinced that the U.S. should delay no longer in going all out to build a hydrogen bomb.

There began then a major debate—within the government at first, later in public. Teller and a few others thought the security of the free world demanded that the U.S. have the Super. The majority of the most influential scientists in America thought such a project would be wrong.

Bethe wrote: "Can we who have always insisted on morality and human decency between nations as well as inside our own country introduce this weapon of total annihilation into the world?" [6]

Teller wrote: "The scientist is not responsible for the laws of nature. It is his job to find out how these laws operate. . . ." [7]

A group of physicists issued a statement saying: "We believe that no nation has the right to use such a bomb, no matter how righteous its cause. This bomb is no longer a weapon of war but a means of extermination of whole populations. Its use would be a betrayal of all standards of morality and of Christian civilization itself. . . ." [8]

Teller wrote: ". . . it is not the scientist's job to determine whether a hydrogen bomb should be constructed, whether it should be used, or how it should be used. This responsibility rests with the American people and with their chosen representatives." [9]

On October 29, 1949, the chief scientific consultants to the Atomic Energy Commission, its General Advisory Committee, recommended unanimously that the Super should "never be produced." (The Chairman of that committee was the influential J. Robert Oppenheimer, the man who had said after Hiroshima, ". . . the physicists have known sin.") But events overruled the scientists.

When, on January 27, 1950, Klaus Fuchs confessed that he had spied for Russia—Fuchs who not only had helped build the fission bomb but who had also discussed with Teller how the fusion bomb might be built—President Harry Truman required only four days, to January 31, to countermand the A.E.C. and order that work on the H-bomb begin.

The question was: How to make it? One of the reasons for the opposition to the project was that no one knew yet whether the Super could be built, and all signs indicated that if it could be, it would drain away precious resources from the fission bomb program. Theory indicated that the fuel most likely to fuse would be tritium, a variety or isotope of ordinary hydrogen, three times as heavy as hydrogen. But the only way known to get tritium was to split the nucleus of the element lithium, and this would be an expensive process. Moreover, there seemed a serious problem, once the fission trigger was pulled, of holding everything else together long enough for fusion to occur.

Teller said once: "A scientific invention consists of six (or some number) of ideas, five of which are absurd but which with the addition of the sixth and enough rearrangement of the combinations result in something no one has ever thought of before." [10]

About the first of February, 1951, at Los Alamos, Teller got his sixth idea. Bethe called it "a brilliant discovery . . . a stroke of genius which does not occur in the normal development of ideas." [11] The Elugelab shot of November 1, 1952, was proof that Teller had been right, and subsequently the H-bomb was even made relatively simple and inexpensive. Lithium was split not in reactors before the explosion but in the bomb itself, and the resulting tritium fused in the intense heat. It was found that ordinary uranium would serve as the jacket holding everything together while fusion occurred. Then the plentiful atoms of $U^{238}$ in this jacket were split by the neutrons released in the fusion. So the H-bomb was really a three-step fission-fusion-fission series of chain reactions. Because there was no critical mass of lithium or natural uranium, which could not be exceeded without danger of premature explosion, there seemed no limit to the size of H-bomb that could be built.

Teller went on to lobby for and then organize a second nuclear weapons laboratory, this one at Livermore, California, near San Francisco. There and at Los Alamos, during the fifties, thousands of scientists and engineers continued to develop more and more of more and more types of fission and fusion bombs, and there, as he had at Los Alamos, Teller decorated his office wall with a little poem lettered in gold:

> "Providence, who watches over children and
>     drunkards and fools
> With silent miracles and other esoterica,
> Continue to suspend the customary rules
> And protect the United States of America." [12]

Dwight Eisenhower spent much of his time as President trying to find a way to guarantee that nuclear weapons never would be used. On December 8, 1953, addressing the United Nations General Assembly, he proposed a plan that came to be called "Atoms for Peace" by which each nation with nuclear power would give up some of its fissionable material to an international agency that would use it in peaceful ways. In 1955, in Geneva, at a meeting of the top men of the U.S., Britain, France, and Russia—a meeting, as Winston Churchill had put it, at the "summit"—President Eisenhower put forward his "Open Skies" plan whereby the U.S. and Russia each would permit the other to take aerial photographs of its territory. The idea was that such pictures could reveal any preparations for surprise attack, thus warning the other side. There were endless disarmament conferences, more than seventy of them in fifteen years. But none succeeded because each side too often seemed to want to disarm the other more than itself. More important, the secretive Russians, with their ancient suspicion of foreigners, would never agree to effective international inspection of any disarmament agreement, charging that inspectors really would be spies; but without inspection, no one could be sure the Russians were not cheating.

Therefore, the arms race continued, relentlessly, and it was President Eisenhower's delicate job to defend the West without concessions to the Communists and without using the bomb.

Eisenhower's Army training, which had taught him to delegate authority, made it natural for him as President to give his Secretary of State great trust and power. The man he chose for this job, the man who became the symbol of U.S. power and intent, was a learned, vigorous, Puritanical lawyer and churchman, John Foster Dulles. Even more than Eisenhower, Dulles came to personify the West's dilemma: he was religiously devoted to the goals of peace and freedom for all men; yet to pursue these goals in the thermonuclear age, he had to risk the lives of the same people he was trying to serve.

Foster Dulles, as he was known, was born in Washington, D.C., February 25, 1888, and raised in Watertown, New York, where his father was the pastor of the First Presbyterian Church. His family background gave him his life's orientation, both religious and worldly. As the grandson of one Secretary of State and the nephew of another, Dulles grew up on stories of diplomacy. He also was raised in strict religious discipline: attendance at church three or four times a week, with Sundays, after church, devoted to memorizing hymns, poetry, and the Bible.

Dulles studied philosophy at Princeton and graduated Phi Beta Kappa and valedictorian of the class of 1908. He intended to become a minister like his father, but, apparently, the call was not clear. After studying philosophy for a year in Paris, he came home to become a lawyer, going through George Washington University law school in two years and then taking a job with the great New York law firm, Sullivan and Cromwell.

Thus began Dulles's brilliant career, first as an international lawyer, then as an architect and builder of American foreign policy. He became a senior partner in his firm, one of the highest paid attorneys in the world. Then about 1937, as Hitler and Mussolini threatened war, Dulles began devoting more and more of his time to his church and especially to the study of how Christian standards might be applied to help achieve a lasting peace. He also became the leading foreign policy adviser to the Republican party and, as such, he was President Eisenhower's obvious choice as Secretary of State.

Perhaps no man in modern America ever has been better prepared for the job to which Dulles was appointed. As secretary to his grandfather, he had attended his first international conference when he was nineteen and had been an adviser to those writing the Treaty of Versailles ending World War I. In later life, as an influential Republican who might help recruit G.O.P. support for the agreements ending World War II, Dulles was chosen by Democratic administrations to be a senior adviser to the U.S. delegation at the U.N. conference in San Francisco and the author of the U.S. Peace Treaty with Japan. For a few months, as an appointee, he had also been a United States Senator.

Dulles was a careful student of the theories underlying both democracy and Communism. On his bedside table, he kept the *Federalist Papers,* the *Bible,* and Stalin's *Problems of Leninism.* His great French friend Jean Monnet said of him: "Dulles had the image of liberty constantly before him. If you apply this key, you will find the answer to all of his actions." [13]

Dulles was not unaware of his qualifications for his new job. He became almost a one-man State Department, sometimes seeming to live in his airplane in order to talk face to face with those with whom he planned Western strategy. During his secretaryship, he traveled 559,988 miles.

There was no question of Dulles's devotion to the goal of peace with freedom. "His religious belief and his love of liberty shimmered through every discussion in one way

or another," said the man who translated his frequent talks
with West Germany's Chancellor, Konrad Adenauer. "One
could see beyond a doubt in these conversations that Dulles
really believed in God, and shaped his policy accordingly." [14]

But the very faith that made Dulles so opposed to what
he normally called "atheistic Communism" also made him
seem to many persons too moralistic, too much the unbend-
ing Puritan. Moreover, his tendency to imply more than he
meant in his public statements led many people to assume
that Dulles was a dangerous cold warrior. He became feared,
particularly in Western Europe, for three slogans that were
associated with his name: "rollback," "massive retaliation,"
and "brinksmanship."

To Dulles, mere containment of Communist power was
not enough. He considered it immoral not to go beyond
containment to a more aggressive policy of trying to liberate countries under Communist domination. He wrote in
1950: "It is time to think in terms of taking the offensive
in the world struggle for freedom and of rolling back the
engulfing tide of despotism." [15]

"Massive retaliation" became famous in a Dulles speech
to the Council on Foreign Relations in New York, on January 12, 1954. "Local defense will always be important,"
said the Secretary of State, referring to the need for a ring
of force on Communism's borders. "But there is no local
defense which alone will contain the mighty land power of
the Communist world. Local defenses must be reinforced
by the further deterrent of massive retaliatory power . . .
a great capacity to retaliate, instantly, by means and at
places of our choosing. . . ."

Finally, there was "brinksmanship." In an interview published in 1956, Dulles said, "You have to take chances for
peace, just as you must take chances in war. Some say that
we were brought to the verge of war. Of course we were
brought to the verge of war. The ability to get to the
verge without getting into the war is the necessary art.

If you cannot master it, you inevitably get into war. If you try to run away from it, if you are scared to go to the brink, you are lost." [16]

Actually, there was nothing new about what Dulles really meant in any of these statements. Massive retaliation had been implied U.S. policy ever since the nuclear age began, and brinksmanship was as old as diplomacy. Moreover, Dulles later qualified many of his remarks: rollback, he insisted, did not imply the use of force. Nevertheless, there was something about the Dulles language and manner that did not ease the fearful climate of the times, and the U.S. did threaten to fight more than once.

In 1953, Dulles passed the word that unless the Chinese agreed to a truce in Korea, the U.S. would do as General MacArthur had recommended and fight to win. Soon afterwards, there was an armistice.

In 1954 and 1955, and again in 1958, the Chinese shelled the little offshore islands of Quemoy and Matsu, which were held by Chiang Kai-shek's forces from Formosa. The U.S. made it clear that if the Chinese were thinking of attacking Formosa, they would have to fight the U.S. as well. Eventually, the shelling stopped.

But the realities of the cold war in the thermonuclear age also forced the U.S. back from the brink more than once. In 1954, Dulles gave serious consideration to going to war alongside the French in Indo-China. For seven years, the French had been tied down there, fighting Communist-led nationalists who wanted to run their own country free of French rule. With so many new nations in the world, the U.S. did not want to be on the unpopular side in a colonial war, but President Eisenhower subscribed to what was called the "domino theory"; referring to what would happen to all the other nations of Southeast Asia if South Viet Nam were to become Communist, Mr. Eisenhower said at a 1954 news conference: "You have a row of dominoes set up and you knock over the first one, and what will happen to the last one is the certainty that it will go over very quickly." [17] So the U.S. chose anti-Communism over anticolonialism and paid for more than a third of France's Indo-China effort. Even this was not enough, however, and by the spring of 1954, the French were surrounded in a valley called Dien Bien Phu. Should the U.S. go in, too? Many persons feared that it would, perhaps with nuclear weapons. But the New Look had left the U.S. with too few conventional forces to do the job, and no one was eager to use nuclear weapons in Asia again. So the U.S. did nothing —then. Dien Bien Phu fell, and the Communists took half of Viet Nam.

One of the problems of fighting in Viet Nam, and of fighting anywhere, was the danger of what came to be called "escalation." A little war with conventional weapons could escalate, step by step, to world thermonuclear war. In 1956, Suez contained this danger. On June 26 of that year, President Gamal Abdul Nasser of Egypt had decreed that henceforth his government would be the owner of the Suez Canal connecting the Mediterranean with the Red Sea. The British and French had owned the canal, which the French had built and on which both countries depended, especially for shipments of oil. So, when negotiations failed, Britain and France invaded Egypt in retaliation, on November 5. The U.S., however, feared that war in the Middle East might invite Russian participation and that what started relatively small could become suicidally big. Therefore, the U.S. opposed even its traditional allies, putting on enough pressure to force their humiliating withdrawal.

The danger of escalation was an even greater factor in the U.S. decision not to go to the aid of Hungary, also in 1956. There was a revolution in Budapest against Russian rule that appeared as if it might succeed. But then at midnight on November 4, the Russians struck, moving in with overwhelming force. Two hundred thousand Hungarians fled their country. Many observers thought Hungary in

1956 the perfect opportunity for Secretary Dulles to imple-
ment his policy of rollback, but the realities of the nuclear
age seemed to make this impossible. Who could say what
might grow from a meeting somewhere in central Europe
of just one American and one Russian tank? It was the
danger of just such a direct confrontation between the
two great nuclear powers that made West Berlin, too, such
a continuing source of cold war tension.

On each of these occasions—Korea, Quemoy-Matsu, Indo-
China, Suez, and Hungary—one side or both moved back
from the edge in time. But each crisis contained the seeds
of disaster, and with each year of the fifties, thermonuclear
developments in the U.S. and Russia increased the magnitude of that disaster, should it come. Russia tested her
first hydrogen bomb on August 12, 1953, just nine months
after the first U.S. test. Both countries built up fleets
of jet planes to carry their bombs to the other. Moreover,
the power of the H-bomb meant that it could do vast damage even if it were exploded miles from its target. This
fact permitted and triggered a race to develop the intercontinental ballistic missile—the ICBM—which, armed with
a thermonuclear warhead, was to become the "ultimate
weapon" for which neither side had any defense.

Dwight Eisenhower must have thought more than once
during his Presidency about the answers to the questions
he himself had asked in his Inaugural Address. Were we
nearer the light? Or were the shadows of another night
closing in? It sometimes seemed as if the answer to both
questions could be "yes." The new weapons added to world
tensions and thereby made war more likely. At the same
time, they seemed too dangerous to use, and this made war
less likely. Dr. J. Robert Oppenheimer had put the situation graphically in 1953. "The atomic clock ticks faster
and faster," he wrote. "We may anticipate a state of affairs
in which two Great Powers will each be in a position to put

an end to the civilization and life of the other, though not without risking its own. We may be likened to two scorpions in a bottle, each capable of killing the other, but only at the risk of his own life. This prospect," added the man who had built the bomb, "does not tend to make for serenity. . . ." [18]

Winston Churchill also had anticipated this state, calling it "peace through mutual terror." Because neither side could use its new weapons on the other without guaranteeing its own destruction in return, Churchill looked forward to a day in which "by a process of sublime irony . . . safety will be the sturdy child of terror, and survival the twin brother of annihilation." [19]

But—even terrified—could anyone really count on safety and survival? Even if no rational man would start a nuclear war, what about the insane? What about even a sane man who miscalculates and imagines that his enemy will not come all the way to the brink? And might tension become so great that war could start if an H-bomb went off somewhere by accident?

President Eisenhower had lamented, in his Inaugural Address: "Science seems ready to confer upon us, as its final gift, the power to erase human life from this planet." By the end of his Presidency, there was no doubt that this had happened. There existed by then in the nuclear stockpiles of East and West the equivalent of more than ten tons of TNT for every man, woman, and child on earth.

## Chapter Seven

# THE MISSILE DUEL

THE missile and space age began on October 4, 1957, with a fiery rocket launching from Kazakhstan in the south-central U.S.S.R., near the Aral Sea. A 120-foot-high "booster" lifted a 22-inch-wide, 184-pound hollow aluminum sphere up through the earth's atmosphere into the near vacuum of near space. The rocket did its job with such thrust that the little capsule was accelerated to a speed of nearly five miles per second, nearly 18,000 miles per hour. Because this is the speed required to offset the pull of the earth's gravity, the shiny sphere the Soviets called "Sputnik"—in Russian, "fellow traveler"—became the world's first man-made moon, going into orbit around the earth once every ninety-six minutes.

In orbit, when its booster and casing had fallen away, Sputnik's four antennae snapped out into position, and batteries inside began feeding power to two radio transmitters that broadcast a signal back to earth. It was an insistent "beep": a third of a second of tone, then a third of a second of silence, then a third of a second of tone again. At one time or another in the three months Sputnik was in orbit, this "beep-beep-beep" could have been heard in nearly every part of the earth, telling anyone who cared to think about it that in the field of rocketry the Union of Soviet Socialist Republics now led all other countries,

*138*

including the U.S.A. This leadership was a symbol of general scientific and engineering prowess, but it also had special importance in the cold war, for throughout the world it quickly became understood that a nation with rockets which could put a satellite into orbit could use the same rockets to launch intercontinental missiles.

In the United States, many top government officials spoke of Sputnik as if it were of little significance, military or psychological. President Eisenhower said at a news conference, ". . . in itself it imposes no additional threat to the United States." The outgoing Secretary of Defense, Charles Wilson, called the launching "a nice scientific trick." The Chief of Naval Operations described it as "a hunk of iron almost anybody could launch."

But many U.S. scientists and engineers, and many Democratic politicians, reacted as if stunned. One called the achievement "fantastic." Senator Henry Jackson said it was "a devastating blow to U.S. scientific, industrial, and technical prestige." Another scientist said, "We won the first round with the H-bomb, they won the second with the satellite."

The fact was that a nation that had been relatively backward forty years before, and that had had two-thirds of its industry laid waste by war just fifteen years before, had demonstrated in a spectacular way that its scientists, its engineers, and its industrial abilities were by no means second rate.

The American predicament was hardly the fault of lack of scientific theory. The basic principles of rocketry had been known for centuries, ever since the ancient Chinese lit up the sky with high-flying fireworks. Sir Isaac Newton had stated the principles in his Third Law of Motion in 1687: every action, he wrote in the *Principia Mathematica*, has an equal and opposite reaction. A rocket does not move because its exhaust pushes against the air; it moves because a force going out from it one way requires an equal movement the other way. Rockets work best where there is no air.

The British used rockets effectively in their attack on Washington, D.C., in the War of 1812. Describing the siege of Fort McHenry in Baltimore in that war, Francis Scott Key wrote a factual, not an imaginative account when he reported "The Star-Spangled Banner's" survival through a perilous night lighted by the "rockets' red glare," rockets that did indeed carry "bombs bursting in air."

During the early years of the twentieth century, the American Robert Goddard pioneered modern rocket research, and there were major advances in Russia, as well. But it was left to the Germans during World War II to develop the V-1 airplane-like "buzz bomb" and then the V-2 rocket, a lethal, liquid-fuel missile that climbed seventy miles high and then plunged to its target in Belgium or Britain, traveling faster than the speed of sound. (V was the first letter of the German word for "reprisal weapon.")

After the war, both the U.S. and Russia enjoyed the assistance of German rocket experts, and both countries built on the Germans' liquid-fuel experience. The resulting boosters were wonders not only of mathematics and chemistry but also of plumbing. The early U.S. varieties were, really, giant tanks holding kerosene and cold liquid oxygen nicknamed "lox." (A rocket must carry its own oxygen because it climbs to altitudes at which the atmosphere contains too little oxygen for the fuel to burn.) A pump would spray the fuel and oxygen into the rocket chamber, where the mixture would be ignited, and the resulting burning gases—expanding at great speed—would have only one way out: through a nozzle at one end of the chamber. It was this action in one direction that caused an equal reaction in the other. Later, there was more and more use of solid fuel and so-called hypergolic fuel—liquids such as blends of hydrazine that all but explode merely on contact with

another liquid like nitrogen oxide—but, whatever the pro-
pellant, the Newtonian reaction principle remained fundamental.

In both the U.S. and Russia in the late forties, development of an intercontinental missile was more a matter of
engineering effort than of scientific breakthrough. In the
U.S., this effort was not begun until the successful development of the hydrogen bomb made possible a warhead with
force enough to compensate for the aiming errors likely
in a rocket. Moreover, once begun, the U.S. program did
not include an appreciation of the psychological and political value of being first to put a satellite into orbit. "Our
satellite program," said President Eisenhower, "has never
been conducted as a race with other nations." [1]

But Russia started sooner than the U.S., and Russia chose
to develop far more powerful boosters than those built, at
first, by the U.S. Russia did not separate her purely military
and satellite programs, as did the U.S., and Russia was by
no means shy about showing off her "weight-lifting" capability. So, the early part of the race into space was an uneven
contest.

On November 3, 1957, when the U.S. had realized it
was indeed in a race and was hurrying to prove that it,
too, could put something into orbit, Russia launched Sputnik II. This was 1,120 pounds of payload—more than six
times heavier than Sputnik I—and the load included a live
Husky dog named Laika. Special instruments on board the
satellite let scientists on earth monitor Laika's reaction to
being weightless.

Finally, on December 6, 1957, the U.S. was ready to
launch the Navy's Vanguard I. Its job was to put into orbit
a satellite weighing only four pounds, about the size of a
grapefruit; if it were successful, it would put the U.S. into
the race. At Cape Canaveral (later Cape Kennedy) in
Florida, while the world watched, the Vanguard countdown
was completed, the fuel was ignited, the rocket began to

lift off the launching pad, but then—after a flight of little more than two feet lasting no more than two seconds—the whole thing blew up. It was a humiliating failure. At the United Nations, Russian diplomats taunted their American opposite numbers, asking gravely if the U.S. would like Russian technical aid.

Soon afterwards, of course, the U.S. space program matured, with achievements both spectacular and of great scientific and military value. On January 31, 1958, the U.S. launched its first satellite, Explorer I. On May 5, 1961, Commander Alan B. Shepard became the first American astronaut to fly into space. On February 20, 1962, Lieutenant Colonel John Glenn orbited the earth three times.

With its rocket lead, Russia had been the first to put a man into space, "Cosmonaut" Yuri Gagarin successfully orbiting the earth on April 12, 1961. But the U.S. matched and surpassed nearly every Soviet achievement. By 1965, the U.S. had developed hundreds of ingenious spacecrafts to study the weather, relay television signals, watch for nuclear explosions, and photograph the moon and Mars. Moreover, the nation was publicly committed to trying to land two men on the moon and return them safely by 1970.

Nevertheless, there was a time, in the late fifties, when Russia's Sputnik "trick" caused great concern. As the then Senator Lyndon Johnson put it: "We cannot concede outer space to communism and hold leadership on earth." [2]

The man who presided over Russia and Russia's new missile power was a loud, earthy, squat, quick-tempered, sometimes engaging, always shrewd politician, Nikita Sergeyevich Khrushchev. For most of his life, his was a dazzling success story, Soviet style.

Khrushchev was born on April 17, 1894, in the village of Kalinovka near the town of Kursk in southern Russia, near the Ukraine. His father was a coal miner, and Khrushchev in his turn became a miner. At other times, he was also a shepherd and a metal worker. In 1918, after the revolution, Khrushchev joined the Communist party. He had had very little formal education, but the party accepted him in one of its new three-year high schools for adults. From that time on, Khrushchev's life was devoted to the brutal, fearful, uncertain world of the party. He became what was known then as an "apparatchik," a man of the party apparatus, moving nimbly and luckily from one rung to the next up the ladder, doing whatever was required of him, including helping Stalin carry out the terrible purges by which he killed or imprisoned those of whom he was suspicious.

There are, in a sense, two governments in the Soviet Union. One is the formal one of ministries and government-owned industries and farms. The other is the party. At nearly every level, from the Kremlin to the individual factory, a party official not only keeps his eye on what is going on but also helps run things. The top party man at each major level is the First Secretary.

Khrushchev became First Secretary for the city and region of Moscow, then First Secretary for the huge and productive Ukraine. When the Germans attacked in 1941, Khrushchev helped organize resistance and became a Lieutenant General, the party man attached to various Soviet armies. After the war, he helped rebuild the Ukraine, and then, in 1949, he was recalled by Stalin to his old job as First Secretary for Moscow.

On March 5, 1953, at the age of seventy-three, Stalin died, and as one of the top men in all Russia then, Khrushchev was one of Stalin's pallbearers and the man in charge of his funeral. There is in Russia no orderly or constitutional way by which one dictator succeeds another. The survivors just have to fight it out. Stalin had been top man in both government and party, but his successors had to share power—at first. No one of them was strong enough to take over by himself. So Georgi Malenkov became the top government man, the Chairman of the Council of Ministers. And, on September 13, 1953, Nikita Khrushchev succeeded Stalin as First Secretary of the party.

Khrushchev and Stalin's other heirs were thoroughly ambitious and competitive men. All their party lives, they had done whatever they had been told to do, in order to succeed. But by 1953, they had had enough of Stalin's terror. They did execute the head man of the secret police, Lavrenti Beria. But they also permitted throughout the Soviet Union an easing of fear and total party control, an amnesty for many political prisoners, more freedom for writers and artists and scientists and scholars. The author Ilya Ehrenburg gave a name to this time of new hope when he called a book about it *The Thaw*.

In the Kremlin after Stalin's death, "collective leadership" worked for a while, but gradually Khrushchev, with his control of the party, became first among equals. In early 1955, Malenkov resigned as Chairman of the Council of Ministers, to be replaced by one of Khrushchev's friends, Nikolai Bulganin. On March 27, 1958, Khrushchev had lined up enough support to be elected Chairman himself. Like Stalin before him, he now had both of Russia's top jobs.

As a student of Communism as well as power, Khrushchev knew that traditional Marxist-Leninist theory held that war between Communism and capitalism was inevitable. Lenin had written: "The existence of the Soviet Republic side by side with imperialist States for a long time is unthinkable. One or the other must triumph in the end. And before that end supervenes a series of frightful collisions between the Soviet Republic and the bourgeois States will be inevitable." [3] But Khrushchev was also a realist who knew that war with modern missiles and the hydrogen bomb would destroy not only capitalism but Russia, too. After such a war, he said, the living would envy the dead. At the Twentieth Congress of the Communist Party of the Soviet Union, in 1956, Khrushchev insisted, ". . . war is not a fatalistic inevitability." He went on to preach what he called "peaceful coexistence" with non-Communist countries.

As Khrushchev saw the world, Communist nuclear, air, rocket, and ground power was or soon would be enough to deter the West from attacking Russia. With China now a Communist country and nation after nation cutting their colonial ties, Khrushchev thought the world balance of power was shifting to the Communist side. Moreover, Khrushchev insisted that Soviet economic growth was continuing at a pace that would permit Russian production to overtake that of the U.S. by 1970. There was in Khrushchev's doctrine no deviation from the Marxist-Leninist goal of a Communist world. (Khrushchev said that objective would be abandoned only when the shrimp learned to whistle.) What was changed was the means to the end. At a Kremlin reception on November 17, 1956, Khrushchev shouted to a group of visiting Westerners, "Whether you like it or not history is on our side. We will bury you." He explained later that this did not mean physical interment. "I believe I did use that expression once," he admitted, but he insisted he was speaking figuratively. By the "laws" of history, said Khrushchev, communism would replace capitalism just as capitalism had replaced feudalism, "and capitalism thereby would be, so to speak, buried." [4]

But who in the West could be sure that if the balance of military power shifted to the Communists, they would not abandon "peaceful coexistence" and try to have their way suddenly by surprise attack? And even though Khrushchev in a speech to party organizations in 1961 called the prevention of thermonuclear war "the most burning and vital problem for mankind," who could be sure that a small anticolonial war, a war Khrushchev called one of "national liberation" and the kind of war he considered "sacred," could not escalate into all-out disaster?

In the West, a worried minority of persons felt that the survival of the human race demanded the destruction of U.S. and British nuclear weapons even if Russia would not do the same and even if this invited Communist takeover. As they put it: "Better Red than Dead." The prevailing view, however, was that it would be folly to disarm unless the West could be sure Russia were doing the same, and that until such a time came, the only chance of preventing war lay in trying to stay stronger than the Communists.

So, the arms race continued. By 1958, the U.S. government was spending, annually, forty-five billion dollars on defense alone, more than it had spent on defense and everything else just ten years before. This was about 10 percent of the value of all the goods and services produced in all the country. In total, in the first fifteen years of the cold war, the U.S. spent about half a trillion dollars on defense.

In the early fifties, a few American officers had spoken of the desirability of "preventive war": the U.S. should attack and destroy Russia, they argued, before Russia became powerful enough to attack and destroy the U.S. It was true that whichever side could make the first strike would have a great advantage. But a world in which each side thought the other was planning a surprise first strike would be certain to produce one. Therefore, the U.S. chose to build forces capable of what was called a second strike.

In World War II, the U.S. had been able to mobilize after Pearl Harbor, but the missile age demanded mobilization in advance. Moreover, what mattered as a deterrent would be not what force existed before an attack but what force could survive an enemy first strike and still be able to launch a devastating second strike in reply.

To make Russia believe in American second strike capability, the U.S. developed an elaborate military machine. Some of the jet bombers of the Strategic Air Command were kept in flight at all times. Some of the others were on such taut alert on the ground that their crews became able to take off in less than three minutes, B-52's rolling down the runways fifteen seconds apart, each in the wash of the one before. In the early 1960's, missiles began replacing planes, and of these perhaps the most important were the Minutemen. Their fuel was a gray rubber-like solid always ready for firing in less than a minute after the decision to launch had been made. Each Minuteman was sunk into a silo made of twelve tons of steel and concrete, each silo capable of withstanding blast pressure of at least a hundred pounds per square inch. The plan was to scatter a thousand of these across the U.S., making it almost impossible for an enemy attack to destroy the contents of every one.

Even more secure were the Navy's Polaris missiles, again solid-fuel rockets but mounted in nuclear-powered submarines instead of silos. Each submarine carried sixteen missiles, and each could lie quietly in the oceans around Russia's borders, undetected and secure. There were to be forty-one such ships by 1967.

Polaris, Minuteman, and all the other complex and expensive elements of American security were, of course, begun under President Eisenhower. Before the second Eisenhower term came to an end, Washington officials also came to see the need for more conventional forces to enable the U.S. to fight at any level, "brushfire" as well as thermonuclear wars. But in the frightened reaction to Sputnik, it became possible for Democrats in the U.S. to mount a telling campaign in 1960 on the issue of America's apparently declining world power and prestige. The man who led that campaign, the man who became the Thirty-fifth President of the United States, the man who went to the brink of war and won a missile showdown with Nikita Khrushchev, was John Fitzgerald Kennedy.

John F. Kennedy was a tall, graceful, well-educated child of privilege who, as they said of him in his native Boston, had "class." He was also a tough, cool, and intensely practical politician. One of his grandfathers, John F. ("Honey Fitz") Fitzgerald, had been mayor of Boston, well known during campaigns for his renditions of "Sweet Adeline." John Kennedy was not too far removed from his Irish immigrant forebears to be unable to play the political game hard and happily.

Kennedy was restrained, sparing of gesture and emotion. According to his brother Robert, injuries and sickness caused him to be in physical pain at least half of his life. Yet neither pain nor responsibility subdued a dry, often devastating wit.

As a student and writer of history, Kennedy insisted on a life of action and excellence, frequently quoting an ancient Greek definition of happiness as "the exercise of vital powers along lines of excellence in a life affording them scope." Of the lure of the Presidency, he said once: "This ability to do things well, and to do them with precision and with modesty attracts us all." [5] He was also fond of quoting Dante on the subject of personal commitment: "The hottest places in Hell are reserved for those who, in a time of great moral crisis, maintain their neutrality."

Yet Kennedy had no illusions about his or anyone else's ability to change human nature. Even as he led the country, he sometimes seemed almost a bemused spectator, taking no one, including himself, too seriously. To one of his great friends, he once gave a silver beer mug on which was inscribed: "There are three things which are real: God, human folly and laughter. The first two are beyond our comprehension. So we must do what we can with the third." [6]

Kennedy was intelligent, eloquent, and courageous. It was not just tragic but also absurd that he should have been murdered.

He was born May 29, 1917, in Brookline, Massachusetts, a suburb of Boston. His father was a highly successful financier, later U.S. Ambassador to Great Britain. There were nine Kennedy children, reared in an atmosphere both of great family loyalty and of intense competition. John Kennedy was the second of the nine.

At Harvard, Kennedy hurt his spine playing football, made the swimming team, won sailing races with his older brother, and wrote a senior thesis on prewar Britain that was good enough to be published, in 1940. It was called *Why England Slept*.

During World War II, Kennedy was a lieutenant in the Navy in command of a motor torpedo boat in the Solomon Islands in the Pacific. In August of 1943, his PT-109 was hit and sliced in two by a Japanese destroyer. Kennedy swam three miles to shore, towing one of his wounded crewmen by a lifebelt he held in his teeth. Eventually, he and his men were rescued, but in the ordeal Kennedy suffered serious enough injuries to be sent home to Massachusetts to recuperate. It was while he was in the hospital, in 1944, that he got the news that his older brother, Joe, had been killed in Europe.

In the Kennedy family, it had been assumed that Joseph P. Kennedy, Jr., would go into politics. With his death, the second son took over this responsibility. John F. Kennedy ran for Congress in 1946 and was elected. He ran for the U.S. Senate in 1952 and was elected. He ran for the White House in 1960 and was elected. At forty-three years of age, he was the youngest man ever chosen President of the United States.

One reason why Kennedy could climb so swiftly was his family's money and help. But in the end, it was he himself who made the decisive difference: he had the ability to overcome handicaps. In 1954, when he was bedridden for six months recuperating from a spinal operation, he used the time to write a series of short biographies, *Profiles in Courage,* which won a Pulitzer Prize. In 1960, when many thought him too young for the job he sought, he denied his inexperience with an impressive command of fact and argument in television debates with his opponent,

Vice-President Richard Nixon. And with straightforward statements throughout the campaign, Kennedy tried to change the minds of those whose prejudices forced them to suspect that a Roman Catholic as President might find his loyalty to his country challenged by his loyalty to his church.

On November 8, 1960, Kennedy became the first American Catholic ever elected President.

Kennedy had spoken in his campaign of "Getting America Moving Again," urging the country to meet the responsibilities and opportunities of what he labeled the "New Frontier." Now, in the bright, bitter-cold noon day of January 20, 1961, Kennedy stood in front of the Capitol, shouting out his inaugural challenge to his countrymen and to the world: "Let the word go forth from this time and place," he said, "to friend and foe alike, that the torch has been passed to a new generation of Americans, born in this century, tempered by war, disciplined by a cold and bitter peace, proud of our ancient heritage, and unwilling to witness or permit the slow undoing of those human rights to which this nation has always been committed, and to which we are committed today at home and around the world.

"Let every nation know, whether it wishes us well or ill, that we shall pay any price, bear any burden, meet any hardship, support any friend, oppose any foe to assure the survival and the success of liberty."

The new President spoke of the need for negotiation between East and West, of the dangers of the arms race, of the need for a world of law and plenty. "All this will not be finished in the first one hundred days," he said. "Nor will it be finished in the first one thousand days, nor in the life of this Administration, nor even perhaps in our lifetime on this planet. But let us begin.

"In the long history of the world," he said as he neared the end of his speech, "only a few generations have been granted the role of defending freedom in its hour of maximum danger. I do not shrink from this responsibility; I welcome it. I do not believe that any of us would exchange places with any other people or any other generation. The energy, the faith, the devotion which we bring to this endeavor will light our country and all who serve it, and the glow from that fire can truly light the world.

"And so, my fellow Americans, ask not what your country can do for you; ask what you can do for your country.

"My fellow citizens of the world, ask not what America will do for you, but what together we can do for the freedom of man."

Eloquent as was much of President Kennedy's Inaugural Address, he would have been the first to insist that rhetoric is no substitute for action. Now that the torch had been passed, how was Kennedy to cope with the balance of terror and the brink of war?

Just nine days after he had spoken with such enthusiasm of defending freedom in its hour of maximum danger, John F. Kennedy returned to the Capitol to give his State of the Union address. This time the realities of the Presidency in the missile age made him speak in a somber mood. "No man entering upon this office," he told the Congress, "could fail to be staggered upon learning . . . the harsh enormity of the trials through which he must pass. . . ."

Kennedy ordered a speed-up in the number of missiles to be built, even though it turned out that the missile gap to which he had pointed with such alarm during the campaign of 1960 was a myth: Russia had not built as many missiles as American officials thought she could. What did exist, and what caused Kennedy great concern, was the problem of not having enough troops and planes and ships to make a carefully measured response, if necessary, to any kind of challenge. Nuclear war was one extreme. But what about lesser actions? What about what came to be called "salami tactics," by which the Communists might slice away the free world piece by piece, each too small by itself to justify war? To try to prevent this, President Kennedy ordered a major increase in U.S. conventional power, the Army alone growing from eleven to sixteen divisions. He explained: "We intend to have a wider choice than humiliation or all-out nuclear action." [7]

The first major confrontation between John Kennedy and Nikita Khrushchev came in Berlin in the summer and fall of 1961. Khrushchev had long been restless with the situation in Berlin. He wanted East Germany and East Berlin to be a dependable Communist barrier to the reviving West Germany. But how could he achieve this when, out of wartime agreements, the U.S., Britain, and France maintained troops in West Berlin, and West Berlin, 110 miles inside the Communist world, remained a bright island of freedom and prosperity? Khrushchev called West Berlin a "bone in his throat" and tried to force the West out so Communists could take over.

In early June of 1961, Kennedy and Khrushchev met in Vienna, Austria, to take each other's measure, and there the Russians demanded, as they had done before in 1958, that all Berlin become what they called a "free city," free at least of troops from the West. There was no offer of any deal: it was merely one more example of the Communist technique that Western diplomats paraphrased as "What's mine is mine, what's yours is negotiable."

Kennedy's response was a flat "no" and an attempt to make it clear that the freedom of the 2.2 million West Berliners was such a "vital interest" that the U.S. would, in fact, fight rather than let it go. The Kennedy Administration did not use the word "brinksmanship," but this was the technique it practiced. The military budget was increased. So were draft quotas. Reserve units were called to active duty. American and Soviet tanks faced each other in the center of Berlin, and—apparently—the Communists were convinced and the crisis passed.

During it, however, there was created perhaps the most

ugly of all symbols of the cold war. When the crisis began, in June of 1961, thousands of East Germans decided to take what might be their last chance to flee to West Berlin and, from there, to the West. Since 1949, more than two and a half million East Germans had done this, "voting with their feet" in the greatest voluntary migration in European history. Now, in August of 1961, the stream grew to a torrent of two thousand refugees a day. To stop this, the Communists built a wall. Early on August 13, 1961, they moved up trucks and troops and laborers and created a hideous barrier only the bravest and luckiest could breach. For twenty-seven miles, the wall snaked through the city, dividing East and West Berlin, Communist and Free. The West protested, but to the intense disappointment of many West Berliners, there was no attempt to knock the wall down.

During the Kennedy years, there were indirect confrontations with the Communists in the Congo and in Laos. In late 1961, the U.S. began increasing its aid to the government of South Viet Nam, trying to put down a Communist-led "war of national liberation." But the great Kennedy-Khrushchev battle, what many Americans thought shortly afterwards was the victorious end of the cold war with Russia, came over Cuba in 1962.

Cuba is a lush, long Caribbean island whose capital city, Havana, is just ninety miles from Key West, Florida. Early in 1959—after years of guerrilla fighting—a young revolutionary named Fidel Castro took over the government and began moving his country further and further toward Communism. Thousands of Cubans fled to the U.S., many of them eager to organize a counterrevolution. The U.S. equipped and trained a small invasion force, and on April 17, 1961, this little group—about two thousand men—went ashore on Cuba's south coast in the Bay of Pigs. The attack was a complete failure: there were too many invaders to slip in undetected and too few to overcome Castro's forces;

the U.S. provided no air cover, so every man who went ashore was either killed or captured. After the Bay of Pigs landings, Castro became, understandably, even more anti-American than he had been, and by the summer of 1962, he had agreed to be a party to a major and secret move by Nikita Khrushchev to upset the world nuclear balance of terror.

Beginning about the middle of July, 1962, and continuing into the fall, U.S. intelligence reported a steady build-up of Russian military supplies and men in Cuba. The Soviet explanation was that all this was for purely defensive purposes. But on October 14, 1962, a high-flying U.S. U-2 reconnaissance plane brought back pictures of one-thousand-mile-range missiles in place in Cuba, with a two-thousand-mile missile site under construction. Clearly, when the missiles became operational, much of the U.S. would be more vulnerable than ever to Soviet "nuclear blackmail." Clearly, to President Kennedy and his top advisers, the missiles had to go.

The question was: How to get rid of them? An air attack would do the job, but it might also provoke a Russian attack some place else, and it could trigger all-out war. An alternative seemed wisest.

On Monday night, October 22, President Kennedy went on television to report what the Russians were doing, to demand that the missiles be removed, and to announce that beginning on the morning of the twenty-fourth the U.S. would blockade Cuba and sink any ships trying to carry in any more offensive weapons.

"We will not prematurely or unnecessarily risk the cost of world-wide nuclear war in which even the fruits of victory would be ashes in our mouth," he said, "but neither will we shrink from the risk at any time it must be faced." Privately, the President told friends it seemed to him as if the crisis could go "either way." [8] Robert F. Kennedy, the President's brother, who was then Attorney General and one of those who helped him decide the U.S. response, said later: "We all agreed in the end that if the Russians were ready to go to nuclear war over Cuba they were ready to go to nuclear war and that was that. So we might as well have the showdown then as six months later." [9]

The U.S. moved into position to fight. The Strategic Air Command was alerted. More than forty ships converged on the Caribbean. Marines put to sea, and extra planes and troops marshaled in Florida and other southeastern states.

Now it was Russia's move. The U.S. "quarantine" went into effect as announced on the morning of October 24 with about twenty-four Russian ships then on their way to Cuba. But by the afternoon of that day, it became apparent that the ships were not going to try to run the blockade. In Washington, Secretary of State Dean Rusk turned to a colleague and said: "We're eyeball to eyeball, and I think the other fellow just blinked." [10]

The crisis continued for several more days. An American U-2 was shot down over Cuba, and another was shot at. U.S. intelligence reported that work on the Cuban missiles continued. But by the end of the week, Nikita Khrushchev took the necessary step back from the brink. On Sunday, October 28, he agreed to crate up his missiles and take them home if the U.S. would promise that Cuba would not be invaded. The deal was made. Khrushchev, the realist as well as the Communist, explained later, ". . . there began to be a smell of burning in the air." [11]

The Cuban missile crisis forced Russia to accept, at least temporarily, the realities of American power. The Cuban missile crisis also forced East and West to look again at the arms race and see if there were some way, at last, to slow it down. In fifteen years of effort and expense, the total time required to transport a bomb from Moscow to Washington or vice versa had been reduced from sixteen hours to thirty minutes. Total war, it was estimated, would kill nearly 300 million persons in the U.S., Europe, and the Soviet Union. Moreover, there was the ever-growing danger of the spread of nuclear weapons to more and more countries. How safe would the world be if China, West Germany, Israel, Egypt, etc., etc., had the bomb?

President Kennedy had told the United Nations on September 25, 1961: "Today, every inhabitant of this planet must contemplate the day when this planet may no longer be habitable. Every man, woman and child lives under a nuclear sword of Damocles, hanging by the slenderest of threads, capable of being cut at any moment by accident, or miscalculation or by madness. The weapons of war must be abolished before they abolish us."

All through the cold war, there had been efforts to do this. But it took the Cuban crisis to bring a real beginning. On June 10, 1963, in a speech at American University in Washington, President Kennedy urged that the U.S. reexamine its attitudes toward the Soviet Union and toward peace. "Our problems are man made," he said. "Therefore, they can be solved by man." He urged that there be established a direct teletype link between Washington and Moscow, for fast and accurate communication in time of crisis. This "hot line" might help prevent war by accident. Kennedy also announced that talks soon would begin aimed at agreement, at last, on a treaty banning nuclear weapons tests. "Confident and unafraid we labor on," he said, "not toward a strategy of annihilation but toward a strategy of peace."

The "hot line" was installed, and the U.S., Britain, and Russia did agree to ban all but underground nuclear weapons tests. Relations between Russia and the West seemed to enter a new phase, and the world began going about other business as if it thought it had been freed, at least for a while, from the terror of the cold war.

Appealing for public support for the test ban treaty, President Kennedy said: "According to the ancient Chinese proverb, a journey of a thousand miles must begin with a single step . . . let us take that first step. Let us, if we can, step back from the shadows of war and seek out the way of peace. And if that journey is a thousand miles or even more, let history record that we, in this land, at this time, took the first step." [12]

A secure world free of the danger of war did seem a long way away, but the world had come a long way, too. As Russian ships carried the missiles east from Cuba, the earth began to seem safer and, in a sense, wider: where the world of the cold war had had just two capitals, Washington and Moscow, now there were, once again, many.

*Part Three*
*North and South*

Atomic bomb of the type dropped on Hiroshima. It is 28 inches in diameter, 120 inches long, and weighs about 9,000 pounds. *(Los Alamos Scientific Laboratory)*

Hiroshima, Japan, after August 9, 1945. *(Atomic Energy Commission)*

Vladimir Ilyich Lenin. *(United Press International Photo)*

Joseph Vissarionivich Stalin. *(Sovfoto)*

George Catlett Marshall, June 28, 1939. *(Wide World Photos)*

Petrograd (now Leningrad) during the terror preceding the Bolshevik seizure of power, May, 1917. *(Wide World Photos)*

U.S. plane airlifting food and coal to blockaded Berlin, 1948. *(Wide World Photos)*

U.S. troops advance through a snow-covered rice paddy toward a Communist-held hill in Korea, February 4, 1951. *(U.S. Army Photograph)*

U.S. Marine in Korea. (*David Douglas Duncan*, © **Life** *Magazine, Time Inc.*)

General Douglas MacArthur returns to the Philippines, October, 1944. (*U.S. Army Photograph*)

Sun Yat-sen, 1923. *(United Press International Photo)*

Generalissimo and Madame Chiang Kai-shek, 1960. *(United Press International Photo)*

Mao Tse-tung, 1964. *(Eastfoto)*

General Dwight D. Eisenhower with U.S. paratroopers just before they drop behind Normandy beaches, June 5, 1944. *(U.S. Army Photograph)*

Edward Teller testifies before Senate Committee, August 20, 1963. *(Wide World Photos)*

Dwight David Eisenhower, October 25, 1956. *(Wide World Photos)*

John Foster Dulles, January 22, 1951. *(United Press International Photo)*

*Chapter Eight*

# THE END OF COLONIALISM

On the evening of August 14, 1947, in New Delhi, the political leaders who in a few hours would take over full control of their country gathered in the garden of the man who would become independent India's first President, Dr. Rajendra Prasad. As women chanted hymns, those who had helped lead the long fight for India's freedom passed before a Hindu priest, who sprinkled them with holy water. An old woman placed a dot of red powder, for luck, on each man's forehead, and then they all went to the Council of State Building to wait for midnight and independence.

They would need hymns and holy water and luck, these men. Most of the people of their subcontinent were not only poor and hungry and sick; they were also bitterly divided, Moslem against Hindu. Furious religious riots still raging would take half a million lives before they stopped. Moreover, the astrologers reported that August 15 was not an auspicious day, and in India, astrologers were influential.

Nevertheless, August 15 had been set as Independence Day, and in honor of it, temples were strung with lights, hundreds of thousands of people packed the streets, even bullocks' horns and horses' legs had been painted with the national colors, bright orange, white, and green.

The Indian flag was everywhere. Inside the Council of

State Building, where the political leaders gathered to assume power, flags occupied the gilt frames along the walls where once had hung the portraits of former British Viceroys.

At 11 P.M., just one hour before independence, three women sang the national anthem. Then Dr. Prasad spoke, calling for two minutes of silence "in memory of those who died in the struggle for freedom in India and elsewhere." Next Jawaharlal Nehru, India's first Prime Minister, rose to say: "At the stroke of the midnight hour, when the world sleeps, India will awake to life and freedom. A moment comes, which comes but rarely in history, when we step out from the old to the new, when an age ends and when the soul of a nation long suppressed finds utterance."

Now the hands of the clock overlapped, and those about to rule their own country listened in silence as the hour chimed. As the last note died away, someone blew on a conch shell, the kind used in Hindu temples to summon the gods to witness a great event. A cheer went up. India was free.

In every city, there were celebrations far into the night: sirens, whistles, bells, and fireworks. In Delhi, a group of students burned a paper coffin labeled "British Imperialism." But this was exceptional. Generally, Indians were polite— even affectionate—with the British they met. In Bombay, an Indian bandleader felt it was not quite suitable to play "God Save the King," but he did see fit to order "God Save the Prince of Wales."

Throughout India, on Independence Day itself, there were more than three hundred separate flag-raising ceremonies, the main one in New Delhi. Britain's last Viceroy, Lord Louis Mountbatten, was driven to it, inch by inch through the throngs, in a coach pulled by six chestnut horses with sixteen outriders before and behind, dazzling in white uniforms, gold and blue turbans, and gold sashes.

It spoke well for Britain, giving up power, and for India, taking it, that Mountbatten was cheered as much as Nehru.

So many people had come to Delhi for this occasion that there was no room for the Army and Navy to pass in review, as had been planned. But the Air Force flew over, speeches were made, and—in a light rain—as the Indian flag rose on its staff, a rainbow appeared in the afternoon sky. Perhaps this good omen would offset the message of the stars. Again and again came the shout, "Jai hind! Jai hind!"— "Long Live India!"

There were a host of other signs, large and small, of what had happened. In Bombay, the Royal Yacht Club, to which no Indian ever had been able to go even as a guest, closed its doors because the new government refused to renew its lease. The best hotels took down the signs reading, "Europeans Only." And on August 17, the transport *Georgic* sailed from Bombay with five thousand men, most of them of the Royal Norfolk Regiment, the first British troops to leave after independence. Mountbatten came to the dock to say good-by. As they cast off, the troops sang the predictable "Bless 'em All" and "Auld Lang Syne"; and probably from habit rather than a sense of irony, they also burst forth with "Rule Britannia."

Thus did colonialism end and independence begin in one "new" nation. Nehru said such a moment comes but rarely in history, and that was true in 1947. But since then, the world has been swept by what has been called a "wildfire of independence." By the mid-1960's, more than fifty of the world's nations—nearly half the members of the United Nations—were new: they had not existed as independent countries twenty years before. In Africa, in 1945, there had been just four independent countries: Egypt, Ethiopia, Liberia, and the Union of South Africa. But during the 1950's, eight African colonies became free. In 1960 alone, fifteen more were added, one nearly every other day during the first two weeks of August. By the mid-sixties, there were thirty-five new nations on that one continent. As Thomas Jefferson wrote to General Lafayette in 1820, "the disease of liberty is catching." The shot fired at Concord in 1775 was indeed "heard 'round the world."

Black or brown or yellow, in Africa, the Middle East, or Asia, the people of the new nations had one central emotion in common: they wanted no more colonialism, no more domination by white Europeans who, no matter what benefits they brought, also brought an air of superiority that had become intolerable. With Europe exhausted by World War II, the colonial people could and did make their moves. Occasionally without violence but usually with it, they persuaded their masters to set them free.

About six hundred years ago, most of the people of the world lived in roughly the same kinds of communities: a few men of privilege ruled with absolute authority over the great majority, the very poor, who worked the land. But then, while the rest of the world remained as it was, Western Europe began developing. Towns and cities drew people off the land, and there grew up a middle class of merchants, some of whom were interested in trade overseas.

One man specially concerned with exploration was Prince Henry of Portugal, Prince Henry the Navigator. He was impatient with the Arab monopoly of both the land and sea routes to the spices and cloth of India. So, he encouraged Portuguese sailors and map-makers and mathematicians to try to find another way. Besides, to the East they might discover not only wealth but also the Garden of Eden.

No one knew what mysteries the sea held, and those Portuguese sailors must have been terrified as their caravels crept down the west coast of Africa. There were Arab rumors of a "Green Sea of Darkness" and a widespread belief that the water over which they sailed toward the equator would get warmer and warmer until, finally, it boiled.

But they persevered, and in 1488, Bartholomew Diaz rounded the southernmost tip of Africa, the Cape of Good Hope, and in 1498, Vasco da Gama landed on the Indian coast. Spain joined the search for a new route to the Indies, sponsoring Christopher Columbus in his trip westward to try to get east. Then the Dutch and the British and the French and the Belgians joined the race. By the turn of the twentieth century, the countries of Europe had carved up nearly all the world into colonies or places in which their influence was dominant.

Why did they do it? Some say it is human nature for any powerful people to try to take over their less powerful neighbors. There was the lure of trade and gold and then the need to protect the routes to these riches. Also, with the Industrial Revolution, colonies became sources of raw materials for the home factories and markets for their finished goods; textile men dreamed of the wealth they might earn if they could sell just an inch of shirttail to every Chinese.

But personal or national profit was by no means the sole motivation. Empire-building was adventurous; many men truly believed it their duty to bring what they considered civilization to people they thought backwards; and there was religion: had not Christ said, "Go ye into all the world and preach the gospel to every creature"?

So they went, the adventurers, the missionaries, the merchants, the soldiers, the administrators, the planters, the doctors, and the educators. They took and they gave. In our time, the words colonialism and imperialism have become charged with hostile meaning, but there was a time when they conveyed to Europeans, at least, the highest emotions of duty and pride.

Of all the colonial, imperial powers, none was greater than Great Britain. The sun, literally, never set on the British Empire. The Union Jack flew over at least part of every continent, and—until just after World War II— globes were dominated by the color red, which map-makers, by tradition, reserved for Britain and her colonies.

The map is changed now, but some of the language of empire remains. Asia is the Far East, Asia Minor is the Middle East, and anything luxurious is "posh": former colonial officers recalled that in the days of the long sea trips out to India and back, even through the short cut of the Suez Canal, the cooler and, therefore, fashionable side of a ship on which to reserve a cabin was "Port Out, Starboard Home."

A nineteenth century historian once remarked that the British Empire was acquired in a fit of absent-mindedness. It is true that the first British had gone out to trade, not to conquer. But, trading and conquering, the Empire became for the British a cherished possession, the symbol of their greatness. It was this for Winston Churchill, who, on the night of November 10, 1942, remarked of the growing world demand for independence: "I have not become the King's First Minister in order to preside over the liquidation of the British Empire." [1]

But much as Churchill may have deplored it, his successors—and he himself when he became Prime Minister again in 1951—did oversee just this liquidation. In the twenty years following 1945, Britain granted independence to more than 650 million persons in 21 countries.

One reason not even Britain could control the wildfire of independence was the power of the very ideas British educators had taught: ideas of the fundamental rights of all men. The U.S., first to revolt against British colonialism, had long preached the same rights, urging others to pursue national independence. The Communists also played a part: Russia had known the humiliation of being a backward, at least half-Asian nation in the same world with Western Europe's modern industrial powers. Moreover, Lenin had seen European imperialism as the last stage of capitalism: he and his disciples believed that if colonialism ended, capitalism would end, too.

But as important as all other reasons was the matter of national pride. Britain and the other European powers might have brought to their colonies peace and order, sanitation and schools, parliamentary traditions and Christianity. They might have built roads and hospitals and durable systems of administration and law. But it made no difference. They were still aloof foreigners, who felt superior and unappreciated. Listen to Rudyard Kipling, writing in 1899, when the United States became a colonial power after winning the Philippine Islands from Spain:

> "Take up the White Man's burden
> Send forth the best ye breed
> Go bind your sons to exile
> To serve your captives' need; . . .
>
> "Take up the White Man's burden
> The savage wars of peace
> Fill full the mouth of Famine
> And bid the sickness cease:
> And when your goal is nearest
> The end of others sought,
> Watch Sloth and heathen Folly
> Bring all your hopes to nought.
>
> ". . . Take up the White Man's burden
> And reap his old reward:
> The blame of those ye better,
> The hate of those ye guard. . . ." [2]

Or read George Orwell's essay, "Shooting an Elephant." His hero is a British police officer in Burma. An elephant had escaped, and the Englishman had taken a rifle and gone to find it. When he did, the elephant was doing no harm. There was no reason to kill it. But a crowd had gathered. Orwell writes:

> "Here was I, the white man with his gun, standing in front of the unarmed native crowd—seemingly the leading actor of the piece; but in reality I was only an absurd puppet pushed to and fro by the will of those yellow faces behind. I perceived in this moment that when the white man turns tyrant it is his own freedom that he destroys. He becomes a sort of hollow, posing dummy, the conventionalized figure of a sahib. For it is the condition of his rule that he shall spend his life in trying to impress the 'natives,' and so in every crisis he has got to do what the 'natives' expect of him. He wears a mask, and his face grows to fit it. I had got to shoot the elephant. I had committed myself to doing it when I sent for the rifle. A sahib has got to act like a sahib; he has got to appear resolute, to know his own mind and do definite things. To come all that way, rifle in hand, with 2,000 people marching at my heels and then to trail feebly away, having done nothing —no, that was impossible. The crowd would laugh at me. And my whole life, every white man's life in the East, was one long struggle not to be laughed at." [3]

When the days of Empire were over and retired colonial officers were back in London living out their days, one of their recollections was, "They may not have loved us, but they respected us." It may be true. But just as the British want to be respected, so does everyone else. In our time, on whatever continent, by whatever technique a colonial people has forced its way to independence, the first require-

ment always has been that a revolutionary leader give his
people pride. Once the people of a country respect themselves, they cannot rest until they rule themselves, too.

Of all the new leaders of the new nations, none has
fascinated more people—East and West—than the man who
gave India her self-respect. He was a slight, good-humored
ascetic, a lawyer turned reformer, a revolutionist who
abhorred violence, perhaps the only saintly politician of our
time, Mohandas K. Gandhi.

Gandhi was born October 2, 1869, in Porbandar, one of
India's more than five hundred native states. His grandfather, his father, and his uncle had been, in turn, prime
minister to the prince of Porbandar.

As in Old China, families in Gandhi's India arranged
marriages. Gandhi was engaged at the age of seven, after
two previous engagements to girls who died. He and his
wife for sixty-two years were married when each was thirteen.

Families in India also took care of their own, so—since
his family was relatively prosperous—Gandhi, at the age
of seventeen, was able to leave his wife and infant son for
nearly three years in order to go to London and become a
lawyer.

Back in India, Gandhi was less than a success, so in 1893,
he welcomed an offer to go to South Africa for a year to
settle a lawsuit for an Indian business firm. He did the
job, in the process discovering his life work and beginning
to display the qualities that led Indians to call him "Mahatma," which means "Great Soul."

The white settlers of South Africa had brought in Indian
laborers to work for them. Other Indians had followed, and
all were discriminated against. Gandhi became the cham-
pion of the Indians of South Africa in their campaign for
equal treatment under the laws. For twenty years, he tried
cases and wrote pamphlets and put into practice the idea

of civil disobedience, which he used later with such success to help win independence for India and which has played such an important part in the campaign for equal rights for Negroes in the United States. Essentially, Gandhi's technique was to prevail over an opponent not by force or stealth but by showing him that there was no limit to what Gandhi and his many followers were willing to suffer because of their belief in the justness of their cause. Gandhi led his countrymen in refusing to obey laws they thought wrong and in cheerfully and nonviolently taking the consequences. Gandhi was beaten, insulted, and sent to jail, but before he and his wife and, by then, his four sons sailed for home in 1914, his efforts had produced an end, by law, to the principal Indian grievances. Passive resistance was just too much for the South African authorities, one of whom, Jan Christian Smuts, said, "You can't put 20,000 Indians into jail." [4]

Gandhi's political methods had deep religious roots, for Gandhi was a deeply religious man. He said once: "Men say I am a saint losing myself in politics. The fact is that I am a politician trying my hardest to be a saint." [5]

Gandhi was a Hindu who believed that the saintly life was to be achieved only by overcoming physical desire. All his life, the first target of his reform was himself. Through prayer, meditation, fasting, celibacy (beginning when he was thirty-seven), and whole days of silence, Gandhi tried to perfect, in his words, "the yoga [means] which will deliver the self [soul] from the bondage of the body. . . ." [6]

Nonviolent resistance, which Gandhi preferred to call "Satyagraha," or "truth-force," was rooted in the religious idea that because all life is sacred, violence is wrong and the opponent must be converted, not destroyed. If the opponent could not be converted by patient argument, then perhaps one's own cheerful suffering in the cause of Truth, which Gandhi believed identical with God, would change the opponent's heart and mind. In any event, even one's most persistent enemies were to be loved, not harmed.

Back in India, in 1914, at the age of forty-five, Gandhi founded a little community, or ashram, near the city of Ahmedabad, where he and his family and his closest followers all lived together in monklike simplicity. From this cluster of whitewashed huts, Gandhi transformed the subcontinent. His were no minor causes. He preached and worked for independence from Britain, brotherhood between Hindus and Moslems, and an end to what he called "the hideous system" by which millions of his fellow countrymen were known as "untouchables."

Ancient Hindu tradition had produced in India four major social levels, or castes, with three or four thousand subcastes. Originally, the distinctions were by color, the lightest skinned ruling the darker. (The Hindu word for caste means color. The English word comes from the Portuguese, "casta," which means breed.) The people of each caste used to do certain jobs: at the top were the Brahmins, who were priests and educators; at the bottom were the Sudras, who were workers and servants. But underneath even the Sudras were the untouchables, outcastes, who did jobs others thought unclean, such as sweeping the streets and tanning the hides of animals. They could not use public wells; they could not travel on public conveyances; they could not eat with those of other castes.

To Gandhi, this system was wrong. He invited untouchables to live in his ashram. He adopted an untouchable daughter. He called untouchables "Harijans," or "Children of God." He named his newspaper "Harijan."

Gandhi seemed to know instinctively that in a country as big and diverse as India, any successful political movement had to appeal to the more than 80 percent of the Indian people who lived in the country's nearly 600,000 villages. Once, before the Industrial Revolution began in

England, India's villages had produced cloth that still bears Indian names: khaki, calico, muslin. But then the mills of Lancaster, in England, began their own weaving, and Britain wanted to sell cloth, not buy it. India's village industries declined, as did her income.

Gandhi tried to change this, preaching a boycott of English cloth. At independence meetings, he urged his hearers to hand in their British clothes, which were then set on fire. Gandhi said the Indians should make their own cloth. He himself began spinning for thirty minutes a day, and homespun—as worn by Gandhi—became the patriotic garb of the Home Rule movement.

But principally, Gandhi's method was as it had been in South Africa: civil disobedience, "non-cooperation" with British rule. Indians went out on strike, quit government jobs, refused to pay taxes, intentionally broke the laws.

In 1930, Gandhi decided to protest the lucrative British tax on salt, which Gandhi thought specially evil because it not only helped pay for a foreign government but also affected the poor more than the rich. His method of protest revealed both his technique of civil disobedience and his accomplishments as a showman. With well-publicized advance notice to the British authorities, Gandhi and seventy-eight disciples set out from the Ahmedabad ashram, walking two hundred miles in twenty-four days, finally arriving at the seashore, where Gandhi bathed and then picked up a pinch of natural salt left on the shore by the waves. It was a small gesture, but it violated the law under which the British protected their tax revenues by making it a crime for anyone to possess salt not made by the government monopoly. More important, Gandhi's act inspired thousands of others up and down India's coasts to make their own salt from the sea, thereby inviting arrest.

Perhaps more than any other people would have been, the Indians were receptive to Gandhi's insistence on nonviolence. Most of them shared with him the Hindu heritage that forbade killing even animals and that led a specially strict Hindu sect, the Jains, to ban deep breathing and to wear face masks, for fear they might inhale and kill an invisible insect.

But even with such traditions, Gandhi's campaigns still produced bloodshed, and whenever this happened, Gandhi called them off and undertook a fast as penance for the violence.

Gandhi developed his fasts into potent political weapons. He fasted for Hindu-Moslem friendship, feeling that only if all Indians were united, could they become free. He fasted to get better treatment for the untouchables. Because of his hold on his countrymen, other Indian leaders and British leaders had to pay attention to these fasts: if Gandhi were to kill himself because of their refusal to compromise, no one could predict the reaction of the Indian people.

The year 1930 was a climactic one, with demonstrations, strikes, and arrests all over India. By June 30, 1930, more than 100,000 Indians were in jail for civil disobedience, and the British Viceroy sat down to negotiate with Gandhi a greater voice for Indians in their own rule.

To those in Britain most devoted to the idea of empire, what Gandhi was doing seemed by no means noble. Winston Churchill wrote of "the nauseating and humiliating spectacle of this one-time . . . lawyer, now seditious fakir, striding half-naked up the steps of the Viceroy's palace, there to negotiate and to parley on equal terms with the representative of the King-Emperor." [7] But there was no stopping Gandhi's movement; full independence was now just a matter of time.

By his fasts, by his service, by his showmanship, by his 2,089 days in Indian jails, Gandhi had awakened his people and given them pride in themselves. "What I did was a very ordinary thing," Gandhi wrote of one of his first civil disobedience campaigns. "I decided that the British could not order me around in my own country." Nehru's assessment was: "Gandhi has straightened our backs and stiffened our spines." Louis Fischer, one of Gandhi's biographers, wrote: "The British beat the Indians with batons and rifle butts. The Indians neither cringed nor complained nor retreated. That made England powerless and India invincible." [8]

All this resulted from the leadership of a near-toothless vegetarian, five feet, five inches tall, who at no time in his life weighed more than 112 pounds.

The fruits of Gandhi's life work, however, were bittersweet. When the Indian subcontinent finally became independent, it had to be divided into two nations because the Moslem leaders insisted that they have a separate country, Pakistan. The Moslems were quite willing to use force for their end, so the British had to choose between creating two nations or permitting civil war. They agreed to the Moslem demand.

August 15, 1947, thus became independence day not just for India but for Pakistan, too. Gandhi called it an "inglorious end" and refused to participate in the celebrations.

Gandhi spent the last years of his life trying to end the Hindu-Moslem bloodbath that accompanied partition, continuing to preach tolerance and nonviolence. But he could neither quell nor, as it happened, survive the hatred. On the afternoon of January 30, 1948, in Delhi, just before prayers, a fanatical Hindu who hated Moslems and feared Gandhi's ideas of brotherhood fired three shots at the Mahatma from just two feet away. Gandhi said, "Hey, Rama"—"Oh, God"—and slumped down dead. He was seventy-eight years old.

Nehru told his people: "The light has gone out of our lives. . . ." There was mourning all over the world.

It has been said that liberty is never given but always has to be taken. In our time, this often has seemed the case. In East Africa, in Kenya, the secret Mau Mau with their deadly chopping knives terrorized the country, demanding from the British settlers land and "Uhuru," freedom. In North Africa, the Algerians fought a full war against the French. In the Far East, there was war against the French in what was Indo-China and war against the Dutch in what is now Indonesia.

But freedom has not always required violence. To their great credit, the British learned early from men such as Gandhi that the wildfire of independence could not be contained. So they accepted the inevitable, setting future independence dates for their colonies, gradually letting the people of those colonies take over full power. As a result, the British Empire was succeeded by a loose association of sovereign equals called the Commonwealth, in which most of Britain's former colonies chose to remain. Generally, the transition was peaceful.

On April 18, 1955, there opened in the city of Bandung on the island of Java in Indonesia a conference of the leaders of twenty-nine Asian and African nations. About half of these nations were "new." Together, the twenty-nine included 56 percent of the world's people. Significantly, this was the first major international conference of colored peoples: no white nation was invited.

Nasser of Egypt was there, handsome and immaculate in his British-style uniform. So were Nehru and his proud aide Krishna Menon, Menon wearing Gandhi homespun. The gentle U Nu of Burma was there, a pastel bandana around his head. So was the stately Kojo Botsio of what was about to become Ghana. He was draped in a huge yellow, green, and blue robe.

There were Pakistanis in wool hats, Liberians in striped gowns, Yemenis in white turbans, and the Prince of Saudi Arabia in a flowing black and white burnoose.

This variety of dress merely reflected the deeper differences of history and culture. The Indians knew far more about England than they did about what had been French Indo-China. The delegates from Laos and Cambodia and North and South Viet Nam knew far more about France than about India or Indonesia. But all of them had in common the fact of their color and the history of their domination by white Europeans, and most of them believed that their ancient civilizations had developed spiritual values from which the whole world could benefit.

The delegates met in what had once been a Dutch club, before Indonesian independence. As President of the host nation, Sukarno welcomed them. The nations of Asia and Africa, he told them, are no longer "the voiceless ones in the world . . . no longer the tools of others and the playthings of forces they cannot influence." A new Asia and Africa had been born, Sukarno said, one that could play a significant role in world affairs. In Sukarno's words, "We can mobilize all the spiritual, all the moral, all the political strength of Asia and Africa on the side of peace." [9]

In fact, the Bandung conference quickly became divided by the tensions of the cold war, a minority of delegates favoring a resolution condemning Communism by name as a new form of the old colonialism. But the dominant theme of the conference was independence—independence from the old colonial powers and independence of both sides in the cold war. In his concluding address, Nehru of India put this theme most clearly, speaking both to and for the leaders of what has come to be called the "Third World."

"The countries assembled in the conference are not banded against anyone," said Nehru. "We send our greetings to the great countries of Europe and America. We want to be friends with them and cooperate with them. But Europe and America are in the habit of thinking that their quarrels are the world's quarrels and, therefore, the world must submit to them this way or that way."

Nehru continued: "Why should we be dragged into their

quarrels and wars? I hope we shall keep away from those quarrels. Are we copies of Europeans, Americans, or Russians? We are Asians or Africans and none else. For anyone to tell us that we have to be camp followers of Russia or America or any country in Europe," Nehru insisted, "is not very creditable to our new dignity, our new independence, our new freedom, our new spirit." [10]

Thus did the Bandung Conference become a symbol of the emergence of the new nations—proud and hypersensitive about their independence. But most of these nations of the "Third World" were also desperately poor, and therein lay a continuing threat to their freedom and to everyone's peace.

## NEW NATIONS SINCE 1945

### Asia

| New Name | Old Name | Former Colony, Protectorate, or Trust Territory of | Date of Independence |
|---|---|---|---|
| Philippines | Philippines | U.S.A. | July 4, 1946 |
| India | British India | U.K. | August 15, 1947 |
| Pakistan | British India | U.K. | August 15, 1947 |
| Burma | British India (to 1937), Burma | U.K. | January 4, 1948 |
| Ceylon | Ceylon | U.K. | February 4, 1948 |
| Korea (North) | Korea | Japan | May 1, 1948 |
| Korea (South) | Korea | Japan | August 15, 1948 |
| Laos | French Indo-China | France | July 19, 1949 |
| Indonesia | Netherlands Indies | Netherlands | December 27, 1949 |
| Cambodia | French Indo-China | France | November 9, 1953 |
| Viet Nam (South) | French Indo-China | France | July 21, 1954 |
| Viet Nam (North) | French Indo-China | France | July 21, 1954 |

Both the Republic of Viet Nam (South Viet Nam) and the Democratic Republic of Viet Nam (North Viet Nam) claim earlier independence dates. But there is controversy about these claims. July 21, 1954, is the effective date of the Geneva accords, which formally partitioned the country.

| | | | |
|---|---|---|---|
| Western Samoa | Samoa | Germany, New Zealand | January 1, 1962 |
| Malaysia | Malaya, Singapore, North Borneo, Sarawak | U.K. | September 16, 1963 |

The Federation of Malaya became independent of Britain August 31, 1957. Singapore, Sabah (formerly North Borneo), and Sarawak became independent with the creation of Malaysia, September 16, 1963. Singapore then became a separate state on August 9, 1965.

| | | | |
|---|---|---|---|
| Singapore | Singapore | U.K. | September 16, 1963 |
| The Maldives | Maldive Islands | U.K. | July 26, 1965 |

### NORTH AFRICA

| | | | |
|---|---|---|---|
| Libya | Libya | Italy (to 1941), U.K. | December 24, 1951 |
| Morocco | Morocco | France | March 2, 1956 |
| | | Spain | April 7, 1956 |
| Tunisia | Tunisia | France | March 20, 1956 |
| Algeria | Algeria | France | July 3, 1962 |

### AFRICA SOUTH OF THE SAHARA

| | | | |
|---|---|---|---|
| Sudan | Sudan | U.K. and Egypt | January 1, 1956 |
| Ghana | Gold Coast | U.K. | March 6, 1957 |
| Guinea | French West Africa | France | October 2, 1958 |

## NEW NATIONS SINCE 1945 (Continued)

### AFRICA SOUTH OF THE SAHARA (*Continued*)

| New Name | Old Name | Former Colony, Protectorate, or Trust Territory of | Date of Independence |
|---|---|---|---|
| Cameroon | Cameroons | France | January 1, 1960 |
| | | U.K. | October 1, 1961 |
| Togo | Togoland | Germany, France | April 27, 1960 |
| Mali | French West Africa | France | June 20, 1960 |

Senegal seceded August 20, 1960.

| New Name | Old Name | Former Colony, Protectorate, or Trust Territory of | Date of Independence |
|---|---|---|---|
| Senegal | French West Africa | France | June 20, 1960 |
| Malagasay | Madagascar | France | June 26, 1960 |
| Congo (Leopoldville) | Belgian Congo | Belgium | June 30, 1960 |
| Somali | Somaliland | Italy, U.K. | July 1, 1960 |
| Dahomey | French West Africa | France | August 1, 1960 |
| Niger | French West Africa | France | August 3, 1960 |
| Upper Volta | French West Africa | France | August 5, 1960 |
| Ivory Coast | French West Africa | France | August 7, 1960 |
| Chad | French West Africa | France | August 11, 1960 |

| | | | |
|---|---|---|---|
| Central African Republic | French Equatorial Africa | France | August 13, 1960 |
| Congo (Brazzaville) | French Equatorial Africa | France | August 15, 1960 |
| Gabon | French Equatorial Africa | France | August 17, 1960 |
| Nigeria | Nigeria | U.K. | October 1, 1960 |
| | Cameroons | U.K. | October 1, 1961 |
| Mauritania | French West Africa | France | November 28, 1960 |
| Sierra Leone | Sierra Leone | U.K. | April 27, 1961 |
| Tanganyika | Tanganyika | U.K. | December 9, 1961 |

Tanganyika united with Zanzibar to form Tanzania, April 26, 1964.

| | | | |
|---|---|---|---|
| Rwanda | Rwanda-Urundi | Belgium | July 1, 1962 |
| Burundi | Ruanda-Urundi | Belgium | July 1, 1962 |
| Uganda | Uganda | U.K. | October 9, 1962 |
| Zanzibar | Zanzibar | U.K. | December 10, 1963 |

Zanzibar united with Tanganyika to form Tanzania, April 26, 1964.

| | | | |
|---|---|---|---|
| Kenya | Kenya | U.K. | December 12, 1963 |
| Malawi | Nyasaland | U.K. | July 6, 1964 |
| Zambia | Northern Rhodesia | U.K. | October 24, 1964 |
| The Gambia | Gambia | U.K. | February 18, 1965 |
| Rhodesia | Southern Rhodesia | U.K. | November 11, 1965 |

## NEW NATIONS SINCE 1945 (Continued)

| New Name | Old Name | Former Colony, Protectorate, or Trust Territory of | Date of Independence |
| --- | --- | --- | --- |
| **MIDDLE EAST** | | | |
| Jordan | Trans-Jordan | U.K. | May 25, 1946 |
| Israel | Palestine | U.K. | May 14, 1948 |
| Cyprus | Cyprus | U.K. | August 16, 1960 |
| Kuwait | Kuwait | U.K. | June 19, 1961 |
| **WEST INDIES** | | | |
| Jamaica | Jamaica | U.K. | August 6, 1962 |
| Trinidad and Tobago | Trinidad and Tobago | U.K. | August 31, 1962 |
| **SOUTH AMERICA** | | | |
| Guyana | British Guiana | U.K. | May 26, 1966 |

(*Sources:* U.S. Department of State, Foreign Embassies, National Geographic Society, British Information Service.)

*Chapter Nine*

# THE RICH AND THE POOR

As of the middle 1960's, perhaps the world's greatest irony is that while the people of the rich nations are getting richer, the people of most of the poor nations are getting poorer, and the fundamental cause of both trends is the application of new knowledge. In the U.S., Britain, Europe, and Japan, there is still poverty and hardship for a minority, but generally—especially in the U.S.—the majority enjoys a level of living known in centuries past only by the very rich. In a book published in 1958, Harvard economist John Kenneth Galbraith labeled the U.S. *The Affluent Society*, and since then, the country has become even more prosperous. Indeed, in the 1960's, new knowledge was increasing America's ability to produce at such a rate as to comprise a Second Industrial Revolution.

In hideous contrast to the ever greater abundance of the West, however, is the continuing misery of most of the new nations to the south and east. The U.N. Food and Agriculture Organization reported in 1963 that 10 to 15 percent of the world's people were undernourished and up to half suffered from some degree of hunger or malnutrition or both. (The undernourished are those who get too few calories; the malnourished are those who may get enough calories but who do not get enough protein or vitamins.) According to the best estimates, perhaps 10,000 peo-

ple die of starvation or malnutrition every day. In spite
of the need for more food, however, the FAO revealed
in 1964 not only that there had been no increase in food
production per person for five years but also that in the
growing season of 1963–64 there had been less produced
per person than there had been the year before. In 1965,
a U.S. Department of Agriculture study concluded, "The
less developed world is clearly losing the capacity to feed
itself." [1]

By the middle 1960's, many experts were predicting
widespread famine in the 1970's. In 1965, B. R. Sen, Direc-
tor-General of the FAO, wrote of a "looming crisis" and
called the next thirty-five years "a most critical period in
human history." [2] Thomas Ware of the Freedom From
Hunger Foundation said in June of 1965, "There is a
global food catastrophe now building up on the horizon
which threatens to engulf the free world and the Communist world alike." [3] Swedish economist Gunnar Myrdal
warned of a "world calamity," and Raymond Ewell of the
State University of New York called extensive famine both
"likely" and "the most colossal catastrophe in history."

The chief reason for this shortage of food is the unprecedented growth in world population. Scientists have discovered inexpensive techniques for preventing the dis-
eases that once kept death rates high, but in most of the
world, there has been no comparable adjustment in birth
rates. At the time of Christ, there were perhaps 250 million human beings. With plagues and famines and wars,
it took about sixteen centuries for this population to double
to 500 million. But then it took only another 250 years to
double again, and since 1850, the number of people in
the world has more than tripled. As of the middle 1960's,
the population is 3,300,000,000 and growing by 65,000,000
each year, 180,000 a day, 125 each minute, at which rate it
will be at least 6,000,000,000 by the year 2000.

In general, the fastest growth has come in those areas

least able to afford it, so it is not just food that is lacking for half the human race: it is clothing and shelter and health and literacy and skills and jobs, as well. As the world of the West used to be, the world of the South and East today is backward and underdeveloped, and life for her people, in the words of the seventeenth century English philosopher Thomas Hobbes, is "poor, nasty, brutish, and short."

For centuries, men accepted misery as the normal condition of human life. But in the West, beginning with the Industrial Revolution two hundred years ago, there has developed the conviction that life need not be like this any more. Now the same belief is sweeping the rest of the world, the people of Egypt and Indonesia and the other new nations asking impatiently why they cannot do what Europe and the U.S. and Japan and, now, Russia have done. Why cannot they develop and develop quickly? Have not science and technology—for the first time in human history—made it at least theoretically possible to produce enough for everyone? Why cannot theory become reality? The demands for "more, now" have become as insistent as were the demands for independence itself, and the study of economic development has become the great new frontier of the social sciences.

Beyond the gifts of nature and the willingness of people to work—beyond even good luck—the key to the prosperity of the West is the continuing use of new knowledge to make men more productive. For our time, the process began with the invention of machinery to improve the efficiency of the textile mills of Britain in the middle of the eighteenth century. Then in 1769, James Watt took out his first patent on a steam engine. Capitalists and governments invested in the new devices, and with such equipment it became possible for just a few men to do the work once done by many. With the introduction of each new machine, of course, some men lost their jobs; but over the years mechanization created new jobs, too—usually more than it eliminated—and it permitted society as a whole to produce and earn more with less work.

Steadily, the Industrial Revolution spread—to Belgium and across Europe, then to the United States and Japan, country after country transforming itself from a nation of farmers to a nation of factory workers. Steadily, too, the lonely genius of the inventor grew into the collective skill of trained engineers who apply for practical use the principles scientists reveal. In the United States in the last hundred years, enough new machinery and new processes have been engineered to make the average worker more than four times as productive as he was in 1870.

No change in productivity has been as dramatic as that which science and technology have brought to American farms, where pesticides, new machinery, fertilizer, and improved seeds have permitted a revolution in agriculture. In 1860, one farm worker in the United States could supply farm products for 4½ people. In 1900, it was up to 7. Then from 1900 to 1950, the number more than doubled, to 15, and from 1950 to 1963 it more than doubled again, to 31— 26 in the U.S. and—because the U.S. exported nearly 20 percent of all its farm products—5 abroad. In 1860, 70 percent of the American population was engaged in agriculture; by 1960, this was down to 7 percent.

But it is not just old pursuits to which scientists and engineers apply modern methods: they create new industries, too. Moreover, the time from laboratory to showroom is becoming shorter and shorter. It took nearly a hundred years after its invention for the steam engine to have a wide impact on society. The introduction of electricity required about fifty years. Today, the birth of a new product takes only ten or twenty years: the Du Pont Company reports that over 40 percent of its sales in 1964 came from products that had emerged from the research laboratory during the previous two decades.

The telegraph, the telephone, the internal combustion engine, the airplane, motion pictures, radio, and all the other inventions and developments of the generations just past made life in the United States in the first half of the twentieth century far different from what it had been before. Now, writes the British author and government official Lord Snow (Parliamentary Secretary to the Ministry of Technology), "I believe the industrial society of electronics, atomic energy, and automation is in cardinal respects different in kind from any that has gone before, and will change the world much more." [4]

Nothing better symbolizes this prosperous new society of rapid technological change than the new world of punched cards and magnetic tape, of quiet machines in air-conditioned rooms, of careful logic and miniature parts, of "bits" and "cores" and "programs" and "nanoseconds" —the world of the electronic computer.

Until no more than a few hundred years ago, even many of the world's best-educated men were unable to do what we would consider simple arithmetic. Multiplication tables were not taught in the schools. Since the start of the Industrial Revolution, however, the ability to do mathematical computation has become more and more important, and computation itself has become mechanized. Adding machines have become common in business offices, and as early as 1890, the U.S. Census Bureau used punched cards and machines to help count and analyze the population: the cards were the size of the dollar bill of that era, and the most common of today's punched cards still are.

Like so many other fields of modern technology, the computer industry of the 1950's and 1960's was the child of World War II. The Army needed help computing the trajectories of artillery shells, and mathematicians, physicists, and engineers offered it. Industries such as radio broadcasting had been made possible by the new science of electronics—putting to work the tiny negatively-charged particles in orbit around the nucleus of every atom. Beginning in 1943, it was this science that physicists and engineers at the University of Pennsylvania's Moore School of Engineering in Philadelphia used to help solve the Army's mathematical problem. The machine they built—the first electronic computer—was nicknamed ENIAC, for Electronic Numerical Integrator and Calculator. It used 18,000 vacuum tubes and could do 5,000 addition problems every second.

While electronics made possible the almost unbelievable speed with which modern computers can do arithmetic, it was an idea that made them such an important tool. This was the concept of the "stored program." Like a cook preparing a meal, a computer operator needs a recipe—a program. The men running ENIAC had to wire in new instructions for every new step their machine took, but in the late 1940's, mathematicians and engineers developed systems by which a computer could be loaded with a program in advance so the machine could change its own instructions, whenever and as quickly as necessary.

With this development, the computer revolution came of age. By the early 1950's, the first computers were sold to industry, and by the middle 1960's, there were well over 25,000 computers in use in the U.S. in every type of business and scholarship. More than 100,000 men and women—most of them young—had become trained in the techniques of computer programing. The Federal government alone was using two billion dollars' worth of computers each year.

Until the development of computers, most of the inventions of the Industrial Revolution had extended the power of human muscles. Computers, however, extend the power of the brain. They can receive and store and add and compare and print out immense amounts of information, performing hundreds of thousands of operations per second, switching signals in a billionth of a second—a measure of time called the nanosecond.

The process begins when specially trained analysts break down a problem into its many small logical steps and then translate these steps into the program—the mathematical language—with which the computers work. In our daily life, we use a decimal system of counting—probably because our ancestors many centuries ago began counting on their ten fingers. Most commonly, however, the computer's language is not a decimal but a binary system in which all numbers are expressed by one or more of just two digits. The words "binary digit," in the jargon of the computer operators, become contracted to "bit."

In both the decimal and binary systems, the number "1" is the same, but the decimal number "2" is "10" to the computer; the decimal number "3" is "11"; the decimal number "4," "100." Such a system is ideally suited for computer use because a pulse of electricity passing in one direction can signify a "1," and current passing in the other direction can mean "0."

A computer is fed information, in binary form, from punched cards or punched paper tape, from magnetic tape or discs with a magnetic coating. For temporary storage, each bit of information goes to a tiny core—about one-third the size of a small letter "o" on a printed page—made of a material called ferrite. These cores—more than a million of them in large storage units—are woven on a lattice of tiny wires. Just as electricity or the absence of it turns a light bulb on or off, so when electric current passes through a core, it magnetizes it in one direction or another, "1" or "0," thus making it a storage place for one bit of information.

Even though electricity travels with the speed of light, the computers of the early 1950's were too slow for the demands made on them. There was no possibility of increasing the speed of the signals; therefore, the only way to make computers work faster was to reduce the distance the pulses of current had to travel and to cut down the time required to switch signals.

This was done with transistors—tiny slices of a specially treated solid material, usually silicon or germanium—that could conduct and amplify electricity in far less space than that required by vacuum tubes. In the mid-1950's, these so-called semiconductors permitted the construction of reliable and relatively cool-running computers not the size of a huge room and weighing thirty tons, like ENIAC, but no bigger than an ordinary office desk.

But hardly had this second generation of computer technology been developed than it was replaced by a third. In the mid-1960's, transistors, even though no longer than a quarter of an inch, gave way to smaller (and cheaper) glass-coated chips. Each one was no bigger than the head of a pin; 50,000 of them could be put into an ordinary thimble.

With such miniaturization, the computers of the 1960's became thousands of times faster than those of the 1940's.

Computers can do nothing men do not tell them to do, but they will do whatever their program commands. If given a sloppy program, they will print out a sloppy result: indeed, computer operators developed the slogan "GI-GO" —Garbage In, Garbage Out—to underscore the need for careful and systematic instructions. But when programed imaginatively and precisely, computers can be an invaluable tool, doing as much arithmetic in a minute as a human being can do in a lifetime, thus enormously expanding man's ability to work and even to think.

Computers and their operators were vital to the entire U.S. space program, civilian and military. They revolutionized clerical procedures: processing airline seat reservations, making out payrolls, keeping records, checking income tax returns, counting bank checks. In industry, computers helped make possible the technique that came to be called automation, by which machines were used to help run other machines.

By the mid-1960's, there was hardly a field of scientific research that had not been aided or revolutionized by com-

puters. Engineers found that they could simulate on a computer so many problems of design and construction that
they could test such things as rockets and bridges before
they were built. Many executives were using computers to
help keep track of that which they administered, thus—hopefully—permitting more realistic decisions. Scholars were
helping develop computer programs that could translate
languages. Computers were even being used to help build
new computers, including machines that could, in effect,
"learn"—changing their programs according to their experience.

Like every other major development of the Industrial
Revolution, computers have caused reactions of both hope
and fear. Would they eliminate more jobs than they created? Would they permit ever greater control by the few
over the many? Or would they create a whole new age
of freedom and understanding?

No one can predict all the consequences of computers,
but all observers agree that they will be formidable. "Within
the next decade," wrote the industrial analyst Edwin L.
Harder in 1965, "these machines will affect our lives more
than any other technological development in history." [5] And
it was in a discussion of computers and their effects that
C. R. De Carlo of the International Business Machines
Corporation, the world's largest manufacturer of computers,
said: "I think we've come to accept the notion today that
practically anything is possible." [6]

While the U.S. worried about adjusting to the changes of
a second Industrial Revolution, most of the rest of the
world struggled to begin a first one. But every advance in
productivity was threatened, if not offset, by the soaring
growth in the number of people to be fed and clothed and
housed. In the 1950's, all the underdeveloped countries
increased their total output by about 40 percent but increased
their total number of people by 30 percent. Egypt's great

new symbol of development is the high dam at Aswan, which may irrigate enough new land along the Nile River to increase agricultural production by 45 percent. But this is precisely the figure by which Egypt's population was estimated to increase during the ten years it would take to build the dam, so in terms of more food per person, the immediate net effect of building the dam would be zero.

Perhaps in no country in the world can one see the problems of development and measure the gap between the rich and poor nations as well as in India. Since 1901, public health measures have cut the death rate in India by more than half. But the birth rate has dropped only slightly: the average Indian family in the mid-1960's still has six children. Therefore, since 1901, India's population has nearly doubled, to 460 million, and in early 1965, her chief economic planner forecast another doubling—to nearly a billion people—by the year 2000.

The steady increase in the number of Indians to be fed, however, has not commanded a comparable increase in the total amount of cultivated land or in the total amount of food produced. Therefore, while nutritionists advise that a person living in that part of Asia must have a minimum of 2,300 calories a day, the average Indian consumes only 1,800—compared to the average American's 3,200.

In the United States in 1960, 97.6 percent of the people could read. In India, the comparable figures were 34.5 percent for men and 13 percent for women.

In the U.S. in 1963, a new boy baby could be expected to live to be 66.6 years old, a girl baby, 73.4. In India, life expectancy was just above 40.

In 1964, the average person in the U.S. had income to spend, after taxes, of $2,248. In India, the total average per capita income was about $60, and only half a million people in the whole subcontinent earned enough to pay any income tax at all.

In the U.S., there is one private car for every three people; in India, one for every 10,000. There is one radio for every 250 Indians, one bicycle for every 400.

In short, in every measurable index of wealth, India and the U.S. seem in different worlds, or at least in different centuries. The only thing India has plenty of is cattle—a third of all the cattle in the world. Hindu custom, however, makes cows sacred, so only about a third of India's cattle can be used efficiently. The rest just roam the city streets and eat.

The symbol of all these facts of borderline existence and the real measure of the gap between the world's rich and poor is the ordinary Indian villager—poor, indebted, illiterate, undernourished, sometimes hungry, fatalistic for himself yet wanting something better for his sons, torn in many ways between the traditional and the new. His name might be Mohan Ram.

He would have been born in 1940, the second child of five. There had been a sixth, but she had died at birth: the village midwife never could explain why. Ram's older brother went for four years to the primary school in the next village, seven miles away. He learned to read and write and had become a very junior kind of district official, keeping the records of who owned which land. It was good that he had left home: his position earned him and the whole family a little respect, and besides, he was one less mouth to feed.

Ram became the farmer of the family, raising wheat and sugar cane on the twenty acres his aged father is lucky enough to own. He had always been the son most interested in the land, so he had never gone to school. He is illiterate.

Except for using a plow with a steel tip, rather than a wooden tip, Ram farms exactly the way his father did. Like his father, he has two bullocks and a milk buffalo. Like his father, he thinks he knows better than anyone else when to let a field lie fallow and when to sow it, and how. His labor is worth about $600 a year.

The government wants Ram to use fertilizer so his land will produce more, but Ram is wary. Always the harvest has depended on the rain: when the summer monsoon comes early enough and with enough water, there is enough to eat. When it is too little or too late, there is famine. That is the way it has always been, so that must be God's will. Besides, some people say fertilizer will spoil the land.

There is talk of a government dam to store water and thus help prevent the famines of about one year in five. But the dam would generate electricity, as well, and Ram has heard a politician who opposes the government say making electricity would take the goodness out of the water. So, he is suspicious of the dam.

Ram's land would produce more food if he could use insecticide. But this is not available, and even if it were, Ram's religion would not permit its use: since all life is sacred, all killing is wrong.

Of the five hundred people in Ram's village, about seventy have no land. Therefore, they eat so little, they feel their hunger. Ram does not feel his, except when there is famine. He is just malnourished, as he has always been. That is why he is less than five feet tall.

But lucky as he is, comparatively, Ram is still in debt. His is a generation that has the double expense of serving both the past and the future. One of his biggest expenses is his family's good name. He must try to save money, and if he cannot save enough—as he probably cannot—he must borrow from the moneylender to see that his sister or daughter gets a proper wedding. On the dowry and gifts and the ceremony and food, he may spend a whole year's income, just as his father did. Ram has heard that there are weddings in the cities in which this is no longer done, but in his village, the father or the brother of the bride is insulted if any other family lights a fire for cooking on any day during the wedding celebration: everyone eats with him.

The future makes its claim on Ram, too. His younger brother is seventeen and is still in school. Ram and his older brother each pay about $5.00 a month to help this boy become, perhaps, a lawyer. Sometimes Ram goes without a shirt or a pair of sandals he needs in order that his brother may learn. Some of the men in the government's Community Development Program might think it unfortunate for India and her growth that Ram's brother does not want to become an engineer or a doctor or an expert in scientific farming. But no one in Ram's family has ever seen an engineer or a doctor or an expert in scientific farming. Neither has anyone else in their village. Through all the years of British rule, and perhaps for centuries before that, the most respected man an Indian villager ever saw was a government official or lawyer. To become such a man, to do a job without dirtying his hands, is Ram's brother's dream.

So Ram works and borrows, and when his brother is educated and his sisters are married, there will then be his own children to serve. He and his wife have a son and two daughters now and will probably have two or three more. Ram has heard of government talk of birth control, but children, to him, are a gift of God. Besides, who will look after him and his wife in their old age unless it is their sons, and how can they be sure there will be at least one son who will live long enough to do this unless several are born?

Ram's mother died, exhausted, a few years ago. Ram's father will die, exhausted, soon. Ram and his wife will probably live to be about forty-five. Then they will die, exhausted, too.

Despite computers and automation and the increasing affluence of the West, most of the people of most of the

world are like Mohan Ram, and many are worse off. The
causes of their needs vary from continent to continent, from
the crowding of Hong Kong to the poor soil of much of
Africa. Paul Hoffman, Managing Director of the United
Nations Special Fund, has spoken of "a hundred nations, a
hundred problems." But whatever the variety of specific
problems, the underlying problem is the same: most of the
people of most of the world can produce so little with their
labor that they have nothing left over to save. With no sav-
ing, there is no money to invest. Without investment, there
is no increase in productivity. So, the shortages and the
hunger remain.

No one aware of the needs of the world's many can fail
to be impressed and perhaps troubled by the affluence of
the few. But the U.S. was not backward in sharing the food
it grew but did not need. Under Public Law 480, passed
in 1954, Congress established a program that came to be
called "Food for Peace" and that, by the end of 1962, had
given away or sold, nearly always for local money, not
dollars, $12,000,000,000 worth of surplus corn, sorghum,
butter, cheese, wheat, and rice. This was 102,000,000 tons
of food to 114 nations. By 1965, U.S. surplus food was being
exported by Food for Peace at the rate of $1,700,000,000
worth per year, making possible some kind of supplemen-
tary food ration each day for a hundred million people.
Under this program, India alone was getting 220,000,000
bushels of wheat a year—about a sixth of the entire U.S.
crop.

All this, of course, was just a tiny fraction of what was
required. Food for Peace Director—later U.S. Senator—
George McGovern said, in 1961, that if all the American
food surplus for one year were distributed equally to all
the people in the world who were underfed, it would mean
for each recipient the equivalent of just two teacups full of
rice every seventeen days. B. R. Sen of the Food and Agriculture Organization wrote in 1965: ". . . the total food

supplies of the developing countries will have to be increased fourfold in the next 35 years, to give their vastly increased populations an adequate, though in no sense a lavish diet." [7]

Economists studying the world's food crisis were in general agreement by the middle 1960's that charity—however moral and however immediately helpful—was not the lasting answer. They recalled the Chinese proverb: "Give a man a fish and he will eat for a day; teach him to fish and he will eat for the rest of his days." Therefore, more and more during the 1960's, most of the free world's aid effort became concentrated on helping the underdeveloped countries to help themselves up what American economist Robert L. Heilbroner called *The Great Ascent*.

Together, the rich free nations were giving or loaning to the poor about five billion dollars a year in economic aid—nearly half of which came from the U.S. Aid from the Communist countries was running at just under one and one-half billion a year. In the twenty years following the end of World War II, the U.S. alone provided more than forty billion dollars in economic aid. In 1961, it established the highly successful Peace Corps through which thousands of Americans, especially young ones, gave two years of their lives to other nations' development. By 1965, most of the countries of Western Europe had aid programs; so did Canada and Japan and Israel. The United Nations was deep in the development business, making surveys of resources, teaching people skills with which they could produce more, making loans for dams and factories. Indeed, the U.N. had named the ten years of the 1960's the "Decade of Development."

From all this experience, certain lessons emerged about the process of economic development. The first step is to create the conditions for investment in industry. This means building harbors and docks and roads and sewers and dams and power plants and schools. Such fundamentals may be financed, at least partially, by the U.N. or the developed countries, but the labor comes from within, from some of the people who used to live on the land. Mohan Ram or some of his neighbors must leave their village to build a railroad or port. This will not mean a drop in food production: in most underdeveloped countries, there are too many people on the land, anyway, and what is needed is to have fewer people farm bigger plots.

Then, as the roads and bridges and railroads are built, industrial investment can begin: local and foreign money can be put into fertilizer factories and steel mills. This is stage number two.

Next, hopefully, comes what the economic historian Walt W. Rostow has called the "take-off." It happened in Britain nearly two hundred years ago, and in the U.S. just before the Civil War. It may be beginning in India and China now. The whole economy starts to grow, profits going back into new factories, creating new jobs and new demands for new products made in more new factories. Science and technology make possible large increases in the amount of food or goods each man can produce. The conditions of life should improve.

Along with a theoretical understanding of the development process, however, has come the realization that "the great ascent" to take-off and beyond is no gradual and happy process. Certainly, it is neither automatic nor easy. The experience of every modern underdeveloped nation is that responding to the "revolution of rising expectations" is in itself nothing short of revolutionary. The job requires not only new investment and new skills but also new attitudes and even new beliefs. Who will make Ram or his neighbor move off his land? If he stays, who will teach him that fertilizer and electricity are not dangerous? How will he change his ideas about sacred cows or his custom of spending a year's income on a wedding? How will he and his wife be persuaded to have fewer children? "No division of the problem into parts," writes a group of Massachusetts

Institute of Technology experts, "permits escape from the fundamental proposition that the paramount requirement for the modernization of any society is that the people themselves must change." [8] And such change is no simple matter.

Assuming, however, that change does begin, there then develops what has been called the "revolution of rising frustrations." Before independence, the politicians told Ram that freedom would bring a better life in all ways. Now Ram may be producing more food, and India may indeed be building roads and schools and factories, but Ram does not yet see the benefits of his labor. He may ask: Why do I not have more? Moreover, even when he does begin to see the benefits of development, there is still no guarantee that he will be content. Far from it. A little improvement in a poor man's life usually increases his demand for more.

The hard truth is that development is a long-term and difficult process. Robert Heilbroner estimates that even with a Herculean effort, it will take the underdeveloped world at least twenty-five years to accumulate wealth per person equal to one-tenth of what the average American has now, or an average yearly income equal to an American's for two weeks. Writing in 1963, Heilbroner said all the effort of the previous ten years had raised the average money income in the backward areas by just one dollar a year. Making the most optimistic possible forecasts, he estimated that one dollar could become two dollars within five or ten years, and ten dollars in twenty or thirty years. "In the meantime," Heilbroner concludes, "this generation of the backward lands will have no alternative but to bear the burdens of the past as they labor for a future they will not live to enjoy." [9]

But will this generation be content to work for growth it cannot enjoy? Will it, instead, make impossible demands on its leaders? Will those leaders be forced to become dictators in order to control development's discontents? Might they promote war abroad in order to try to divert attention at home from an unacceptable pace of growth? However the new leaders attempt the job, the West can expect them to do it with toughness, drama, strong words, and the attitudes of soldiers. "Mild men," writes Heilbroner, "will not ride the tiger of development." [10]

The massive frustrating, revolutionary attempt to develop the Third World, in the words of the editor Gerard Piel, "will engage the principal energies of mankind in the second half of this century." [11] There is no assurance whatever that all the poor nations now hoping to achieve take-off will be able to do so. Those that do succeed may also develop intensely nationalistic dictatorships, especially suspicious of nations that are rich and white. The Secretary General of the U.N., U Thant, said, in 1964, "North-South tensions are fundamentally as serious as East-West ones." But in spite of all the predictable insults and disappointments, most students of the development process see no moral, political, or economic reason why the West cannot and should not at least double its economic aid.

There are the arguments of national security and self-interest: without the sincere and generous support of the world's rich, the poor nations seem almost certain to become bitter, aggressive totalitarian breeding grounds of wars into which the great powers would almost certainly be drawn. Moreover, continued misery among the non-white majority would surely heighten its resentment of the rich white minority. In his last speech before his death in 1965, U.S. Ambassador to the U.N. Adlai Stevenson told the U.N.'s Economic and Social Council the survival of the world depends on the resolution of its "vast contradictions." We cannot maintain the world, said Stevenson, "half fortunate, half miserable, half confident, half despairing, half slave . . . [and] half free." [12]

But beyond even arguments of self-interest is the moral

imperative: it seems, simply, wrong for the rich not to do all they can to try to prevent the hunger and sickness and despair that cause so many underdeveloped lives. One of the most effective pleas for such aid came from the British economist Barbara Ward. "This is the ultimate challenge we face," she wrote in 1961: "to extend our vision of the good society to the whole family of man. Our wealth and comfort hold us back. We find it easier—as do the wastrels of any age—to 'sit down to eat and rise up to play.' We can, like the misers of every epoch, argue that even the smallest transfer of our superabundant wealth will face us with bankruptcy and ruin. It is easy for us, as it has been for the lazy and unaware of every generation, to pretend that nothing has changed, that the world is not in flames, that the old ways are better, and that, if the poor lack bread, they can eat cake. Societies, classes, families, all have tried these evasions in the past. Marie Antoinette playing shepherdess at Trianon when the peasants, not the sheep of France, were eating grass; Rome bemused with bread and circuses while the barbarians gathered at the gate; the Cretan kings drinking deep behind the walls of Knossos with Mycenean fleets waiting to take the city in the night— all these are symbols of the fate that awaits the complacent and the comfortable when they let their good fortune stifle their good will. There is no reason to suppose that the fate of the Western peoples will be different if they carry on with their round of fun and distraction. . . . If . . . the Western peoples make no more response than 'to pass by on the other side,' they will not only endure the fate of Babylon or Carthage. They will deserve it." [13]

# Part Four
# The New World (II)

*Chapter Ten*

---

# RUSSIA AND CHINA

ON FRIDAY, March 6, 1953, Radio Moscow began its broad-casting with a roll of drums, then with the Soviet National Anthem, and then with the formal announcement that on March 5 at 9:50 P.M., Moscow time, Joseph Stalin had died. "The heart of the comrade and inspired continuer of Lenin's will," read the announcer, "the wise leader and teacher of the Communist party and the Soviet people, Joseph Vissarionovich Stalin, has stopped beating."

The news was not unexpected. Two mornings before, Radio Moscow had reported that Stalin had had a stroke on the night of March 1; he was partly paralyzed and had lost consciousness. The day before, two more bulletins had revealed that Stalin's health had further deteriorated, that his condition was extremely serious. Now the suspected was confirmed.

Thousands of Muscovites waited in the bitter cold of Red Square for Stalin's body to be brought by on its way from the Kremlin to the nearby hall in which it would lie in state. There, according to reliable estimates, two or three million more people lined up to pay their last respects. Thousands of wreaths were banked along the Kremlin wall, and black-bordered red flags hung from the state buildings.

The funeral, on March 9, was properly solemn and impres-sive. The coffin was rolled on a gun carriage back through

Red Square, then borne by the dead leader's eight top heirs to its place of honor in the tomb that, until then, had been Lenin's alone. Guns fired a salute, and everything movable throughout the Soviet Union came to rest for five minutes. And yet . . .

It became increasingly clear that the single dominant emotion of most of Stalin's heirs was not sadness but relief. The tyrant of whom they had lived in fear for so long was, at last, gone. Nikita Khrushchev recalled later that another long-time Stalin henchman, Nikolai Bulganin, had told him once: "It has happened sometimes that a man goes to Stalin by invitation, as a friend. And when he sits with Stalin, he does not know where he will be sent next, home or to jail." [1] Khrushchev also said later: "Stalin was a very distrustful man, sickly suspicious; we knew this from our work with him. He could look at a man and say, 'Why are your eyes so shifty today?' or 'Why are you turning so much today and avoiding looking me directly in the eyes?' The sickly suspicion created in him a general distrust even toward eminent Party workers whom he had known for years. Everywhere and in everything he saw 'enemies,' 'double-dealers,' and 'spies.' " [2]

Through the twenties and thirties, Stalin had presided over the bloody purges of those he suspected or feared, and even in 1953, it seemed as if a new purge were beginning. Just before Stalin's death, those closest to him must have wondered which "eminent party workers" would be shot this time, and as they placed the tyrant's body in the red granite mausoleum, it must have seemed as if the fatal hemorrhage had come none too soon.

With a ruthless and total terror that surpassed even that of the ancient Czars, Stalin had forced peasant Russia to build a complex industrial machine. In 1917, 80 percent of the people of the new Soviet Union had been illiterate; in 1953—just thirty-six years later—Russian scientists and engineers tested a hydrogen bomb. The industrialization that Stalin forced on his country was, of course, the key to its survival in World War II, but those who lived through it were more apt to remember the murders and the suffering. There may have been enough tanks and guns, but there was too little of all the common necessities: food, housing, clothes, and transportation. Even after the war, there was so little to eat on some of the collective farms that prisoners in the slave labor camps sent food packages back to their villages. Everyone lived in fear of the 3 A.M. knock on the door that meant jail or death. No one dared speak out.

So it was not just the top men of the Communist party who wanted an end to Stalin's rigid ways but the great mass of the people, too. Moreover, the Thaw, as it came to be called, could be justified on the most practical grounds: Russia's sophisticated factories were now dependent for their growth on a "new class" of managers and technicians who wanted continuing and even increasing privileges and whose best work could be done only if they were permitted greater freedom from clumsy central control by those who, too often, did not know what they were doing. Thus, Stalin's heirs had both personal and political incentives to loosen the reins Stalin had held so painfully taut. The problem was (and is): How does a dictatorship give a nation its head without permitting it to run away?

The Thaw began in the Kremlin itself, paradoxically, with one more act of terror. Stalin's successors saw to it that Lavrenti Beria, head of the secret police, was murdered and the fearsome power of the police curtailed. Then thousands of prisoners were sent home from the slave labor camps, the codes of justice were made more fair, and throughout Russia it became possible for people to breathe a little more freely.

Those who breathed most deeply, of course, were the

most sensitive, the writers and artists whose only job, under Stalin had been to grind out propaganda that would encourage production and discipline. In their work, their personal feelings had been taboo, almost the only acceptable hero a young worker dedicated to fulfilling his quota. "Socialist Realism," this had been called. As the Thaw spread, one writer eager for it to spread further said nobody read Soviet poetry and nobody ever would read it as long as it always was about "the same old dam, the same old steam shovel."

Now, however, in the summer and autumn of 1953, the regime permitted Russian writers to publish stories about real human beings with real feelings. Musicians could experiment with a twelve-tone scale, and painters could toy with the abstract. What was truth? What was justice? The young poet, Yevgeni Yevtushenko, said, "Let us give back to words their original meanings."

Nikita Khrushchev had become First Secretary of Russia's Communist party in September of 1953, and as such, he was the single most powerful of Stalin's successors, eventually becoming Chairman of the Council of Ministers, too. At first, he encouraged the Thaw, then cracked down on the writers when they moved beyond new forms and old questions into social criticism, attacking the hypocrisy and abuses of the Stalin system itself. But, significantly, no critics were shot. Then, on February 25, 1956, Khrushchev turned the Thaw into a near flood with one of the most remarkable speeches of our time, a secret speech to the Twentieth Congress of the Communist party of the Soviet Union in which he attacked none other than Joseph Stalin. Apparently, Khrushchev believed the modernization of Russian industry required a degree of freedom that could come only with the destruction of everything associated with Stalin. Apparently, he believed the best way to do this was suddenly and shockingly, in an address to those who had served Stalin the most faithfully.

It must have been one of history's greatest denunciations.

Khrushchev accused his late boss of "brutal violence," of "the most cruel repression," of "grave abuse of power." The heart of the problem, said Khrushchev, was "the Stalin cult," "the cult of the individual," which permitted no deviation from Stalin's personal whim. "Stalin acted not through persuasion, explanation and patient cooperation with people," said Khrushchev, "but by imposing his concepts and demanding absolute submission to his opinion. Whoever opposed this concept or tried to prove his viewpoint and the correctness of his position was doomed to removal from the leading collective and to subsequent moral and physical annihilation."

Then Khrushchev began the terrible documentation of his charges. Stalin nearly cost Russia victory in World War II, said Khrushchev, by disregarding warnings first of the German attack, then of potential tactical problems. He made up false charges against people. "Confessions were obtained through physical pressures against the accused." Just before he died, said Khrushchev, Stalin told the Minister of State Security investigating an alleged "plot": "If you do not obtain confessions . . . we will shorten you by a head." Then he told the judge investigating the case: "Beat, beat, and once again, beat."

Finally, Khrushchev detailed Stalin's cost to the Communist party itself: of the 139 members and candidates elected to the Central Committee in 1934, 98—70 percent of them—had been arrested and shot. At this point, the text of the Khrushchev speech as obtained by the U.S. government carries in parentheses the comment: "Indignation in the hall."

News of the secret speech spread quickly through Russia's Communist party, through all Russia, and into Eastern Europe, where it triggered a successful nonviolent revolution in Poland and then the unsuccessful and violent uprising in Hungary. After this, Khrushchev tightened up again on free expression. The revolution in Hungary never would have happened, said the same man who had deplored the ruthlessness of Stalin, if the government there had had the sense to shoot a few writers. If he had to do so, Khrushchev warned, "My hand would not tremble." [3]

But nothing in the Communist world was the same after Khrushchev began the process called "de-Stalinization," a process that resulted in the actual removal of Stalin's body —in 1961—from Lenin's tomb to a less honored gravesite nearby. De-Stalinization downgraded all Russia's leaders: it was hard to see how there could be again such total one-man rule or how Russians and Russia's satellites could fail to be more independent. When the world sits down to write an epitaph for Nikita Khrushchev, wrote the veteran Moscow correspondent for *The New York Times,* Harrison Salisbury, in 1965, it is likely to read: "Here lies a man who sowed discord within the world Communist movement and brought to the Russian people an atmosphere in which poets again began to sing." [4]

For years, the leaders of the Communist nations had repeated so often their devotion to unity amongst themselves, under Russian leadership, that most people in the West had come to believe these countries really were one bloc of nations, one large and solid monolith. True, Yugoslavia had dared go its own way in 1948, but this did not really undermine Western acceptance of the idea that all Communists were one. It took Stalin's death and the events that followed it to reveal just how many cracks the bloc had. Of these fissures, none was more important than that which opened between Russia and China.

The death of Stalin left Mao Tse-tung the world's senior Communist leader. At least, Mao thought of himself that way. He had been elected head of the Communist party of China during the Long March in 1935. He had been top man in the Chinese government since he proclaimed the People's Republic in 1949. For thirty years, he had been

developing the ideas of Marx and Lenin to fit the needs
of Asia, and by 1956 his propagandists were referring to
him as the leading theoretician of the Communist world.
From Peking, Nikita Khrushchev must have seemed a
coarse latecomer to whom one such as Mao need never defer.

Moreover, just as Russia's Communists carried into power
the traditions of their country, so Mao Tse-tung was at least
as Chinese as he was Communist, impatient to drive out
all foreign influence, to unify his country, to expand it to
its ancient frontiers and make it, once again, the great
Middle Kingdom to which all the barbarians should kowtow.

The key to power in the modern world, of course, is
industry, and Mao's China had little of that. Reliable estimates of China's production per person in 1952 show it
at no more than a fourth of what Russia's had been in 1928.
So, with this underdeveloped base, Mao's task was to produce enough food not only to feed China's relentlessly
increasing population—growing by perhaps fifteen million
a year—but also to have some left over to sell abroad for
money with which to buy the machines that could bring
strength.

The leaders of the Soviet Union thought the way they
had come was not only the best but also the only correct
course for a "Socialist" state to follow. But Mao could and
did disregard their counsel: he had experienced half a lifetime of bad Russian advice, and he saw no need to begin
accepting it now. He did welcome Russian economic and
military aid, but by and large, he proceeded on his own with
his own uniquely Chinese plan.

In perhaps the greatest social upheaval in all history,
Mao Tse-tung tried to remold not just Chinese society but
all the Chinese people, as well. To anyone devoted to the
sanctity of the individual human being, what happened in
China during the 1950's must seem like nothing else so
much as hell.

The first step was to make sure the country and people were under control, and here—even though millions of people were shot—the principal technique was "brute reason" rather than "brute force." Stalin had ruled Russia by the terror of his secret police, but Mao preferred a more sophisticated device, a combination of terror and enthusiasm that came to be called "brainwashing." Instead of killing or confining his enemies, Mao would convert them. He had been working on the technique for many years, experimenting on captured Kuomintang soldiers during the 1930's and on captured Japanese soldiers during World War II. He had said of the process in 1942: "We must begin by administering a shock and shouting at the patient, 'You are ill!' so that he is frightened into a sweat, and then we tell him gently that he needs treatment." [5]

The treatment involved hardship, insecurity, fatigue, indoctrination, threats, and confession. It was effective enough to make some captured American G.I.'s "confess" to germ warfare in Korea. In China, its mission was nothing less than the destruction of the most important Confucian loyalties, substituting for devotion to father and family new ties to Mao and the party.

Everywhere, there were slogans and campaigns, one frenzied drive after another. One was against sparrows, which were known to eat scarce grain. On "Kill the Sparrows Day," literally everyone in a city would go outside or up on top of buildings with whistles and cymbals and sirens and pots and pans—anything to make a noise—so the sparrows would be too frightened to land and would fly around until they dropped, exhausted, to be pounced on and killed. It was estimated such campaigns killed a billion sparrows. Only afterwards did the regime realize that the birds had eaten insect pests, too, and that they may have been a greater asset than a liability. This combination of regimented fervor and bad management dominated China through the fifties.

Unlike Lenin, who had come to power with the support of the new proletariat in the cities, Mao had based his revolution on his country's peasants, four out of every five of China's people. Mao had promised land to each peasant family, and beginning in 1950, he fulfilled that promise— briefly. Three hundred thousand trained party workers carried to every village Mao's special kind of land reform. First, the peasants were forced to list all they owned, and the land of all the gentry and rich peasants was confiscated. Next, the party cadres encouraged complaints: first privately, then in formal accusation meetings, people were urged to "speak bitter" about their neighbors, especially the gentry. Hatred and tension built up. Finally, party judges arrived for public trials of the accused, after which there were quick public executions and then a celebration at which the poor peasants were given deeds to the confiscated land. No one knows how many people were shot, but all estimates are in millions. Thus was China's gentry class eliminated, and thus did the government try to extend its control to every village.

Similar campaigns were conducted in the cities, where everyone was required to join at least one mass organization through which "thought reform" was carried out. Executions were broadcast over street-corner loudspeakers; there were frequent mass demonstrations; and by 1953, Communist rule was secure—inflation stopped, land redistributed, enemies eliminated, foreigners expelled, and, above all, the people controlled. Now Mao could begin to try to build.

In an attempt to get the greater amount of food China needed, Mao decreed even greater control over the peasants. One part of the first Five Year Plan, from 1953 to 1957, was the collectivization of land. Just as the last of the poor peasants were getting their new deeds, the drive began to herd all the peasants into "cooperatives." By the middle of 1956, 90 percent of the peasants had been persuaded to put their land into common ownership.

But the new way did not work. During the first Five Year Plan, there were impressive increases in industrial output: steel production up 325 percent, for instance, and coal up more than 200 percent. But the output of grain went up only slightly, and this with at least 50 million more mouths to feed. Nothing in the ideas of Marx or Lenin or Mao had changed China's ancient imbalance between the people and the land.

Russia had agreed to help China build 211 factories and to train Chinese technicians, but there was little comradely generosity about the deal: China had to pay promptly. By early 1958, it was clear that if Mao were to make China a modern power in a hurry, he would have to do something even more drastic than he had already done. He chose to try, deciding to apply more intensively than ever, especially to the land, his only abundant resource, human labor. In February of 1958, Mao decreed an intended shortcut to Communism that he called a "Great Leap Forward": China would overtake Britain in total production by 1970. Everyone was to work "harder, faster, better, cheaper." Extra steel was to be cooked in back-yard blast furnaces. Above all, the 700,000 collective farms were to be merged into 24,000 huge "communes" in which the regimented peasants would attack the land like troops doing battle.

The year before, Russia had startled the world with the accomplishments of her space and rocket scientists and engineers. Now China would show what her common people could do: not by accident China's first commune was named "Weihsing," which means "Sputnik."

By the end of 1958, all China's peasants had been herded into communes to which they handed over their homes, their livestock, and whatever land they had not already given the cooperatives. Some communes even abolished money. The peasants wakened to whistles, marched to the fields, worked all day and often much of the night, with meetings afterwards, and ate and slept too little. Young men were ordered off to build dams and canals, children were kept in central nurseries, but all the rest, including the women, waged war on the land. Even city intellectuals, especially those of uncertain loyalties, were sent down to "learn from the peasants." In 1958, the *China Youth Daily* published this peasant description of commune life:

> "At the sound of the cease-work bell
> We enter the mess hall to eat.
> Taking one mouthful of rice
> We find sand between our teeth;
> Helping ourselves to the vegetable,
> We find grass stalks in it.
> We lay down the chopsticks
> And go to work again." [6]

Once again Mao's scheme failed, and this time, on a scale as colossal as its goal. Partly, it was mismanagement: for instance, orders to plant rows of grain twice as close together as was healthy. Partly, it was bad weather. Mostly, it was the almost incredible pace that doubled the death rate during the "three hard years" from 1959 to 1962, cut the birth rate by at least 10 percent, and left the survivors exhausted, hungry, and sick. By 1960, grain production had dropped to the same level as it had been in 1952. None of the steel from the 600,000 back-yard furnaces was worth using.

Even before 1958 was over, Mao's regime decided to turn the Great Leap into a great retreat. Decisions about what to plant and when to harvest were returned to "production teams," essentially the former villages. Each peasant was given back his home and was permitted a little land to work and profit from on his own. But the damage had been done: reliable foreign observers estimated that in city and countryside the Great Leap Forward had set

back China's development by at least five and more likely
ten years.

As of 1965, the best of the few reports coming out of
China indicated that, although there was no more famine,
life was still austere in the extreme. The family of the
average Peking worker shared a one-story house with three
or four other families. The man worked a six-day week and
earned perhaps $25.00 to $30.00 a month. Since 1961, the
regime had given agriculture first priority over both heavy
and light industry, so only about half of China's factories
were in operation, and twenty million people living in the
cities had been ordered "down to the countryside" for the
rest of their lives to help the peasants grow more food.

True, the Communists had forced undeniable achievements: foreign observers noted that China had become
cleaner and healthier, more honest and more literate, with
the formerly hopeless poor much better off. But China also
seemed more isolated, with a surplus of indoctrination
and demonstrations. Robert Guillain, a French correspondent who revisited China in 1964, made this grim report:
". . . the great leap forward and the communes succeeded
in pulverizing a whole people into socialism. They are
broken to the discipline of no complaints, no resistance, no
discussion. By force, by habit, or by resignation the Chinese have learned how to dose out applause and silence." [7]

All the evidence suggests that China's leaders will continue to drive their people as quickly as possible to achieve
the new Middle Kingdom. The price of such ruthless development probably will be even more tragic than was Stalin's
price in Russia, but even with the mistakes of the Great
Leap Forward and even with the ever-increasing demands
for food of ever more and more people, there seems no
reason to doubt that China will become a great power.
China's bellicose anti-Americanism may bring another
cold war just as dangerous as the one with Russia.

But there may be ground for hope that China will not always be an enemy. Her people inherited a tradition of compromise and acceptance long before they began singing the praises of Mao and the party. As in Russia, successful industrialization may eventually require the relative freedom of a Thaw. And even though brainwashing seems to have done its job, still there was evidence in the 1950's, at least, that not everyone was as docile as he seemed.

Shortly after the Thaw began in the Soviet Union, Mao invited more discussion in China, saying in May of 1956: "Let a hundred flowers bloom; let the hundred schools of thought contend." What this meant was that there should be expression of opinion and even criticism. Perhaps Mao thought his control over his people so complete that this invitation would produce little response, pleasing the intellectuals without creating any threat to the party. If so, he was wrong. For nearly a year, no one dared "bloom," but finally party exhortations seemed sincere enough, so criticism began. The gray walls of Peking University were papered with protests, demands for more freedom, attacks on Marxism and the party. One sign read: "Communist society makes human beings inhuman." [8] Throughout China, intellectuals wrote critical letters to the newspapers, which printed them. And then it all stopped as suddenly as it had begun. Mao cut off the heady exercise after just six weeks, the *Peking People's Daily* explaining that the project had been a trap to expose those it called "poisonous weeds." Some observers, however, thought the campaign had been stopped because it had so dangerously backfired.

What another such invitation would bring today or five years hence is anyone's guess, but it seems probable that there remain even now people who, while dutifully and prudently shouting Mao's praises, still remember with some fondness the other values that served China for so long. Even more important, as trustworthy an authority as Mao himself confessed sadly to visitors in the mid-1960's that China's young people—despite their indoctrination—had little of the revolutionary fervor of Mao's dying generation.

Through the late fifties, the feud between China and Russia became more and more bitter and more and more obvious. In the summer of 1960, Russia called home all her technicians who had been helping China industrialize: they left factories half finished and took their blueprints with them. By the early sixties, each side was accusing the other of the most serious deviation from the correct Communist path, and in October of 1961, China's Prime Minister, Chou En-lai, even walked out of Russia's Twenty-second Party Congress.

The roots of the feud went deep. As the first nation to make a Communist revolution, Russia thought all others should follow its way and that any who did not were incorrect. Stalin once called Mao Tse-tung a "margarine Communist." [9] But Mao Tse-tung thought Russia knew nothing of how Communism should be applied in Asia. Had not Stalin backed Chiang Kai-shek's Kuomintang through most of the years Mao was fighting it and even after World War II advised Mao to ally with the KMT rather than fight it?

Russia had based its revolution on the workers in the cities; China had based its on the peasants. Russia's Communists had come to power suddenly, in the midst of political chaos; the Chinese Communists had had to fight a long guerrilla war.

Like Yugoslavia, China was independent enough to quarrel with Russia because her revolution had been home-grown not Soviet-imposed. But the major cause of the argument probably was the difference in the two countries' industrial development. By the 1960's, Russia had come far enough to be able to afford to relax a little, but China could not. Mao had no use for de-Stalinization; indeed his own "cult of personality" was at least as fervid as Stalin's ever had been. So, on issue after issue the two nations disagreed.

There was the matter of economic aid. China wanted as much as possible from Russia in order to build herself up. Therefore, her leaders were bitterly resentful of Russian loans to such "bourgeois" governments as those in India and Egypt, when China—a member of the "Socialist" camp —could get no more than she did.

There was also, to the West, the grimly fascinating matter of the "inevitability" of war. Khrushchev often "rattled" his rockets, shouting angry threats of incinerating those with whom he disagreed. But Khrushchev also preached that the Communist nations could and should bring about the downfall of capitalism by peaceful economic competition, not by all-out war. He thought if Communism outproduced capitalism, if it put "more meat in the goulash," it would triumph. Local anticolonial wars of national liberation were proper, he said, but a nuclear "exchange" would destroy all the Russians had suffered so much to build. "Coexistence is the only way," he said in 1960, "the only path to take. Any other way means death and destruction for all of us." Because world war would have "fatal consequences," it could be advocated only by "madmen and maniacs."

China, however, was in all ways more militant. "If the imperialists insist on unleashing another war," Mao wrote in 1957, "we should not be afraid of it." He scoffed at Western power, insisting that it was not what it seemed: all imperialists remained, as Mao had put it in 1946, "paper tigers."

Some observers thought China could be so casual about war because her leaders did not understand the power of nuclear weapons. Others thought the Chinese understood all too well: world nuclear war might cost China several hundred million people, but she would still have several hundred million left, whereas Russia and the U.S. would be ruined. Thus, nuclear war would leave China the "Laugh-ing Third."

Khrushchev threatened to use his intermediate range rockets on Europe at the time of Suez. He walked near the brink more than once in Berlin. But as a general matter, he was unwilling to run as many risks as Mao thought he should. In 1957, just after Russia had launched Sputnik and proved that she had an intercontinental rocket, Mao thought the balance of world power had shifted. He made a speech entitled, "The East Wind Is Prevailing Over the West Wind." But Khrushchev, in Mao's eyes, did not fully press his new advantage.

Nor did Mao approve of Khrushchev's agreement to withdraw his rockets from Cuba in 1962. Khrushchev justi-fied his retreat with the observation that the "paper tiger has nuclear teeth." But Mao was contemptuous, author-izing publication of an indirect but scathing criticism of Russia as having "lost every quality a revolutionary ought to have," and of having become "timid as mice."

In spite of its economic backwardness, China's criticism succeeded in putting Russia on the ideological defensive, challenging its leadership of Communist movements through-out the bloc and among the underdeveloped nations, where Mao's agents used not only the argument of their Marxist-Leninist purity but also—more and more—the racist claim that the world's nonwhite majority should stand together against the white.

On October 16, 1964, there occurred two major events that revealed the changing realities of the Communist world: China's drive for power, Russia's for affluence, and the rivalry between the two. In Moscow, it was announced that Nikita Khrushchev had been deposed; in China, Mao Tse-tung tested an atomic bomb.

China's admission to the nuclear club had been expected for some time. In spite of the hunger of her people, in

spite of Russia's refusal, in 1959, to give her any more
help with nuclear development, the Peking regime had
persevered and succeeded. Indeed, the fissionable material
it used was $U^{235}$, the separation of which from $U^{238}$
requires impressive technological ability. It is one thing,
of course, to test one atomic bomb and quite another to
build hundreds of warheads and rockets, but the first Chinese explosion, at Lake Lop Nor in Sinkiang Province, was
one more example of Peking's determination to achieve a
prominent place in the world, whatever the price.

There were many reasons for Khrushchev's fall, not
least his personal feud with Mao, which made more bitter
the basic differences between the two regimes. But according
to his successors at the time, the most important reason was
that his leadership at home was too impulsive. In a major
editorial in *Pravda* the day after the announcement of
Khrushchev's ouster, Russia's new leaders attacked "hare-
brained schemes, immature conclusions and hasty decisions
and actions divorced from reality, bragging and phrase-
mongering, commandism, unwillingness to take into account
the achievements of science and practical experience . . .
armchair methods, personal decisions and disregard for
the practical experience of the masses." They also implied
that Khrushchev had been guilty of building up his own
"cult of personality."

Khrushchev's immediate successors were far less colorful
men: Leonid Brezhnev as First Secretary of the party,
Aleksei Kosygin, as Prime Minister. But, like Khrushchev,
they pledged themselves to "peaceful coexistence" and
"collective leadership," and then they proceeded to reorgan-
ize the Communist party and much of Soviet agriculture
and industry in order to try to produce more for Russia's
consumers.

In the party program adopted in 1961, Russia had set,
as its goal, turning out as much by 1970 as the U.S. produced in 1960. Khrushchev had boasted of a "world histor-

ical victory," of overtaking the U.S. and all other countries in production per person by 1980. The trouble was
that central planning produced so many inefficiencies that
by 1964 Soviet warehouses were filled with three billion
dollars' worth of goods so shoddy or unattractive that not
even the Russians would buy them.

To make Russia more efficient, Khrushchev had begun
experiments in "creeping capitalism," letting individual
factories produce what their customers wanted rather than
what a Moscow ministry decreed. The new regime continued this and also announced a huge new investment in
agriculture, along with more incentives to farm managers
and workers. Brezhnev and Kosygin seemed far more toler-
ant of the memory of Stalin than Khrushchev had been,
but writers still searched for something beyond the drab-
ness of life around them, youngsters aped Western styles
even down to spike heels and blue jeans, satire flourished,
and there was even a revival of interest in religion. "The
essential fact of our age," claimed the writer, Boris Paster-
nak, just before he died in 1960, "is that a new freedom is
being born." [10]

Nothing about the spirit of Russia's young or the search
for efficiency by her rulers implied that the Soviets would
not try to force the West to its knees if they thought they
could get away with it. Cuba '62 showed that. Nevertheless,
the realities of Western power abroad and increasing prosperity and education at home seemed to have dulled
Russia's revolutionary zeal, or at least made her leaders
more careful.

There was no law that said a fat Communist was less
dangerous than a lean one, and no guarantee that China's
successful economic development would make her embrace
"peaceful coexistence," too. Certainly, it seemed as if it
would be many years before Peking could again invite
a hundred flowers to bloom or let poets sing any tune
other than Mao's own. But for the West, there did seem

to be security not only in its own vigilance but also in Communist prosperity. The Peking of Mao Tse-tung might insist on permanent austerity at home and permanent revolution abroad, but the Peking of Mao's successors could be different: after all, in Moscow by 1961—according to Harrison Salisbury—even the tough old Russian Bolshevik Vyacheslav Molotov had three maids and a wine cellar, a fact that came to light when it became known that one of the girls had been fired because she had been stealing bottles.

*Chapter Eleven*

---

# THE NEW EUROPE

O<small>N MARCH</small> 25, 1957, in the city of Rome, six European
statesmen gathered to sign their names to one of the most
important documents in the history of their continent.
Seated behind a long table in the Hall of Horatii and
Curiatii on the Capitoline Hill, the delegates had before
them a 378-page treaty of 248 articles, 8 protocols, and
3 annexes, but with just one ultimate purpose: to make
war among the six obsolete. Like the Horatii and Curiatii
of Roman legend—two sets of triplets who fought until
only one brother survived—the six nations these men represented, especially France and Germany, had nearly destroyed each other in battle; three times in the last hundred
years German troops had marched into France. But now
the generals' civilian successors with their dark business
suits and heavy glasses took up their pens, one by one, to
try to sheathe the sword, to prevent the pride and ambition of their countrymen from ever again slaughtering
the best of each new generation in Europe and bleeding all
the rest of the world, as well.

Ever since the Rome of the Caesars, men had dreamed
of a united Europe, but always the dream had been inter-
rupted by the clamor of one man or one tribe or one
nation putting what it thought was its own interest ahead
of the interest of all. World War II was the most tragic
and most recent result of such selfishness. But now, on

"Freedom Fighters" during the revolt in Hungary, November, 1956.
(United Press International Photo)

Nikita Sergeyevich Khrushchev. (Sovfoto)

John Fitzgerald Kennedy delivers his Inaugural Address, January 20, 1961. *(Wide World Photos)*

The Berlin wall, 1962. *(Wide World Photos)*

Flag of Ghana replaces the Union Jack as the former British colony of
the Gold Coast becomes independent, March 6, 1957. *(United Press
International Photo)*

Mohandas K. Gandhi, 1925. *(Radio Times Hulton Picture Library)*

Part of a crowd in Calcutta, India, 1954. *(Wide World Photos)*

An IBM System/360 computer configuration, 1964. *(International Business Machines Corp.)*

Jean Monnet, November 11, 1964. *(Wide World Photos)*

General Charles de Gaulle makes a triumphal entry into liberated Paris,
August 24, 1944. *(United Press International Photo)*

Mrs. John F. Kennedy and her two children, Caroline and John Jr., follow President Kennedy's body down the steps of St. Matthew's Cathedral in Washington after the funeral mass. Beside and behind Mrs. Kennedy are the dead President's brothers, Robert and Edward. *(Wide World Photos)*

Lyndon Baines Johnson, 1965. *(Wide World Photos)*

U.S. paratroopers look for a Viet Cong sniper after a helicopter landing north of Saigon, South Viet Nam, 1965. *(Wide World Photos)*

this drizzly day, first Spaak of Belgium, then Pineau of
France, Adenauer of Germany, Segni of Italy, Luns of the
Netherlands, and Bech of Luxembourg signed their names
to a promise of cooperation; the mayor of Rome gave
each man a specially struck gold medal; ancient bells pealed
from the Capitoline tower; a small crowd provided a cheer;
and Rome's school children—whatever their knowledge of
treaties and war—were given the day off.

For an agreement with as noble an ultimate end as the
abolition of war, the Treaty of Rome was most ordinary
in its means. It promised neither powerful police forces
nor sweeping disarmament but a European Economic Community—a Common Market—in which the six members,
over twelve to fifteen years, would eliminate the 30,000
tariffs they charged on each others' goods and would apply
a common tax on imports from other countries.

Humdrum as this might appear at first glance, it was
revolutionary for nations in which most businesses had
been carefully protected from outside competition. Moreover, it disguised an even more revolutionary intent, for a
subtle effect of the Treaty of Rome was its encouragement
of the six not only to cooperate but also, little by little, to
give up some of their sovereign power to the community
as a whole. "We are not in business at all," said one of
the leaders of the Common Market, Walter Hallstein of
Germany, "we are in politics." [1] The goal was a United
States of Europe.

The idea of what the Europeans call "integration" had
been gathering force all during World War II, becoming
by 1945 a full-fledged movement with appeal both to the
practical and to the idealistic. Its foremost attraction, of
course, was its promise of peace by making France and
Germany partners instead of enemies. But the European
movement also promised prosperity comparable to that
of the United States. In the U.S., an automobile manufacturer in Michigan need pay no tax to Illinois when he

ships a car to Chicago for sale; a resident of New Jersey is free to find work in New York; there is no restriction on a Texan investing money in California. The states of the U.S.A. have always formed a common market, and now, with nearly two hundred million Americans, they also enclose a mass market which permits the mass production that is the key to low consumer prices: the more items a manufacturer can turn out, the cheaper the cost of each one. It is precisely this system—mass production for a mass market with free movement of goods, labor, and capital—that was the economic goal of the Treaty of Rome.

But beyond even peace and prosperity, there was in the European movement still another lure: the rebirth of European power. The ancient nations of Europe had once been the most influential in the world, their people accustomed to pre-eminence; now, after the war, it was humiliating for the same people to fear Russia and look for protection to America. Perhaps, they thought, the costs of World War II and the loss of the colonies made it impossible for any one nation of Europe by itself to regain its old dominance, but surely if the nations of Europe could unite . . .

France's Secretary of State for European Affairs, Maurice Fauvre, minced no words when he asked the French National Assembly to ratify the Treaty of Rome. He said some men might pretend that all the Allies of World War II were still great powers, but this was no longer the case. "Actually, there are only two," said Fauvre, "the United States and Russia. Tomorrow there will be a third—China. It is up to you to decide whether or not there can be a fourth—Europe. If you fail to make this choice you will condemn yourselves to walk backward into the future."

As did all the others, the French Assembly voted "aye."

After the war, the first great push toward an integrated Europe came from Winston Churchill, who urged, in 1946, that France and Germany become the nucleus of a United States of Europe. The U.S. pursued the same goal: in 1947, one of the conditions of the Marshall Plan was that the Europeans themselves decide how U.S. aid should be divided. The resulting Organization for European Economic Cooperation did accomplish what its name implied.

Then on May 9, 1950, Europe itself took the movement a step further. Robert Schuman, Foreign Minister of France, proposed that France and Germany integrate the basic industries on which aggression had depended, coal and steel, so that, in Schuman's words, war would be "not only unthinkable but impossible." [2] If tariffs on coal and steel were abolished, according to the theory of the Schuman Plan, France and Germany and others who joined the European Coal and Steel Community would become dependent on each other, and those who were interdependent could no longer fight.

France and Germany did join, and so did Belgium, the Netherlands, Luxembourg, and Italy, and on August 10, 1952, the first trainload of German finished steel rolled across the French border duty-free. But at least as important as the growing economic cooperation was the political trust: each member of the ECSC agreed that a High Authority of European civil servants should have the power to make and enforce the decisions on which the plan would depend for success. This surrender of sovereignty by each individual nation to something bigger than itself inspired bold words from those most intimately aware of the process. "This new Community," said the first President of the High Authority, "is a revolution in Europe, perhaps the greatest Europe has known. We are embarked," he prophesied, "upon a liberation of Europe from its past." [3]

The man who said that was the spiritual father of both the Coal and Steel Community and the Common Market, a short, hard-working, self-effacing, practical, but optimistic Frenchman named Jean Monnet (zhawn maw-NAY).

Monnet was born November 9, 1888, in the town of Cognac in southwestern France, where his grandfather had founded a famous brandy firm, J. G. Monnet & Company. Monnet was a poor student who dropped out of school at the age of sixteen to go to work in the family business, traveling over much of the world as a brandy salesman. But during World War I, when he was rejected by the Army because of poor health, Monnet became a junior official in the French government and began to demonstrate his now-famous ability to develop and carry out massive plans. He devised a method by which Britain and France would cooperate rather than compete in buying war supplies and so impressed his elders that, after the war, he was appointed a Deputy Secretary of the League of Nations when he was just thirty-one years old. Monnet served briefly, then resigned to revive his family business, which had suffered during the war, and then he began a career as an international financier, becoming a partner in a Wall Street investment firm, planning—among other projects—new systems of money for Poland and Rumania and a railroad reorganization in China. When France fell to the Germans in 1940, Monnet came to Washington on behalf of the British, his passport signed personally by Prime Minister Churchill. He helped the U.S. supply war matériel to Britain, actually thinking up the phrase President Roosevelt used to describe what he hoped the U.S. could become, "the great arsenal of democracy."

Then, after France was liberated, it was Monnet, back in Paris, who devised the plan by which French industry went back to work; it was Monnet who thought up what became known as the Schuman Plan for the European Coal and Steel Community; and it was Monnet who became the first President of the ECSC High Authority.

How did a brandy salesman with no formal higher education become one of the world's most respected economists and financiers, a "world broker of ideas?"[4] Obviously, Monnet had a brilliant mind. He was willing to let others enjoy whatever credit his labors received. But most of all, he was practical enough to move toward great objectives by simple and undramatic steps—one at a time.

Monnet resigned his job as head of the ECSC High Authority in 1955 to return to the kind of work he does best: planning and persuading. In Paris, he formed a lobby, the name of which, unlike many lobbies, did not disguise its purpose: Monnet called it the Action Committee for a United States of Europe. As President of this Action Committee, Monnet helped design and build the Treaty of Rome, constantly promoting the movement he has called the "quiet revolution," convinced that the Europe he loved must either federate or perish.

John Kennedy wrote Monnet in 1963, ". . . under your inspiration, Europe has moved closer to unity in less than twenty years than it had done before in a thousand." [5]

His Wall Street partner, George Murnane, once called Monnet ". . . one of the most gifted negotiators God ever put on this earth. . . . If I wanted to merge Russia and the United States," said Murnane when the cold war was its most frigid, "I would leave it in Monnet's hands." [6]

The columnist Walter Lippmann once described Monnet as a man whose purpose in life was to "cajole men to work together for their own good." Lippmann called Monnet "the most effective planner and engineer of human unity whom we have known in our time." [7]

Monnet's friend, George Ball, U.S. Under Secretary of State, said of him and his dream of a united Europe: ". . . he has demonstrated anew the ancient adage that a resolute man, plus the truth, can become a majority." [8]

From the beginning, the Common Market was a brilliant economic success. In the five years after January 1, 1959, when the six made their first 10 percent cut in tariffs on industrial goods moving between them, the EEC became the world's largest single trading community, importing and exporting to the rest of the world more than the U.S. In the same five years, trade among the six increased by 75 percent. In 1962, the big Paris department store, Galeries Lafayette, put on display sixty-two products, each with tags revealing how tariff cuts and mass production had affected prices. Before 1959, a woman's raincoat from Italy had sold for the equivalent of $22.00; now it sold for $8.00. An alarm clock from Germany had been $7.00; now it was $4.00. A cotton blouse from the Netherlands had been $4.00; now it was $2.50. A vacuum cleaner made in France had been $46.00, but with the bigger market and stiffer competition, it was now down to $22.

By 1965, the six had lowered their tariffs on each other's manufactured goods by 70 percent and planned to wipe them out completely by July of 1967, three years ahead of the original schedule. Moreover, even though it had required the most heroic negotiations, the six had also agreed to begin moving toward common policies not just in manufacturing but in agriculture, as well.

Of course, much of Europe's postwar prosperity could be traced to the ability and industry of her people and to the new machinery with which the Marshall Plan replaced that destroyed in the war. But at least as important was the new Common Market of 180 million consumers. The quaint, quiet old Europe of bicycles and sausages was shouldered aside by the noisy, new "Americanized" Europe of traffic jams, supermarkets, vending machines, and diets. It was exhilarating for most Europeans and instructive for the rest of the world, for in a manner that mocked all that Karl Marx had predicted, the capitalists of Europe were cooperating, not fighting, and as a result, the economies of the six were growing in a way that made them the envy of most of their neighbors.

To men such as Jean Monnet, of course, the political developments of the Common Market were at least as important as the economic ones. The EEC was administered by a nine-man Commission with headquarters in Brussels, Belgium. It was the job of these men and the 2,700 other "Eurocrats" employed by the Community to work for the best interests of the six as a whole, not for their own countries. A Council of Ministers, one from each of the six, had to pass on all the Commission's proposals. Nevertheless, the Commission gradually acquired power and became what appeared to be the embryo of an executive branch of a federal government, with a seven-man Court of Justice in Luxembourg and a 142-member Parliament in Strasbourg, France, forming what might be the beginnings of the other major branches.

The new European civil servants saw to it that their children were taught the one-Europe idea. By 1964, they had established six schools in which each of five thousand students, at age eleven, was required to choose French or German as his basic language, and in which all children—whatever their nationality—studied a common European history.

The implications of all this—the promise of peace and unity and even brotherhood—inspired many of Europe's most gifted men. Perhaps no one better expressed the essential sentiment of the movement than the Spanish philosopher, Salvador de Madariaga. He wrote: "Above all, we must love Europe: . . . this Europe to whom La Gioconda for ever smiles, where Moses and David spring to perennial life from Michelangelo's marble, and Bach's genius rises spontaneous to be caught in his intellectual geometry; where Hamlet seeks in thought the mystery of his inaction, and Faust seeks in action comfort for the void in his thought, where Don Juan seeks in women met the woman never found, and Don Quixote, spear in hand, gallops to force reality to rise above itself; . . . this Europe must be born. And she will, when Spaniards will say 'our Chartres,' Englishmen 'our Cracow,' Italians 'our Copenhagen'; when Germans say 'our Bruges,' and step back horror-

stricken at the idea of laying murderous hands on it. Then
will Europe live. . . ." [9]

Like de Madariaga, many Americans had a sentimental
interest in a united Europe. After all, what had worked
well for the U.S. should be equally beneficial for others. But
during the Kennedy administration, the top men in the U.S.
government developed an interest in a united Europe that
went well beyond mere sentiment. No one wanted American salesmen to be barred from Europe by a new tariff
wall around the six. More positively, if the U.S. and the
new Europe could become true partners, allied with Japan
to the east and Latin America and Africa to the south,
there could be created a formidable bulwark against Communism and a massive economic power equal to the massive needs of the poor nations. This partnership idea came
to be called "The Grand Design."

In 1962, Congress passed a Trade Expansion Act, permitting the President to negotiate sweeping mutual tariff
cuts with the six so Americans could continue to compete
inside the Common Market. And on July 4, 1962, President
Kennedy outlined the broader dream in a speech at Independence Hall in Philadelphia. He praised the movement
toward a United Europe, calling it "a vast new enterprise"
on which the U.S. looked with "hope and admiration." Then
he promised, "I will say here and now, on this day of Independence, that the United States will be ready for a declaration of interdependence, that we will be prepared to
discuss with a United Europe the ways and means of forming a concrete Atlantic partnership, a mutually beneficial
partnership between the new union now emerging in
Europe and the old American union founded here 173 years
ago. All this will not be completed in a year, but let the
world know it is our goal."

Most observers agreed that the first major step toward
Atlantic partnership would be the admission of Britain to

the European Community. The British people had never thought of themselves as part of Europe, and their government had acted in both a traditional and a representative way when it turned down invitations to join first the Coal and Steel Community and then the Common Market itself. But as the six began to prosper and become more and more efficient and build their common tariff wall against outsiders, it became obvious to the British that they were going to have to join Europe or lose their continental customers, and as a nation dependent on trade, Britain could not afford such a loss.

Therefore, on July 31, 1961, Prime Minister Harold Macmillan announced to the House of Commons that the government had decided that Britain should try to join the EEC. Negotiations began in Brussels on November 8, 1961, and continued throughout 1962. There was a severe problem about British agriculture: Britain subsidized her farmers in a different way than the six did theirs. There was an even more severe problem about the nations of the Commonwealth, whose goods Britain imported duty-free: would the price of British membership in the EEC be economic disaster for such countries as New Zealand, which was dependent on its sales of butter and cheese and meat to the British? Many times the negotiations faltered, but they did not break down, and by the end of 1962, it appeared that there was a good chance that the six soon would become the seven. But then France said "no." On January 29, 1963, the French Foreign Minister made it clear that his government did not want Britain in the Community. The Brussels negotiations concluded in failure and recrimination.

Spaak of Belgium called what the French had done a "monstrous thing" and "a defeat for the movement for a United Europe." "The community's spirit," he said, "will be gravely and perhaps mortally wounded." [10]

Erhard of Germany said: "This is a black day for Europe.

The Common Market is now only a mechanism, and no longer a living thing." [11]

Monnet called the setback "very grave." [12]

Macmillan of Britain went on television the next day to tell his people that what had happened in Brussels was "bad for us, bad for Europe, and bad for the whole free world." France, said Macmillan, had ended the negotiations "brutally" and "not because they were going to fail but, curiously enough, because they were going to succeed."

Everyone placed the blame for the failure on one towering man. He was the President of France, a proud, aloof soldier who seemed almost contemptuous of such criticism, so convinced was he that his idea of what Europe should become was far wiser than Monnet's and Kennedy's. Moreover, he saw his vision of Europe as the most likely to serve the glory of France, and in a manner that seemed both mystical and old-fashioned, he had devoted his life to this glory. He was a prophet, an historian, above all a leader . . . a man, said the writer André Malraux, of "the day before yesterday and the day after tomorrow" . . . Charles André Joseph Marie de Gaulle.

Charles de Gaulle (sharl duh GOLE) was born in his grandfather's home in Lille on November 22, 1890. His father was a professor of philosophy in a Jesuit college in Paris, where de Gaulle grew up in an austere home in which religion and scholarship commanded great respect. As a boy, de Gaulle steeped himself in the history and legends of France, especially military history. The fate of France, he wrote later, interested him above everything. "I was convinced," he said, "that France would have to go through gigantic trials, that the interest of life consisted in one day rendering her some signal service, and that I would have the occasion to do so." [13]

De Gaulle decided to become a soldier and went to France's West Point, St.-Cyr (san-SERE), carrying with him the schoolboy nickname his six-feet, four-inch height had

brought him, "The Big Asparagus." He graduated among
the top ten in his class, just in time for World War I. Three
times de Gaulle was wounded and, the third time, captured. In two years of imprisonment, he made five unsuccessful attempts to escape. Finally, the war ended, and
after a brief assignment fighting the Bolsheviks who had
just seized power in Russia, de Gaulle returned to France
to study and teach military strategy.

In 1934, de Gaulle published a book called *Army of
the Future,* in which he put the case for mobile, armored
warfare. His countrymen paid hardly any attention, but
the Germans did, organizing just the kind of force for which
de Gaulle argued. In 1940, that force swept around the
static French defenses and into Paris itself, compelling the
government of France to surrender.

Charles de Gaulle, however, refused to give up. Even
though he was just a relatively unknown Army General, he
flew to London and there persuaded the British to recognize him as the head of the Free French, a kind of one-
man government in exile. He took for his symbol the
double cross-pieced Cross of Lorraine, the ancient symbol
of another French liberator, Joan of Arc. In a famous broadcast to France on June 18, 1940, de Gaulle told his people
they had lost only a battle, not the whole war. He asked
Frenchmen outside France to join him and continue the
fight. "Speaking in full knowledge of the facts," he said,
"I ask you to believe me when I say that the cause of
France is not lost." [14]

De Gaulle badgered the British government for supplies
for his tiny but growing force, never admitting that he
represented anything less than all forty million Frenchmen,
always insisting on the respect due a great power. Winston
Churchill was said to have complained, "The heaviest
cross I have to bear is the Cross of Lorraine." To which de
Gaulle was said to have answered, "If we consider that
the other crosses Churchill had to bear were the German
army, submarine warfare, the bombing of Britain and

the threat of annihilation then when he says that the heaviest of all these was de Gaulle it is quite a tribute to a man alone, without an army, without a country, and with only a few followers." [15]

Thus did de Gaulle become a legend, acting as if he were France incarnate, even referring to himself in the third person, leading and inspiring French resistance until D-Day and liberation.

On August 25, 1944, de Gaulle re-entered Paris in triumph, a national hero so admired by his countrymen that he was made Prime Minister of the first postwar government. But then there reappeared the problem that had plagued France since her revolution in 1789. How does any nation, especially one of fierce individualists, achieve the proper balance between freedom and authority? As de Gaulle once put it, "How do you expect anyone to govern a country that has 246 different kinds of cheese?"

De Gaulle did not want to become another Napoleon, but he did want the political parties to give him the power to govern. When they refused, returning to the bickering he scorned as "sterile games," de Gaulle resigned—on January 20, 1946. He left Paris and retired to a fourteen-room house in the little town of Columbey-les-deux-Eglises, one hundred and fifty miles from Paris. There he wrote his war memoirs and he waited.

The postwar years were difficult for the French, who needed success and achievement to offset the humiliation of their collapse in 1940. Instead, the anticolonial revolution brought more and more defeat or, at least, lack of victory. There was disaster in Indo-China in 1954 and frustration in Suez in 1956. Then came the bitter and dangerous climax of the war in Algeria, which nearly brought civil war in France itself and which did bring de Gaulle back to power.

Algeria lies due south of France, across the Mediterranean in North Africa, between Tunisia and Morocco. The French had seized it from the Turks in 1830; by the 1950's, it was home for a million European settlers and was considered a legal part of "metropolitan France." However happy and prosperous an arrangement this was for the French "colons," it was intolerable for many of the leaders of Algeria's nine million Moslems, who saw the French as intruders in their country. In 1954, encouraged by the "wildfire of independence" elsewhere in the world, they began their own fight for self-rule.

It became a vicious war. In classic guerrilla style, the 30,000 men of the Algerian F.L.N. (in English, National Liberation Front) terrorized the civilian population in order to guarantee its support. They found supplies and sanctuary across the borders with Morocco and Tunisia and —by 1958—were tying down 400,000 French troops.

French officers, however, were determined not to suffer another defeat. They studied and applied the lessons of guerrilla warfare they had learned too late in Indo-China, even resorting to torture to get information from prisoners. They tried to seal the borders. By 1958, they thought they could win—if only their government in Paris would remain resolute.

But it could not. As had happened so often before in French history, the parties could not agree on anything long enough to permit a government to do its job. Moreover, an increasing number of Frenchmen were becoming convinced that the only hope of ending the war—and the casualties—was negotiation.

To try to prevent negotiations and bring about a stronger government, French generals seized power from the civilians in the city of Algiers—on May 13, 1958. Parachutists also took over the island of Corsica. It was a clear if unadmitted rebellion, and the government in Paris was powerless to quell it.

The hero of the generals and their fellow-conspirators —the man they wanted back in office—was the man who had been waiting confidently for just such a moment for twelve years. On May 15, 1958, Charles de Gaulle drove to Paris from his home in the country to announce that he was ready once again to lead France. The only alternative seemed civil war—perhaps invasion of France by its own army—so on June 1, 1958, the politicians let de Gaulle take over the government.

As de Gaulle saw it, his first job was to make sure he had the power to govern. He presented to the French electorate a new Constitution giving far more authority than before to the President: in September of 1958, it was approved by an overwhelming 80 percent of the voters.

Then de Gaulle went on to try to end the Algerian war. He had never promised the generals and settlers that he would keep Algeria part of France, although they thought he had implied this. Now, when de Gaulle offered to all the people of Algeria self-determination, the right to choose their own political future, the generals thought they had been betrayed. They organized the O.A.S. (in English, Secret Army Organization) to perpetrate new terror and attempt new insurrections. But, gradually, de Gaulle arrested the most mutinous of the officers and opened negotiations with the F.L.N. On July 3, 1962, Algeria became independent.

Simultaneous with his effort to end the war, de Gaulle pursued his dream of achieving for France the greatness and grandeur that, he believed, were essential for national unity. He had explained his purposes on the very first page of his *War Memoirs.*

"All my life," wrote de Gaulle, "I have thought of France in a certain way. This is inspired by sentiment as much as by reason. The emotional side of me tends to imagine France, like the princess in the fairy stories or the Madonna in the frescoes, as dedicated to an exalted and exceptional destiny. Instinctively I have the feeling that Providence has created her either for complete successes or for exemplary misfortunes. If, in spite of this, mediocrity shows in her acts and deeds, it strikes me as an absurd anomaly, to be imputed to the faults of Frenchmen, not to the genius of the land. But the positive side of my mind also assures me that France is not really herself unless in the front rank; that only vast enterprises are capable of counterbalancing the ferments of dispersal which are inherent in her people; that our country, as it is, surrounded by the others, as they are, must aim high and hold itself straight, on pain of mortal danger. In short, to my mind, France cannot be France without greatness." [16]

As General de Gaulle saw it, France could be great again only if she were totally and unquestionably independent. "Greatness cannot be shared," he had written in 1934, and this became the foundation of his postwar policies. He spoke of France's obligation "to play our own role, to allow nobody the right to act and to speak for us, to recognize no law not desired by us. . . ." [17]

First of all, there was the question of defense. At one time, it had been essential that France be protected by American arms, and the U.S. had been happy to offer that protection and France to accept it. But it was undeniable that the alliance was one-sided: the U.S. wanted to keep its nuclear weapons under its own control, encouraging Europe to contribute only conventional forces. France felt like a junior partner, especially when the U.S. was willing to share its nuclear knowledge with Britain but not with France. Moreover, in the missile age when the U.S. itself was vulnerable to attack, who could be sure that in a time of crisis the U.S. would be willing to risk its own destruction in order to come to the aid of Europe? De Gaulle could not. On February 13, 1960, in the Sahara desert, France exploded her first atomic bomb, and General de Gaulle went on to build a jet airplane striking force called a "force de frappe" with which to deliver similar bombs. The purpose, he told a cheering crowd in

Lyons in 1963, was "so that nobody else can become the
master of our destiny." [18] France, he promised, would not
"turn over to the Anglo-Saxons all our chances of life and
all our chances of death." [19]

Next, there was the European Community. Even though
he had not been in power when the Treaty of Rome was
signed, de Gaulle had no quarrel with the cooperative
tariff cuts. But he was stubbornly opposed to the idea of
political integration, of giving up any of France's sovereign
power to those Eurocrats he scorned as "simpletons." A
Europe of independent fatherlands, said de Gaulle, was
proper, but the six had no business "annihilating themselves in nobody-knows-what integration that would deliver
up a Europe 'without soul, without backbone and without
roots' to one or the other of the two foreign hegemonies," [20]
the U.S. or Russia. France would not be governed by anony-
mous and stateless committees. Thus, in 1965, when the
EEC Commission tried to force France to give the European Parliament power to distribute farm subsidies, de
Gaulle refused, ordering France's delegate on the Council
of Ministers back to Paris, blocking all further EEC action,
since all decisions still had to be taken by unanimous vote.

Finally, there were Britain and America—or, in de Gaulle's
scornful term, the Anglo-Saxons. De Gaulle was resentful
of the huge American investment in Europe—five billion
dollars by 1965—and he feared that Britain in the Common Market might be little more than America's "traveling salesman." Moreover, in his news conference of January 14, 1963, de Gaulle made clear his additional fears
about a diluted Common Market. "It is foreseeable," he
warned, "that in the end there would appear a colossal
Atlantic Community under American dependence and
leadership which would soon completely swallow up the
European Community. This," said de Gaulle, "is not at
all what France wanted to do and what France is doing,
which is a strictly European construction."

The fact was, of course, that President de Gaulle had his own grand design for Europe, quite different from President Kennedy's. The General had a vision of Europe as a Third Force in the world, equal to but independent of both the U.S. and the Soviet Union. Someday, when the cold war had melted into history, such a Europe might stretch, as it had once before, from the Atlantic to the Urals.

Whose Europe, then, was it to be? Integrated or confederated . . . Atlantic partnership or Atlantic bounded . . . to which Grand Design would it be built? Economically and technically, the nations of the six, and indeed the whole Western world, were moving closer and closer together. Politically and militarily, however, de Gaulle was leading what one American diplomat called a "counter-revolution of nationalism."

Charles de Gaulle's pursuit of grandeur was in obvious competition with Jean Monnet's idea of integration, making a United States of Europe seem still a distant dream. No one could say which view would prevail or what compromise would develop. But as of the middle 1960's, it was undeniable that however Europe would change in years to come, its people were back again in their traditional place at the center of the world stage—prosperous and proud and, mercifully, peaceful. In 1965, for the first time in the twentieth century, twenty-five years had gone by without world war beginning somewhere in Europe.

*Chapter Twelve*

# THE U.S. AND THE WIDER WORLD

THE President of the United States sat in the back of his long blue Lincoln with his wife on his left and a bouquet of red roses between them. Governor and Mrs. John Connally of Texas sat on the "jump seats" just in front. With election day of 1964 less than a year away, the Chief Executive was on a frankly political trip, trying to unite the Democratic party in the Lone Star state. He had made appearances in San Antonio and Houston the day before, and in Fort Worth that morning. Now he had just received a tumultuous welcome in downtown Dallas and was on his way to a luncheon a few miles away where he was to speak again. It was 12:30 P.M. Central Standard Time on Friday, November 22, 1963.

Dallas was so sunny and warm that day (76 degrees when the President arrived), there was no need for the limousine's plastic "bubble top." The bullet-proof windows also were rolled down, in order to permit the crowds to have a better view. Naturally, those most responsible for the President's safety wished the demands of democracy were a little less dangerous, but the President was fatalistic: that same morning he had remarked to his friend and assistant, Kenneth O'Donnell, that the assassination of a President would not be difficult because ". . . all one had to do was get on a high building someday with a telescopic rifle, and

*242*

there was nothing anybody could do to defend against such an attempt." [1]

The President's car had just passed a high building and was moving at 11.2 miles per hour down a slight incline toward a highway underpass. With the cheers of the lunchtime crowds just behind them, Mrs. Connally turned to the President and said, "You can't say that Dallas isn't friendly to you today." [2]

At that moment there were three shots. Governor Connally was hit in the back, the wrist, and the thigh. He seemed to spin to the right, and his wife pulled him down into her lap. The President was hit first in the neck and then in the head, where the bullet erupted through a massive wound five inches wide. As he fell, his wife cradled him and said, "Oh, my God, they have shot my husband. I love you, Jack." [3]

The Secret Service agent driving the President's limousine sped to a nearby hospital, where the Governor and the President were taken to emergency rooms. Governor Connally was operated on through much of the afternoon, regained consciousness the next day, and lived. But the President could not be saved. Two priests administered the last rites, and just after one-thirty an assistant White House press secretary announced: "President John Fitzgerald Kennedy died at approximately one o'clock." The chief surgeon at the hospital said later, "I am absolutely sure he never knew what hit him." [4]

The President's assassin was a lonely, confused, frustrated twenty-four-year-old named Lee Harvey Oswald. Partly hidden behind a pile of boxes, he had waited for the Presidential motorcade beside a sixth floor window of the Texas School Book Depository, where he worked. His weapon was a second-hand Italian carbine, with telescopic sight, which he had bought through the mail from Chicago.

At one time when he was a child, Oswald had been described by a social worker as "emotionally starved" and "affectionless." A doctor had recommended psychiatric treatment, calling the boy "quite disturbed." But there never was such treatment, nor was Oswald ever confined in an institution. He never confessed to the assassination, even though the evidence against him was overwhelming. He never tried to explain his feelings or his motive. Whether he might have done so someday remains unknown because on Sunday morning November 24—while the police were transferring him from one jail to another—Oswald himself was shot and killed by the proprietor of a cheap Dallas night club, Jack Ruby, who thought it his responsibility to avenge the murder of the President.

As the news of President Kennedy's assassination was flashed across the country and around the world, the overwhelming reaction was stunned unbelief. It all seemed so incredibly senseless and wasteful. The Prime Minister of Britain, Sir Alec Douglas-Home, spoke for many when he said, "Everything in one cried out in protest."

The reality of the tragedy began to come home to millions of Americans early Friday evening when they watched on television as the doors of the Presidential plane opened in Washington revealing the bronze casket. Early that morning in Fort Worth, Mr. Kennedy had apologized to a crowd because his wife was not yet with him. "Mrs. Kennedy is busy organizing herself," he had said. "It takes a little longer, you know, but then she looks so much better than we do." Now she stood beside the coffin in the harsh floodlight, her husband's bloodstains still on her skirt and stockings.

Thus unfolded a series of pictures so vivid they are still sharp in the memory of those who endured that long, grieving weekend: Oswald grimacing with pain as he was murdered . . . the solemn slow march from the White House to the Capitol, the flag-draped casket on the same caisson as the one that bore Franklin Roosevelt's body a generation earlier . . . once again, the muffled drums . . .

Mrs. Kennedy and her daughter, Caroline, kneeling beside the bier in the rotunda of the Capitol . . . the people, especially the many young ones, waiting in line for hours to pay their last respects . . . the full-dress funeral march itself, kings, presidents, chancellors, prime ministers, foreign ministers and hundreds of other dignitaries from all over the world walking to St. Matthew's Cathedral behind the Kennedy family . . . the riderless horse, boots reversed in the stirrups . . . John F. Kennedy, Jr., on his third birthday, saluting his father's casket . . . the flame burning beside the new grave on the flower-strewn hillside in Arlington.

President Kennedy was a man with special appeal to reporters and writers, many of whom mourned him with the best of their talent. Mary McGrory of the *Washington Star* wrote, on November 23, "He brought gaiety, glamour, and grace to the American political scene in a measure never known before. . . . When the ugliness of yesterday has been forgotten, we shall remember him, smiling." [5] E. B. White commented in *The New Yorker,* "It can be said of him, as of few men in a like position, that he did not fear the weather, and did not trim his sails, but instead challenged the wind itself, to improve its direction and to cause it to blow more softly and more kindly over the world and its people." [6] Daniel P. Moynihan, an author and Assistant Secretary of Labor, said in an interview, "We all of us know down here that politics is a tough game. And I don't think there's any point in being Irish if you don't know that the world is going to break your heart eventually. I guess we thought that we had a little more time. So did he." [7]

In the chaotic minutes after Oswald's bullets found their target, no one could be sure that the shots were not part of a conspiracy to wipe out all the top men in the U.S. government. Governor Connally cried out as he slumped over, "My God, they are going to kill us all." [8] So it was mere line of duty for the Secret Service to give immediate extra protection to the Vice-President of the United States who, because Texas was his native state, was also in the Dallas motorcade, two cars behind the President's. The agent assigned to him covered him with his own body as their car, too, raced to Parkland Hospital. There, the Vice-President was surrounded by Secret Service men and urged to return to Washington as soon as possible.

When the word came that the President was dead, the Vice President was taken to the airport in an unmarked police car. He waited inside the Presidential plane for Mrs. Kennedy to arrive with her husband's body, and there at 2:38 P.M. Central Standard Time that Friday, November 22, 1963, he took the oath of office and became the Thirty-sixth President of the United States.

Lyndon Baines Johnson is a six-foot-three-inch Texan whose tremendous physical strength and many contradictions of character make him seem almost larger than life. He is restless, impatient, and capable of a degree of work that would exhaust most men. He can campaign, for instance, all day and half the night, shouting until his voice becomes hoarse, shaking hands ("Pressing the flesh," as he puts it) until the voters' clawing fingernails reopen the old scars on the backs of his hands. "Always," wrote one of his friends and biographers, William S. White, "there has been a controlled hurricane about him; this is his standard operating procedure." [9]

There is also about Johnson a deep complexity. "From gushers within him," wrote other less friendly biographers, in 1964, "spouted torrents of sudden generosity, towering rage, touching compassion, vindictive abuse, overwhelming kindness, biting cruelty." [10] He is careful, seeking the advice of every possible interested party; yet he can also act with great boldness and speed. He is personally vain, ostentatiously fond, for instance, of the initials "L.B.J."; yet he can also be deeply sensitive to the moods and needs of others. With his drawl and colloquialisms, he has no polished eloquence; yet he can both entertain and, frequently, inspire an audience with which he is face to face.

In short, Lyndon Johnson is a powerful man of exaggerated contradictions.

He was born on August 27, 1908, in the dry hill country of southwest Texas, in a five-room house on the banks of the little Pedernales (PUR-din-AL-ice) River. His father was a member of the state legislature, but his grandfather saw in the infant the promise of even greater achievement: the day of his birth, according to legend, the older man saddled up a horse and rode through the countryside shouting, "A United States Senator was born today."

The boy rode a mule to grade school and graduated from high school in 1924, the president of his class of six. His mother wanted him to go to college, but he refused: with several friends he set out in an old "flivver" for California to seek what turned out to be an elusive fortune. Johnson picked fruit and washed dishes and ran out of money and then hitchhiked home, where he took a job on a road-building gang. Finally, he consented to try some more schooling and went to Southwest Texas State Teachers College in San Marcos, where he began to mature. He worked as a part-time janitor and a part-time secretary to the college president; he took one entire year off to make a little money teaching; and still he finished the four-year course in three-and-a-half years.

In 1931, Johnson was teaching in Houston when there was a special election for Congress. He helped campaign for the winner, who rewarded him with the chance to go to Washington as his secretary.

Then, as now, Washington, D.C., was a city of breathtaking mobility. An aggressive, personable, bright, inquisitive, brash, and hard-working young man could attract both the attention and the approval of the top men of the Federal government. Johnson was such a man, and he commanded just such attention. In 1935, President Roosevelt appointed him head of the National Youth Administration in Texas, where he made or found jobs for 30,000 young men who otherwise might have remained unemployed and who later formed the backbone of the Johnson political organization.

In 1937, there was another special election to Congress, this one in Johnson's own home district. He filed and ran as a 100-percent Roosevelt New Dealer, thus drawing the fire of the nine other more conservative candidates and thus quickly making himself the best-known man in the field. He won and was rewarded for his loyalty to the President with appointment to the prestigious House Committee on Naval Affairs.

In 1941, two days after Pearl Harbor, Johnson became the first member of Congress to volunteer for service in the armed forces, becoming a Lieutenant Commander in the Navy and serving in the Pacific until Roosevelt called all Congressmen in uniform back to the Capitol.

Johnson had tried to get the Democratic nomination to the U.S. Senate in 1941 and had failed. In 1948, he tried again, and this time he won—by eighty-seven votes out of nearly 900,000 cast. His opponent charged that there had been fraud in the ballot count, but the courts upheld Johnson.

For a newcomer to the Senate, even one with long prior service in Congress, Johnson was accepted by his new colleagues with unusual cordiality. His fellow Democrats elected him their second in command in 1951, and their leader in 1953, and it was as Majority Leader of the U.S. Senate that Johnson first made a national mark.

He was particularly "effective"—one of his favorite words —in personal negotiation with other men, negotiation so persuasive that it came to be called the Johnson "treatment," negotiation that produced an impressive record of bills passed. He liked to win his legislative battles, but he knew that no bill passed by too narrow a majority or after too bitter a fight would ever become a workable law. Therefore, he was no stranger to compromise. This concern for consensus earned Johnson a reputation among casual observers as nothing more than a shrewd political operator, but it also earned for him the deep respect of those most intimately familiar with the mechanics of government. William S. White called his biography of Johnson, *The Professional.*

It was always hard to classify Johnson in the political spectrum, and he himself always tried to avoid such labeling. "I am a free man, an American, a United States Senator, and a Democrat, in that order," he wrote in 1958. He added: "I am also a liberal, a conservative, a Texan, a tax-payer, a rancher, a businessman, a consumer, a parent, a voter, and not as young as I used to be nor as old as I expect to be—and I am all these things in no fixed order." [11] He said once: "My great strength in politics has been that people who think of themselves as liberals tend to think of me as a liberal, and people who think of themselves as conservatives tend to think of me as a conservative."

Johnson's record, however, revealed the goals to which he was devoted. As a Southerner who had felt the sting of regional prejudice, he believed in national unity. ". . . the ideal of one nation is perhaps the strongest force in his political life," [12] wrote White. As Majority Leader, Johnson prided himself particularly on passage of two major civil rights bills, in 1957 and 1960. His whole career in Congress was concerned with military preparedness, and as a man who had grown up in hard country, Johnson believed in growth and development. He wrote, again in 1958: "I regard achievement of the full potential of our resources —physical, human, and otherwise—to be the highest purpose of governmental policies next to the protection of those rights we regard as inalienable. . . ." [13]

As President, Johnson used all his energy and expertise and power to hurry through Congress perhaps the most impressive package of major legislation since the early days of the New Deal—Federal aid for schools, health insurance for the aged, protection of Negro voting rights, and much more. But as with all his predecessors since the New Deal, it was the world overseas that quickly commanded his major attention and confronted him and the country with the tests by which they would be judged.

As he sits in his office in the west wing of the White House, a President of the United States can turn and look through the windows just behind his desk across the long south lawn, with its splendid old trees and graceful fountain, to the sturdy white obelisk that is the Washington Monument. Or the President can look through the French doors to his right into the elegant garden that was the special pride of President and Mrs. Kennedy. Most of the time, however, the President's view is far less tranquil, for most of the time he must concentrate solely on the papers and sounds that bring to his desk in relentless succession the problems of the less classical, less beautiful, and far less tidy wider world.

In the mid-1960's, after a generation of cold war, the view from that oval office still began with the fact of Communist power and the threat it still posed to the United States. True, since the Cuban missile crisis of 1962 and the nuclear test ban treaty that followed it, the cold war with Russia seemed far less dangerous than it once had. But China had become a militant opponent now, beginning to build nuclear weapons of her own; one could predict a long new cold war with the new Middle Kingdom.

As an ideology, Communism seemed far different in the 1960's than it had in the 1930's and 1940's. Then it had appeared to many as the "wave of the future," a frightening combination of fervor and terror that might indeed sweep the world. But the years had treated it unkindly, as, indeed, they had treated most ideologies. Communism came to seem merely a device by which one nation could try to subvert and control another and a technique by which a backward nation could be forced to industrialize quickly. But so obvious was Communist imperialism that, even with all their craving for immediate modernization, by 1965 only a handful of new nations had become Communist, and then usually because of the pressure and proximity of China or Russia. The rest might have been poor, but they were also proud. Moreover, in no country had the Communists been able to grow food efficiently, and in Russia—once it had developed a sophisticated economy—traditional Communist techniques were proving far too cumbersome.

But however more life-sized Communism might seem and however more stable the cold war had become, the fact of Russian power remained. So in early 1965, the United States felt it necessary to have in sunken silos 854 intercontinental ballistic missiles, and on nuclear-powered submarines 416 Polaris missiles. With an intercontinental bomber force still numbering nearly a thousand planes, this gave the U.S., according to officials in Washington, a superiority of from three or four to one over the Soviet Union.

Such power, combined with the widespread belief that the U.S. would use it if attacked, had proved an effective deterrent. Moreover, American conventional military power and proven willingness to use it had contained most conventional Communist aggression. Now, however, the U.S. faced a new threat. In Asia, Latin America, Africa, and the Middle East—in every former colony impatient to modernize—revolution or the threat of it had become commonplace. Indeed, it was often the case that economic progress required political instability. But it was open Communist policy to try to support and take over such revolutions, slipping in from a neighboring sanctuary arms and men trained in the arts of insurrection.

The United States wanted the radical changes necessary

everywhere for economic growth, but it did not want what the Department of State came to call "concealed aggression," revolutions over which the Communists had gained control. How could the U.S. promote development without risking subversion? Ideally, whenever there was a need for forceful peacekeeping, the United Nations should be the agency to act. But when the U.N. was too divided to do so, the U.S. felt a responsibility as "residual peacekeeper," using its own power—by itself, if necessary—to try to prevent or put down Communist-led uprisings. But where and when should the U.S. intervene in other nations' revolutions? If it did intervene, how could it help but seem to be on the side of the rich who wanted no changes while the Communists seemed on the side of the poor who did? How could it keep from seeming to be an old-fashioned white colonial power dangerously out of place in an independent nonwhite new nation? Above all, if the U.S. intervened in a local war, how could it prevent more Communist intervention on the other side, which could start an escalation up to a global danger nobody wanted?

All these problems, indeed almost all the major problems of our time, were combined in the multiple tragedy of the war in South Viet Nam.

Viet Nam curls like a ragged "S" along the southeasternmost edge of Southeast Asia, nine thousand miles from California. Viet is the traditional name for the people of this area; Nam, in Chinese, means "south." Altogether, about thirty million people live in Viet Nam, most of them crowded together in the fertile deltas of the Red River in the north and the Mekong River in the south, making a population map of the country look a little like a bar bell.

In the days of European empire, Viet Nam was part of French Indo-China, but as it did in so many other parts of the world, World War II brought the end of traditional colonialism. When the Japanese occupied Viet Nam,

Vietnamese patriots, some of them also Communists, organized guerrilla resistance, and by 1945, with the approval and even the help of the United States (which thought French rule should end), the guerrillas were strong enough and popular enough to take over the country before the French could return.

The top man of the new government was one of the world's most experienced Communists, a frail but tough, much-traveled, multilingual revolutionary who had taken the name of Ho Chi Minh—"He Who Enlightens." On September 2, 1945, in the northern city of Hanoi, Ho proclaimed the Democratic Republic of Viet Nam, Asia's second-oldest Communist state, after Outer Mongolia.

What Ho might claim and what the French were willing to accept, however, were two different things: French troops came back to reclaim their colony, and in December of 1946, the "first" Indo-China war began. The French forces fought with conspicuous bravery but without a real understanding on the part of most of their leaders of the nature of the hit-and-run guerrilla war in which they were engaged. The French had troops enough to control the major cities and certain strong points, but they did not have enough to dominate the countryside, where Ho's forces, with their reputation as patriotic independence fighters, were able to command the loyalty of the peasants. With this support, and following and even developing Mao Tse-tung's teachings on protracted war, Ho's troops were able to prevail.

After 1949, when the Chinese Communists extended their control down to the Vietnamese border, Ho had a "sanctuary" to the north where he could train and resupply his men, and after the end of the Korean War, in 1953, China was able to increase her aid to Ho. So, by 1954, the stage was set for a decisive battle that came in the bowl-shaped valley of Dien Bien Phu, on the northern part of the border between Laos and Viet Nam. Over mountain trails, Ho's Communists packed in heavy artillery on their backs and on bicycles, ringing and dominating the airstrip around which the French forces were concentrated. After a fifty-five-day seige, Dien Bien Phu fell on May 8, 1954.

Altogether—in seven-and-a-half years—the French forces, including the Foreign Legion and non-Communist Vietnamese, had lost 172,000 men killed. They had received two billion dollars in U.S. aid; and still they had been defeated.

The day after the fall of Dien Bien Phu, a conference opened in Geneva, Switzerland, of nations most interested in the fate of Indo-China. Its participants agreed to divide the old French colony four ways: the western half, Laos and Cambodia, remained two independent countries; and Viet Nam itself was formally divided at the 17th parallel, with Ho Chi Minh and his Communists retaining the northern half, most of which they already controlled, and the non-Communist Republic of Viet Nam established in the south. The whole area was to be neutral, with no outside interference, and in both halves of Viet Nam, in 1956, there were to be elections to choose one government for the whole country.

The man who became top man in South Viet Nam was a shy, austere, stubborn, devout aristocrat named Ngo Dinh Diem (Noh Ding Zyem). As in China so in Viet Nam, the family name is the first one written. But because the Ngo family had so many influential members, it became customary among Westerners to refer to Ngo Dinh Diem by his "first" name. Like a mandarin of old, Diem believed absolutely in his moral right to govern. But the same heritage that gave him such confidence also made him aloof from most of his fellow countrymen. For nearly ten years, he managed to survive the intrigues of his rivals, but at no time was he able to extend to the South Vietnamese people the reforms and protection that were necessary to command their allegiance. Quite to the contrary, his regime became notorious for favoritism, corruption, and a police-state authoritarianism that rivaled even Ho's Communist state in the north.

The United States compounded Diem's shortcomings by failing to learn the lessons for which the French had paid so dearly. Seeing South Viet Nam as one link in an anti-Communist chain circling China from South Korea to Pakistan, the U.S. gave Ngo Dinh Diem massive economic and military aid. But U.S. advisers in Diem's capital, Saigon, insisted on preparing the South Vietnamese army to fight a conventional Korea-type war, rather than the guerrilla war for which Ho had already become well known. Therefore, when the "second" Indo-China war began, the South Vietnamese were unprepared.

After the Geneva "accords" of 1954, those Vietnamese in the north who wanted to come south were able to do so, and vice versa. But perhaps five thousand of Ho's best-trained and best-indoctrinated men stayed behind in the hamlets and villages of South Viet Nam until they might be needed. They greased and buried their weapons and bided their time. When Ngo Dinh Diem refused to permit elections in 1956, for the good reason that most observers thought Ho would win, Ho apparently decided that the time had come to revive his guerrilla operations. (North Viet Nam also violated the Geneva "accords" by increasing the size of its army.)

Ho's first targets were the district and village chiefs who represented Diem's government to the four out of five South Vietnamese who lived outside the cities. In 1957, more than 700 local officials were murdered. By 1964, the total was up to perhaps 13,000. The rate, if applied to the greater population of the U.S., would have meant the killing of 20,000 American mayors, city councilmen, and governors every year.

Simultaneously, Communist agents preached to the peasants land reform, independence, and—above all—peace. After a generation of almost continual war or occupation, most South Vietnamese peasants wanted nothing so much as to be left alone. The Communists promised this; they tried to make every local grievance their own; and they augmented their numbers by steady infiltration from North Viet Nam by sea and down through Laos along what came to be called the Ho Chi Minh trail. Soon Diem and the U.S. faced a situation dangerously similar to that the French had known: the cities and main roads were relatively safe by day, but the Vietnamese Communists—the Viet Cong—controlled most of the countryside, especially at night.

Like the French before them, U.S. troops in South Viet Nam developed a deep professional respect for the Viet Cong. They seemed the epitome of Mao Tse-tung's metaphor about the guerrilla "fish" living in the peasant "water." They could hit an Army of the Republic of Viet Nam unit, then ambush a relief force coming to the rescue of the first, and then "melt" into the countryside. In the canals of the Mekong Delta, they were known to hide underwater, breathing through reeds, enduring even the gripping sting of leeches. They carved sandals from truck tires and made discarded perfume bottles into tiny lamps. Like guerrillas everywhere, they had more mobility, more intimate knowledge of the countryside, and better intelligence than conventional forces. Above all, they were able to intimidate or inspire or enlist at least the passive support of most South Vietnamese peasants, their leaders understanding from the beginning that the war was more political than military and that the prize, in the words of a famous British general, was "the hearts and minds of the people." By day, government troops might sweep into a village, asking questions, helping themselves to chickens or a pig, and then returning to their barracks. But by night the "V.C." might return to punish anyone who had informed on them and to lecture yet again about the evils of Ngo Dinh Diem.

In Washington in 1961, President Eisenhower's "falling domino" theory still had many advocates, top U.S. officials believing, as Mr. Eisenhower had put it, that the loss of South Viet Nam would be "just incalculable to the free world." [14] Therefore, as the realities of the situation in South Viet Nam began to become known, there were recommendations for much more U.S. assistance. However, there was also in Washington a group of high-ranking veterans of Korea, nicknamed the "Never Again" group, who believed that the U.S. should never again permit itself to be drawn into a land war in Asia without being able to use nuclear weapons. The problem was how to shore up the Diem government without risking such involvement.

In the autumn of 1961, President Kennedy decided to do everything possible to help Diem short of committing U.S. troops to combat. The number of American "advisers" in Viet Nam was increased from about 600 to more than 8,000 in mid-1962, and to more than 16,000 by mid-1964, and more and more armed U.S. helicopters permitted Diem's troops to move more quickly than before to places where Viet Cong had been reported. But the Viet Cong gradually learned how to adapt to the new helicopter tactics; there was more and more infiltration down the Ho Chi Minh trail; and not even the new U.S. and South Vietnamese military power could solve the fundamental political problem of the lack of loyalty to Diem.

Of course, the United States tried to insist on reforms within South Viet Nam as a condition for its new help. But Diem found such change unappealing, and if he disapproved, the U.S. was stymied: one American correspondent summed up U.S. policy with the slogan, "Sink or swim with Ngo Dinh Diem."

By spring of 1963, Diem had become so isolated from his people and the grievances of his people had become so intense that open protests began. Seventy percent of the people of South Viet Nam are Buddhist, and their leaders claimed that Diem, the strict Roman Catholic, had favored his minority of fellow Catholics at the expense of the Buddhists. There were mass demonstrations and then the flaming public suicides of seven Buddhists who set themselves on fire in gruesome but dramatic acts of protest. Diem's police responded with increasing brutality, including even raids on the major Buddhist pagodas, and finally, by autumn, the Vietnamese generals (and the U.S.) had had enough. On November 1, 1963, Diem was overthrown by his own top military men. He and his influential brother, Ngo Dinh Nhu, fled the Presidential Palace through a secret tunnel first to the home of a wealthy friend, then to a small Catholic church nearby. There they were discovered and arrested and put into an armored car to be taken to General Staff headquarters. But en route they were murdered.

Then began in Saigon a parade of successors, one coup succeeding another. Obviously, there was no improvement in the basic problem of the relationship between the regime and the people it was supposed to govern. Meanwhile, the United States became steadily more committed, the American responsibility coming to seem to U.S officials not only one of helping an ally defend itself, but also one of stopping what the Department of State called "a totally new brand" of Communist aggression as dangerous for the future throughout the underdeveloped world as the threat of missile and conventional attack had seemed in the past. From 1960 to 1964, according to U.S. officials, the North Vietnamese had slipped into South Viet Nam approximately 39,000 men. By mid-1965, according to the U.S. Secretary of Defense, the Viet Cong "main force" numbered 65,000 men, with the part-time force perhaps another 100,000 for a total of perhaps 165,000 men. "Agression from the North," the State Department called its booklet documenting the infiltration, and U.S. officials spoke with great concern of the Communist-led, Chinese-influenced guerrilla wars that might develop elsewhere in Asia, in Latin America, and in Africa if the U.S. could not contain this "new kind of war" in South Viet Nam. Therefore, as the Viet Cong committed more and more troops, so did the U.S., and the war began to escalate. President Johnson ordered in another 5,000 troops in mid-1964; the Viet Cong then increased its attacks on U.S. bases; the U.S. began to bomb military targets in North Viet Nam and then permitted its troops to fight first alongside the South Vietnamese and then independently. Each new Viet Cong move brought a U.S. countermove. By the end of 1965, nearly 200,000 American troops were in South Viet Nam in the greatest U.S. commitment anywhere since the war in Korea.

Along with the military action, of course, the United States continued its economic aid, building schools and offering a massive plan for the development of the Mekong River. But neither firepower nor money was a substitute for the dedicated Vietnamese who were needed to win back the support of the villagers. So the U.S. found itself in what one student of the war called a "shadowland between unattainable victory and unacceptable surrender." [15] The North Vietnamese showed no interest in negotiation, apparently because they thought they would win. In late 1965, top officials in Washington could see no honorable and responsible alternative to hanging on and fighting and hoping for the best.

However frustrating and dangerous it might be, the war in Viet Nam did dramatize many of the facts of life in the 1960's. Anticolonialism and nationalism, for instance, were powerful forces, which local Communists found easy to use.

There were deeply felt demands for economic and social reforms throughout the underdeveloped world. There was no guarantee of stability if such reforms were carried

through, but there seemed a guarantee of instability if
they were not.

Temporarily, at least, there was a delicate nuclear stalemate, but there had developed under this "umbrella" a new
kind of insecurity: in 1964, Attorney General (later Senator) Robert F. Kennedy, the late President's brother,
called this ". . . the age of nails in the street and the plastic bomb; . . . the age of arson, sabotage, kidnapings and
murder for political purposes; . . . the age of hit-run ter-
rorist activities coordinated on a global scale." [16] In 1965,
the Chief of Staff of the U.S. Army, General Harold K.
Johnson, said he expected "to see the pattern of Communist effort in Viet Nam repeated again and again." [17]

With the rise of China, the United States faced two major
Communist powers, rather than one, and the Western
Pacific and South and Southeast Asia began to seem more
than ever the front line of the cold war. True, Russia and
China had many disagreements as each pursued what
seemed best for itself as a nation. But major U.S. com-
mitments against Communist-led insurgents, as in Viet Nam,
threatened to force Russia and China closer together and
to destroy the "peaceful coexistence" with Russia that had
emerged since Cuba 1962.

The war in Viet Nam revealed the relative impotence of
the United Nations as a peacekeeping force. The U.N. had
done much along this line—in the Middle East and in the
Congo—and South Korea had been defended under the
blue U.N. flag. But almost from the start, the Security
Council of the U.N. had been paralyzed by the vetoes of
the cold war, and in the mid-1960's, the General Assembly
was unable to act because of a big-power argument over
dues paying. Moreover, the U.N. had become so dominated
by new nations hypersensitive to any hint of colonialism
that many Americans felt a U.N. solution in Viet Nam might
satisfy only Ho Chi Minh.

Nor were the major U.S. allies, especially France, eager

to help in Viet Nam. Like the nations of the Communist world, they pursued their individual national interests as they saw them, and these interests were not always the same as those of the U.S.

The war in Viet Nam also revealed the ignorance of many Americans, even some in high places, of life in the wider world. With the clear vision of hindsight many observers wished that the U.S. had been able to carry out different policies. What might have happened, for instance, if instead of Diem, there had emerged an anti-Communist South Vietnamese leader who in spirit and deed could have enlisted the support of the peasants? What might have happened if the U.S. had prepared the South Vietnamese army for counter-guerrilla rather than conventional war?

Beyond all these questions and conditions, however, remained even more fundamental problems. The first was the whole matter of force and its use. The danger of nuclear war by miscalculation or accident or runaway escalation remained as intense as ever, especially with more nations joining the nuclear club. Therefore, the need for international arms control remained as pressing as ever. And beneath the problem of nuclear war, there was the dilemma of any use of force. Beginning with the world's toleration of the Japanese invasion of Manchuria in 1931, the whole history of our time taught that aggression anywhere could grow into war everywhere and that all local wars contain the seeds of holocaust. What alternative might there be for those who demand change? How could the world prove wrong Lenin's conviction that "great historical questions can be solved only by violence?" More than ever before—because of nuclear weapons—the need for enforceable international law was immediate.

Side by side with the problem of force, there was the equally pressing problem of the growing gap between the world's rich and poor. It was not difficult to predict that as long as this gap continued to widen, the world would remain unstable and dangerous. "Human beings," it has been noted by many observers, "do not indefinitely leave alone the man in the big house on the hill." But beyond even considerations of national security, many observers felt that the rich had a moral obligation to increase their foreign aid and adapt their trade to help the poor nations match the growth of their economies to the growth of their populations.

Another major problem was the racial one, both within the U.S. and in the wider world. Chinese agents, especially, were trying to pose as champions of the nonwhite majority against the white minority. The U.S. and the other predominantly white nations would have to learn to live not only with tolerance but also with respect for their nonwhite neighbors.

Finally, there was the ever growing need for more and more accurate information about the world and its people. The U.S. could not afford mistakes of intervention or nonintervention, aid or no-aid, based on ignorance or prejudice. Scholars and journalists and artists and all observers bore a new responsibility as teachers whose reports could enable their countrymen to adjust to sudden and breathtaking change.

Looking back at the major developments of the preceding twenty years, an American living in the late 1960's could find many reasons to be proud of what his country had done. U.S. scientists and engineers had extended the edges of all that was known about the natural world and how to control it, making possible unprecedented benefits as well as terrible threats. For the first time ever, nuclear weapons gave men the power to destroy all human life, but productivity—also for the first time—made it at least theoretically possible to wipe out all material want. No people of any age ever had such an opportunity to enrich and liberate their fellowmen.

An American could be proud, too, of the way his country

had responded to the challenges that followed World War II. With victory won, the people of the U.S. might have liked to withdraw to the isolationism of the 1930's, but they had learned the costly central lesson of the war—that appeasement is folly. Therefore, when the Soviet Union began trying to push its influence into Western Europe and beyond, the U.S. assumed the leadership of the free. At great cost in life and money, America stretched its concern to every part of the globe.

This new American sense of responsibility was expressed through two old national traits: generosity and bravery. With massive economic aid, the U.S. helped Europe recover from the wounds of war and then went on to help others all over the world start up the long road of development. Meanwhile, it did not flinch from the deadly realities of the cold war, walking steadily and more than once to the brink of nuclear war, when that seemed the only alternative to surrender.

Also, in spite of the frustrations of Korea and Viet Nam, the U.S. showed more patience than ever before, persevering whether it liked it or not with the grim necessities of containment.

Anyone reflecting on the major developments of these violent but promising twenty years could make certain relatively safe predictions about the years to come: for instance, that China would play an ever greater role in world affairs; that science and technology would have more and more influence on everyday life; and that the problems of economic development in the new nations would remain invitations to chaos.

One could also predict the most urgent demands of the near future—for arms control and international law and the improvement of life in the Third World. To cope with these demands, the U.S. would need to continue to apply the same generosity and courage that had served it so well in the past. In addition, it probably would have to learn to negotiate and cooperate with other countries to an unprecedented degree. Like each of the nations of the European Economic Community, the U.S. might have to join other nations in giving up some of its precious sovereignty to the causes of peace and plenty. But no matter what the changes and demands of the future—no matter how sudden or difficult they might be—Americans could anticipate them with confidence: the U.S. record in the twenty years since 1945 was convincing assurance that free men could do whatever was required.

# NOTES

INTRODUCTION

1. Bronowski, J., *The Common Sense of Science,* Cambridge, Harvard University Press, 1953, p. 40.
2. Ley, Willi, *Ten Steps Into Space,* Philadelphia, The Franklin Institute, 1958, p. 11.
3. Johnson, Lyndon B., Speech at Johns Hopkins University, April 7, 1965.
4. Snow, C. P., *The Two Cultures and the Scientific Revolution,* London, Cambridge University Press, 1959, p. 40.

CHAPTER ONE

1. Schlesinger, Arthur M., Jr., *The Crisis of the Old Order,* Boston, Houghton Mifflin Company, 1957, p. 406.
2. *The New York Times,* April 13, 1945, p. 3. © 1945 by The New York Times Company. Reprinted by permission.
3. *The New York Times,* April 15, 1945, p. 3. © 1945 by The New York Times Company. Reprinted by permission.
4. *The New York Times,* April 13, 1945, p. 3. © 1945 by The New York Times Company. Reprinted by permission.
5. *Ibid.*
6. *The New York Times,* April 14, 1945, p. 4. © 1945 by The New York Times Company. Reprinted by permission.
7. Daniels, Jonathan, *The Man of Independence,* Philadelphia, J. B. Lippincott Company, 1950, p. 90. Copyright 1950 by Jonathan Daniels.
8. *Ibid.,* p. 27.
9. Strasser, Otto, *Hitler and I,* London, Jonathan Cape Ltd., 1940.
10. Bullock, Alan, *Hitler, A Study in Tyranny,* New York, Harper and Row, 1952, p. 282.
11. *Ibid.,* p. 322.

12. Churchill, Winston S., Speech to the House of Commons, May 13, 1940.
13. Churchill, Winston S., Speech to the House of Commons, June 18, 1940.
14. Churchill, Winston S., Speech to the House of Commons, August 20, 1940.
15. Churchill, Winston S., *Their Finest Hour*, Boston, Houghton Mifflin Company, 1949, title page.
16. Churchill, Winston S., Speech at Harrow School, October 29, 1941.
17. Churchill, Winston S., Speech to the House of Commons, June 4, 1940.
18. Churchill, Winston S., BBC Broadcast, February 9, 1941.
19. Roosevelt, Franklin D., Fireside Chat, December 30, 1940.
20. Mauldin, Bill, *Up Front*, New York, Holt, Rinehart and Winston, 1945, p. 14.
21. McCormick, Anne O'Hare, *The New York Times*, April 26, 1945, p. 5. © 1945 by The New York Times Company. Reprinted by permission.

CHAPTER TWO

1. Lamont, Lansing, *Day of Trinity*, New York, Atheneum, 1965, p. 235. Copyright © 1965 by Lansing Lamont. Reprinted by permission of Atheneum Publishers.
2. Farrell, Brigadier General Thomas F., *Memorandum for the Secretary of War*, July 18, 1945.
3. Laurence, William L., *Dawn Over Zero*, New York, Alfred A. Knopf, 1947, pp. 10–11.
4. Lamont, Lansing, *op. cit.*, p. 244.
5. Seaborg, Glenn T., "Science, The Third Revolution," Speech at George Washington University, June 6, 1962.
6. Snow, C. P., *op. cit.*, p. 14.
7. Einstein, Albert, *Ideas and Opinions*, New York, Crown Publishers, 1954, p. 205. Copyright 1954 by Crown Publishers, Inc.
8. Jungk, Robert, *Brighter Than a Thousand Suns*, New York, Harcourt, Brace and World, 1958, p. 46.
9. *The New York Times*, April 19, 1955, p. 25. © 1955 by The New York Times Company. Reprinted by permission.

10. Samuels, Gertrude, "Einstein at Seventy-Five Is Still a Rebel," *The New York Times Magazine,* March 14, 1954, p. 13. © 1954 by The New York Times Company. Reprinted by permission.
11. Jungk, Robert, *op. cit.,* p. 118.
12. *Ibid.,* p. 178.
13. *The New York Times,* April 19, 1955, p. 24. © 1955 by The New York Times Company. Reprinted by permission.
14. Jungk, Robert, *op. cit.,* p. 87.
15. "Eternal Apprentice," *Time,* November 8, 1948, p. 77, and J. Robert Oppenheimer, letter to the author, August 21, 1964.
16. Eatherly, Claude, *David Brinkley's Journal,* NBC Television, December 10, 1962.
17. Truman, Harry S., Statement announcing the development of the atomic bomb, August 6, 1945.
18. Oppenheimer, J. Robert, Speech at Columbia University, December 26, 1954.
19. Seaborg, Glenn T., Speech at University of Kentucky, April 26, 1963.

CHAPTER THREE

1. *The New York Times,* April 28, 1945, p. 4. © 1945 by The New York Times Company. Reprinted by permission.
2. Wolfe, Bertram D., *Three Who Made a Revolution,* New York, The Dial Press, 1948, p. 11.
3. *Ibid.,* p. 229.
4. *Ibid.,* p. 116.
5. Wilson, Edmund, *To the Finland Station,* New York, Doubleday and Company, 1940, p. 384. Copyright 1940 by Edmund Wilson. Reprinted by permission of Doubleday and Company, Inc.
6. Khrushchev, Nikita S., Speech to the Twentieth Party Congress, February 25, 1956.
7. Stalin, Joseph, *Problems of Leninism,* Moscow, Foreign Languages Publishing House, 1940, p. 366.

CHAPTER FOUR

1. Churchill, Winston S., Speech at University of Zurich, September 19, 1946.

2. Churchill, Winston S., Speech at Royal Albert Hall, May 14, 1947.
3. Kennan, George ("X"), "The Sources of Soviet Conduct," *Foreign Affairs,* July 1947, p. 575. © Council on Foreign Relations, Inc., New York.
4. "General Marshall," *Life,* October 4, 1943, p. 92.
5. *Current Biography,* New York, The H. W. Wilson Company, 1947, p. 425.
6. *Ibid.,* p. 427.
7. *The New York Times,* October 17, 1959, p. 12. © 1959 by The New York Times Company. Reprinted by permission.
8. MacArthur, Douglas, *Reminiscences,* New York, McGraw-Hill Book Company, 1964, pp. 57–58. © 1964 by Time, Inc. Used by permission of McGraw-Hill Book Company.
9. MacArthur, Douglas, Speech to the Corps of Cadets, May 12, 1962. Reprinted courtesy of *Life* and Major General Courtney Whitney.

CHAPTER FIVE

1. Paloczi-Horvath, George, *Mao Tse-tung,* New York, Doubleday and Company, 1962, p. 54. Copyright © 1962 by George Paloczi-Horvath. Reprinted by permission of Doubleday and Company, Inc.
2. Close, Upton, "The Sun Yat-sen That China Worships," *The New York Times Magazine,* March 10, 1929, p. 12. © 1929 by The New York Times Company. Reprinted by permission.
3. Paloczi-Horvath, George, *op. cit.,* p. 78.
4. *Ibid.,* p. 79.
5. *Ibid.,* p. 3.
6. *Ibid.,* p. 127.
7. *Ibid.,* p. 129.
8. Mao Tse-tung, *On Guerrilla Warfare,* translated and with an introduction by Brigadier General Samuel B. Griffith, New York, Praeger, 1961, p. 46.

CHAPTER SIX

1. Eisenhower, Dwight D., *Crusade in Europe,* New York, Doubleday and Company, 1948, p. 14. Reprinted by permission of Doubleday and Company, Inc.

2. Gunther, John, *Eisenhower, the Man and the Symbol,* New York, Harper and Row, 1951, p. 19.

3. *Ibid.,* p. 41.

4. *Ibid.,* p. 42.

5. Teller, Edward, with Brown, Allen, *The Legacy of Hiroshima,* New York, Doubleday and Company, 1962, p. 8. Copyright © 1962 by Edward Teller and Allen Brown. Reprinted by permission of Doubleday and Company, Inc.

6. Bethe, Hans, "Hydrogen Bomb," *Scientific American,* April, 1950, p. 21.

7. Teller, Edward, "Back to Laboratories," *Bulletin of the Atomic Scientists,* March 1950, p. 71. Copyright 1950 by the Educational Foundation for Nuclear Science, Inc.

8. Allison, S. K., *et al.,* "Let Us Pledge Not to Use the H-Bomb First!" *Bulletin of the Atomic Scientists,* March 1950, p. 75. Copyright 1950 by the Educational Foundation for Nuclear Science, Inc.

9. Teller, Edward, *op. cit.,* p. 71.

10. Shepley, James, and Blair, Clay, Jr., *The Hydrogen Bomb,* New York, David McKay Company, 1954, p. 103.

11. Lapp, Ralph E., *Kill and Overkill,* New York, Basic Books, 1962, p. 32.

12. Teller, Edward, with Brown, Allen, *op. cit.,* p. 54.

13. Drummond, Roscoe, and Coblentz, Gaston, *Duel at the Brink,* New York, Doubleday and Company, 1960, p. 18. Copyright © 1960 by Roscoe Drummond and Gaston Coblentz. Reprinted by permission of Doubleday and Company, Inc.

14. *Ibid.,* p. 43.

15. Dulles, John Foster, *War or Peace,* New York, The Macmillan Company, 1950, p. 175.

16. Shepley, James, "How Dulles Averted War," *Life,* January 16, 1956, p. 78. © 1956, Time Inc.

17. Eisenhower, Dwight D., Presidential News Conference, April 7, 1954.

18. Oppenheimer, J. Robert, "Atomic Weapons and American Policy," *Foreign Affairs,* July 1953, p. 529.

19. Churchill, Winston S., Speech to the House of Commons, March 1, 1955.

CHAPTER SEVEN

1. Eisenhower, Dwight D., Presidential statement, October 9, 1957.
2. Johnson, Lyndon B., Speech to the Aero Club, Washington, D.C., December 17, 1959.
3. Lenin, V. I., *Works,* Volume XXIX, New York, International Publishers, 1927.
4. Khrushchev, Nikita S., Remarks to the National Press Club, Washington, D.C., September 27, 1959.
5. Wicker, Tom, "Kennedy Without Tears," *Esquire,* June, 1964, p. 109.
6. *Ibid.,* p. 141.
7. Kennedy, John F., Report to the nation on the Berlin Crisis, July 25, 1961.
8. *The New York Times,* November 3, 1963, p. 7. © 1963 by The New York Times Company. Reprinted by permission.
9. Bartlett, Charles, and Alsop, Stewart, "The White House in the Cuban Crisis," *The Saturday Evening Post,* December 8, 1962, p. 16.
10. *Ibid.*
11. Khrushchev, Nikita S., Speech to the Supreme Soviet, December 12, 1962, as reported in *The Washington Post,* December 16, 1962.
12. Kennedy, John F., Broadcast to the nation, July 26, 1963.

CHAPTER EIGHT

1. Churchill, Winston S., Speech at Lord Mayor's Banquet, London, November 10, 1942.
2. Kipling, Rudyard, "The White Man's Burden," *Five Fingers.* Reprinted with the permission of Mrs. Bambridge, The Macmillan Co. of Canada, Methuen & Co. Ltd., and Doubleday and Company.
3. Orwell, George, "Shooting an Elephant," *Shooting an Elephant and Other Essays,* New York, Harcourt, Brace & World, 1950, pp. 6–7, and Martin Secker & Warburg, London.
4. Fischer, Louis, *The Life of Mahatma Gandhi,* New York, Harper and Brothers, 1950, p. 116.
5. *Ibid.,* p. 103.
6. *Ibid.,* p. 35.
7. *Ibid.,* p. 277.
8. *Ibid.,* p. 275.

9. *The New York Times,* April 18, 1955, p. 6. © 1955 by The New York Times Company. Reprinted by permission.

10. Nehru, Jawaharlal, Speech to the Bandung Conference, April 24, 1955.

CHAPTER NINE

1. Brown, Lester R., "Increasing World Food Output," *Foreign Agricultural Economic Report No. 25,* Washington, U.S. Department of Agriculture, 1965, p. vi.

2. U.N. Food and Agriculture Organization, *The State of Food and Agriculture 1965,* Rome, F.A.O., 1965, p. 4.

3. Ware, Thomas, Statement to the Subcommittee on Economic and Social Policy, Senate Foreign Relations Committee, June 29, 1965.

4. Snow, C. P., *op. cit.,* p. 28.

5. Harder, Edwin L., "The Myth of the Giant Brain" ("The Information Revolution" supplement), *The New York Times,* Section 11, May 23, 1965, p. 5. © 1965 by The New York Times Company. Reprinted by permission.

6. "The Computer and the Mind of Man," National Educational Television, Program 6, November 27, 1962.

7. U.N. Food and Agriculture Organization, *op. cit.,* p. 3.

8. Millikan, Max F., and Blackmer, Donald L. M., *The Emerging Nations,* Boston, Little, Brown and Company, 1961, p. 23. Copyright © 1961 Massachusetts Institute of Technology. Reprinted by permission of Little, Brown and Company.

9. Heilbroner, Robert L., *The Great Ascent,* New York, Harper and Row, 1963, p. 142.

10. *Ibid.,* p. 157.

11. Piel, Gerard, *Science in the Cause of Man,* New York, Alfred A. Knopf, 1962, p. 57.

12. Stevenson, Adlai E., Speech to U.N. Economic and Social Council, Geneva, Switzerland, July 9, 1965.

13. Ward, Barbara, *India and the West,* New York, W. W. Norton and Company, 1961, pp. 251-2. Copyright © 1961 by W. W. Norton & Company, Inc.

CHAPTER TEN

1. Khrushchev, Nikita S., Speech to closed session of the Twentieth Congress of the C.P.S.U., February 25, 1956.

2. *Ibid.*
3. Crankshaw, Edward, *Khrushchev's Russia,* Harmondsworth, Penguin Books Ltd., 1959, p. 114.
4. Salisbury, Harrison, "What the World Owes Khrushchev," *The New York Times Magazine,* April 25, 1965, p. 109. © 1965 by The New York Times Company. Reprinted by permission.
5. Paloczi-Horvath, George, *op. cit.,* p. 231.
6. *Ibid.,* p. 331.
7. Guillain, Robert, "The 700 Million: A New Look at Red China," *The Washington Post,* October 19, 1964, p. A14.
8. Mehnert, Klaus, *Peking and Moscow,* New York, G. P. Putnam's Sons, 1963, p. 213. © 1963 by George Weidenfeld and Nicholson Ltd. and G. P. Putnam's Sons.
9. Feis, Herbert, *The China Tangle,* Princeton, Princeton University Press, 1955, p. 140.
10. Billington, James H., "Soviet Youth Is Getting Out of [Party] Line," *University: A Princeton Quarterly,* Winter 1965–1966, Number #27, p. 13. Copyright 1965 Princeton University.

CHAPTER ELEVEN.

1. Hallstein, Walter, "Economic Integration and Political Unity in Europe," Speech to Joint Meeting of Harvard University and the Massachusetts Institute of Technology, May 22, 1961.
2. Heilbroner, Robert L., "Forging a United Europe," *Public Affairs Pamphlet No. 308,* New York, Public Affairs Committee, 1961, p. 9.
3. Schoenbrun, David, *As France Goes,* New York, Harper and Brothers, 1957, p. 302.
4. *Ibid.,* p. 299.
5. Kennedy, John F., Message to Freedom House Dinner, January 23, 1963.
6. Drummond, Roscoe, and Coblentz, Gaston, *op. cit.,* p. 57.
7. Lippmann, Walter, Speech to Freedom House Dinner, January 23, 1963.
8. Ball, George, Speech to Freedom House Dinner, January 23, 1963.
9. Madariaga, Salvador de, *Portrait of Europe,* New York, Roy Publishers, 1952, pp. 3–4.

10. *The New York Times,* January 30, 1963, p. 3. © 1963 by The New York Times Company. Reprinted by permission.
11. *Ibid.,* p. 1.
12. *The New York Times,* January 31, 1963, p. 1. © 1963 by The New York Times Company. Reprinted by permission.
13. De Gaulle, Charles, *The Call to Honor (War Memoirs,* Volume I), New York, Simon and Schuster, 1956, p. 4.
14. *Ibid.,* p. 83.
15. Gary, Romain, "The Man Who Stayed Lonely to Save France," *Life,* December 8, 1958, p. 150. © 1958, Time, Inc.
16. De Gaulle, Charles, *op. cit.,* p. 3.
17. *The New York Times,* September 29, 1963, p. 40. © 1963 by The New York Times Company. Reprinted by permission.
18. *Ibid.*
19. *Ibid.*
20. *Ibid.*

CHAPTER TWELVE

1. *Report of the Warren Commission on the Assassination of President Kennedy,* New York, Bantam Books, 1964, p. 57.
2. *Four Days: The Historical Record of the Death of President Kennedy,* New York, American Heritage Publishing Company and United Press International, 1964, p. 14.
3. *Report of the Warren Commission, op. cit.,* p. 62.
4. *Four Days, op. cit.,* p. 25.
5. McGrory, Mary, unsigned editorial in the *Washington Star,* November 23, 1963.
6. White, E. B., *The New Yorker,* November 30, 1963, p. 51.
7. Moynihan, Daniel P., interview with *WTOP News,* November 24, 1963.
8. *Report of the Warren Commission, op. cit.,* p. 63.
9. White, William S., *The Professional: Lyndon B. Johnson,* Boston, Houghton Mifflin Company, 1964, p. 25. Copyright © 1964 by William Smith White.
10. Wheeler, Keith, and Lambert, William, "The Man Who Is President," *Life,* August 14, 1964, p. 26. © 1964, Time, Inc.
11. Johnson, Lyndon B., "My Political Philosophy," *The Texas Quarterly,* Volume I, No. 4, Winter, 1958, p. 17.
12. White, William S., *op. cit.,* p. 167.

13. Johnson, Lyndon B., *op. cit.*, p. 19.
14. Eisenhower, Dwight D., Presidential News Conference, April 7, 1954.
15. Fall, Bernard B., "Our Option in Viet Nam," *The Reporter*, March 12, 1964, p. 22. Copyright 1964 by The Reporter Magazine Company.
16. Kennedy, Robert F., Speech to the Graduating Class of the International Police Academy, Washington, February 28, 1964.
17. Johnson, Harold K., Speech to the Army Civilian Aides Conference, Fort Bliss, Texas, March 22, 1965.

# AN ANNIVERSARY ALMANAC

*January*

1. 1956 Sudan independent
   1959 Castro takes power in Cuba
   1960 Cameroon independent of France
   1962 Western Samoa independent
4. 1948 Burma independent
15. 1908 Edward Teller born
20. 1953 Dwight D. Eisenhower becomes Thirty-fourth President
    1961 John F. Kennedy becomes Thirty-fifth President
21. 1924 Lenin dies
22. 1905 "Bloody Sunday," St. Petersburg, Russia
24. 1965 Winston S. Churchill dies
26. 1880 Douglas MacArthur born
30. 1882 Franklin D. Roosevelt born
    1948 Mohandas K. Gandhi assassinated
31. 1958 U.S. launches Explorer I

*February*

4. 1948 Ceylon independent
13. 1960 French explode first atomic bomb
18. 1965 Gambia independent
20. 1962 John Glenn orbits the earth three times
24. 1948 Communists seize power in Czechoslovakia
25. 1888 John Foster Dulles born
    1956 Nikita Khrushchev makes secret speech denouncing Stalin

*March*

2. 1956 Morocco independent (of France)
4. 1933 Franklin D. Roosevelt becomes Thirty-second President
5. 1946 Churchill makes "Iron Curtain" speech, Fulton, Mo.
   1953 Stalin dies

*275*

6. 1957   Ghana independent
12. 1925   Sun Yat-sen dies
    1947   Truman asks Congress for aid to Greece and Turkey
14. 1879   Albert Einstein born
15. 1947   Congress approves $400 million aid to Greece and
           Turkey
20. 1956   Tunisia independent
25. 1957   Treaty of Rome establishes European Economic Com-
           munity

*April*

3. 1948   Foreign Assistance Act (Marshall Plan) becomes law
   1949   U.S. and eleven other nations sign the North Atlantic
          Treaty
4. 1960   Senegal independent
7. 1956   Morocco independent (of Spain)
11. 1951   Truman fires General MacArthur
12. 1945   Franklin D. Roosevelt dies
           Harry S. Truman becomes Thirty-third President
    1961   Yuri Gagarin becomes first man in space
17. 1894   Nikita Khrushchev born
    1961   Cuban exiles try to invade the Bay of Pigs
18. 1955   Albert Einstein dies
           Afro-Asian conference begins, Bandung, Indonesia
20. 1889   Adolf Hitler born
22. 1870   Lenin born
    1904   J. Robert Oppenheimer born
25. 1945   U.S. and U.S.S.R. troops meet in Germany
           U.N. conference opens, San Francisco
26. 1964   Tanzania formed
27. 1960   Togo independent
    1961   Sierra Leone independent
28. 1945   Benito Mussolini shot
30. 1945   Adolf Hitler commits suicide

*May*

1. 1948   North Korea independent
5. 1818   Karl Marx born
   1961   Alan Shepard becomes first American in space
7. 1945   Germany surrenders

8. 1884 Harry S. Truman born
   1954 Dien Bien Phu falls
12. 1949 Russia lifts Berlin blockade
14. 1948 Israel independent
25. 1946 Jordan independent
26. 1966 Guyana independent
29. 1917 John F. Kennedy born

*June*

5. 1947 Secretary of State Marshall offers U.S. aid to Europe
6. 1944 D-Day in Normandy
19. 1961 Kuwait independent
20. 1960 Mali independent
   Senegal independent
23. 1940 France surrenders to Germany
24. 1948 Russia blockades Berlin
25. 1950 North Korea invades South Korea
26. 1945 U.N. charter signed
   1948 West begins Berlin airlift
   1956 Egypt nationalizes Suez Canal
   1960 Malagasay Republic independent
27. 1950 U.N. votes use of force to stop invasion of South Korea
30. 1960 Congo (Leopoldville) independent

*July*

1. 1960 Somali independent
   1962 Rwanda independent
   Burundi independent
3. 1962 Algeria independent
4. 1946 Philippines independent
6. 1964 Malawi independent
16. 1945 First atomic bomb tested, Alamogordo, New Mexico
19. 1949 Laos independent
21. 1954 Geneva "accords" signed: Viet Nam divided
23. 1952 Revolution in Egypt
26. 1965 Maldive Islands independent
27. 1953 Truce signed ending Korean War

*August*

1. 1960 Dahomey independent

2. 1939   Einstein writes "atom bomb" letter to Roosevelt
3. 1960   Niger independent
5. 1960   Upper Volta independent
6. 1945   Atomic bomb dropped on Hiroshima, Japan
   1962   Jamaica independent
7. 1960   Ivory Coast independent
9. 1945   Atomic bomb dropped on Nagasaki, Japan
11. 1960  Chad independent
12. 1953  Russia tests first hydrogen bomb
13. 1960  Central African Republic independent
    1961  East Germans build Berlin wall
14. 1945  Japan surrenders unconditionally
15. 1947  India and Pakistan independent
    1948  South Korea independent
    1960  Congo (Brazzaville) independent
16. 1960  Cyprus independent
17. 1960  Gabon independent
23. 1939  Russia and Germany sign nonaggression pact
27. 1908  Lyndon B. Johnson born
29. 1949  Russia tests an atomic bomb
31. 1962  Trinidad and Tobago independent

*September*

1. 1939   Germany invades Poland
2. 1945   Japan signs surrender, Tokyo Bay
3. 1939   Britain and France declare war on Germany
16. 1963  Malaysia independent
          Singapore independent
22. 1960  Mali independent
28. 1820  Friedrich Engels born

*October*

1. 1949   Chinese People's Republic proclaimed
   1960   Nigeria independent
   1961   Cameroon independent of Britain
2. 1869   Mohandas K. Gandhi born
   1958   Guinea independent
4. 1957   Russia launches Sputnik I
9. 1962   Uganda independent
10. 1911  Revolution begins in China

12. 1939 Alexander Sachs interests Roosevelt in atomic bomb
14. 1890 Dwight D. Eisenhower born
    1962 U-2 discovers Russian missiles in Cuba
16. 1964 China tests an atomic bomb
         Kremlin announces Khrushchev ouster
20. 1944 MacArthur returns to Philippines
22. 1962 U.S. announces Cuban blockade
24. 1962 U.S. blockades Cuba; Russian ships turn back
    1964 Zambia independent
28. 1962 Khrushchev agrees to remove Cuban missiles
30. 1961 Twenty-second Congress Soviet Communist party approves removal of Stalin's body from Lenin's tomb
31. 1887 Chiang Kai-shek born

*November*

1. 1952 U.S. tests a hydrogen bomb
   1963 Ngo Dinh Diem overthrown
4. 1956 Russians crush Hungarian revolution
5. 1956 British and French invade Egypt
7. 1917 Bolsheviks seize power in Russia
9. 1953 Cambodia independent
11. 1965 Rhodesia declares independence
22. 1890 Charles de Gaulle born
    1963 John F. Kennedy assassinated
         Lyndon B. Johnson becomes Thirty-sixth President
28. 1960 Mauritania independent
30. 1874 Winston Churchill born

*December*

2. 1942 First sustained nuclear chain reaction, Chicago
7. 1941 Japan attacks U.S., Pearl Harbor
9. 1961 Tanganyika independent
10. 1963 Zanzibar independent
12. 1963 Kenya independent
21. 1879 Joseph Stalin born
24. 1951 Libya independent
26. 1893 Mao Tse-tung born
27. 1949 Indonesia independent
31. 1880 George C. Marshall born

# INDEX